I0812715

IMAGES
of America

RAILROADS OF DUBUQUE

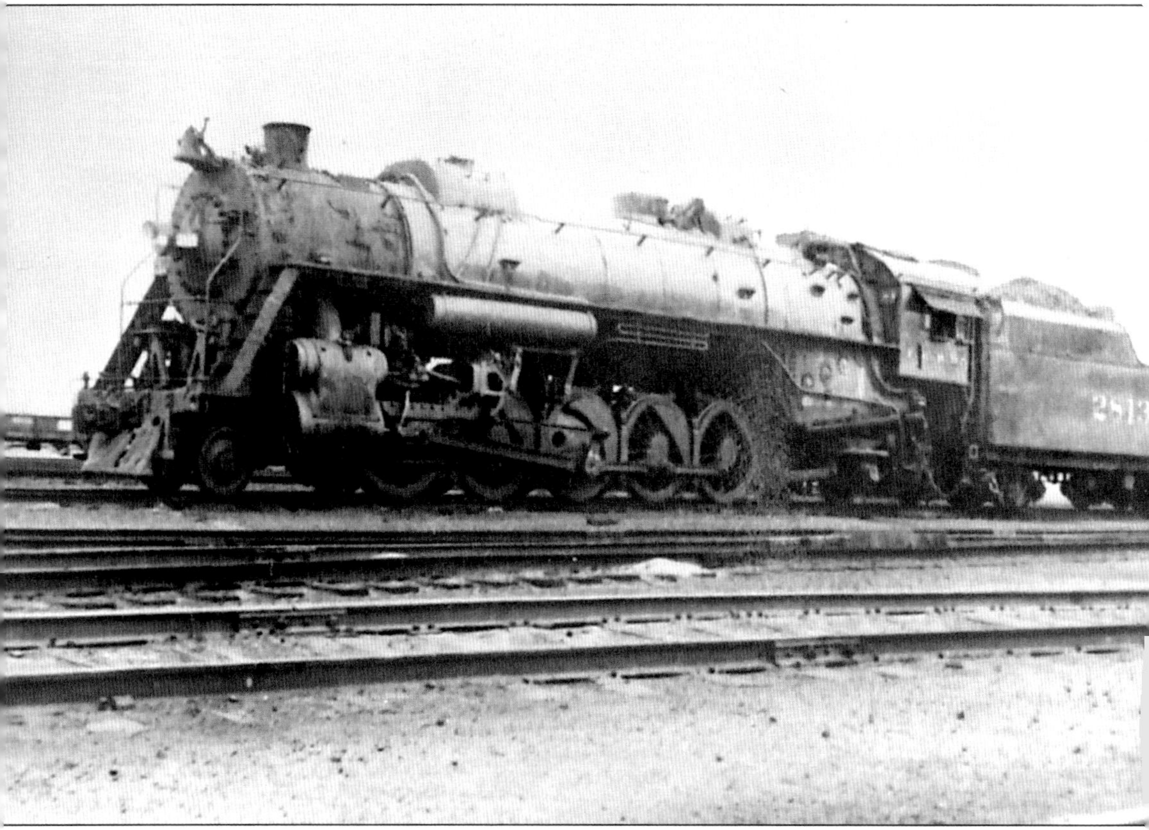

This image shows one of the Illinois Central System's 2-10-2 locomotives, which were the most powerful two-cylinder locomotives in the world.

IMAGES
of America

RAILROADS OF DUBUQUE

John Tigges and James Shaffer

ARCADIA
PUBLISHING

ISBN 978-0-7385-3957-7

Published by Arcadia Publishing
Charleston, South Carolina

Printed in the United States

Library of Congress Catalog Card Number: Applied for

For all general information contact Arcadia Publishing at:
Telephone 843-853-2070
Fax 843-853-0044
E-mail sales@arcadiapublishing.com
For customer service and orders:
Toll-Free 1-888-313-2665

Visit us on the Internet at http://www.arcadiapublishing.com

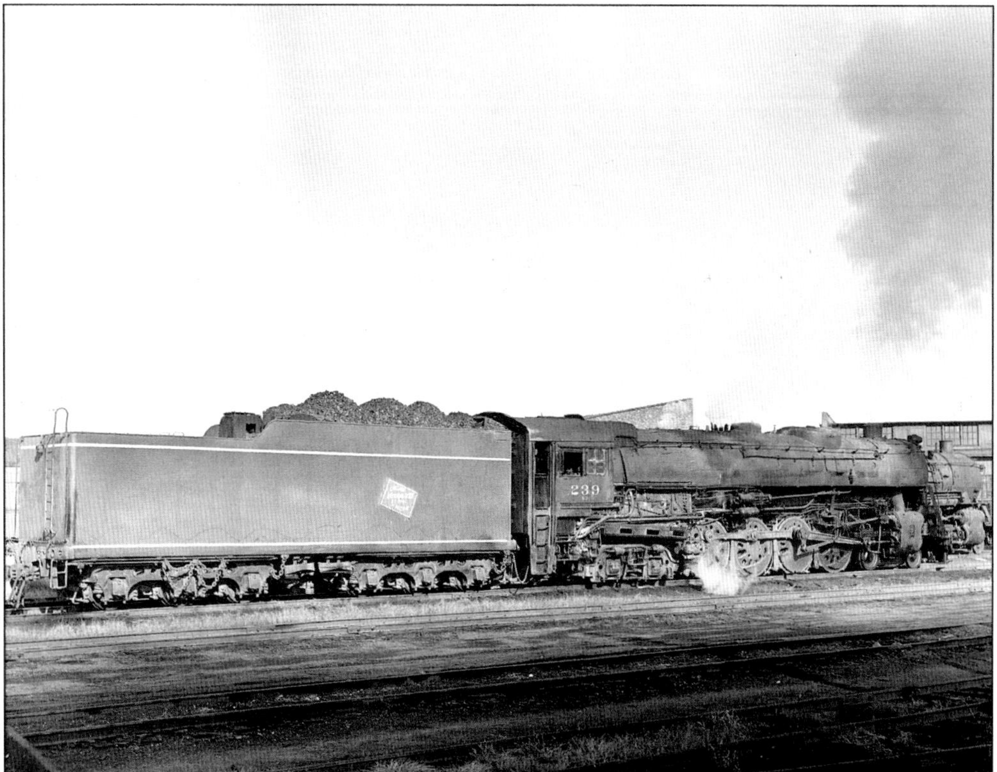

The Milwaukee Road's S-2, 4-8-4 Northerns were the largest locomotives on that road.

Contents

ACKNOWLEDGMENTS

The authors would like to credit and thank the following: the John Tigges Collection, the James Shaffer Collection, the Charles Finch Collection, the John Adney Collection, Robert Courtney, Fred Uthe, the R.G. Corben Collection, the Bill Kohler Collection, the Illinois Central Railroad, the Chicago, Milwaukee, St. Paul & Pacific Railroad, the Chicago, Burlington and Quincy Railroad, the Chicago Great Western Railway, the Plamodom Collection, Frank (Sonny) Widmann, Bette Shaffer, and Kathy Tigges.

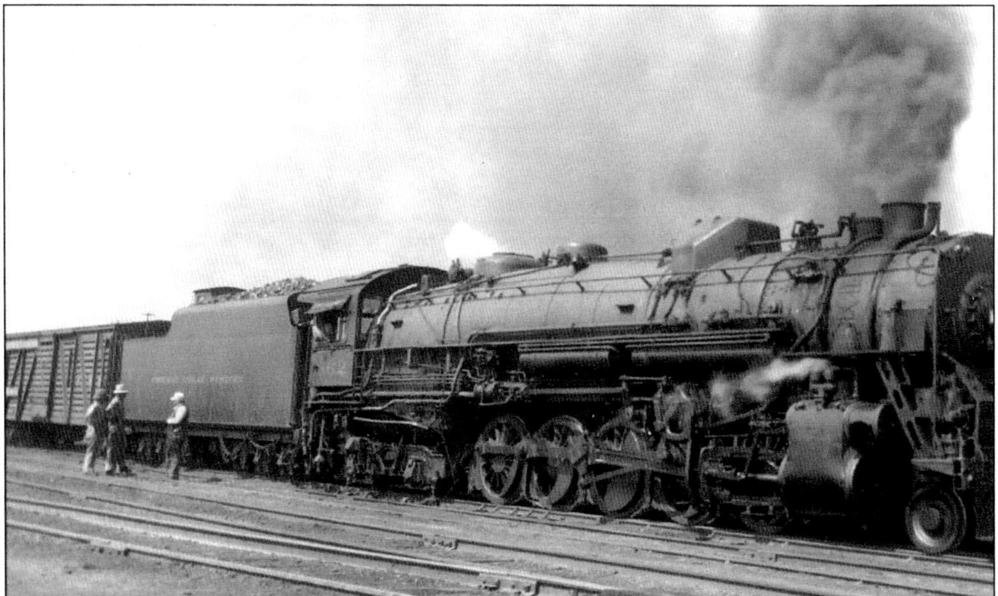

The Chicago Great Western Railway's Texas-type 2-10-4s were capable of pulling 80 to 100 freight cars over hilly terrain.

INTRODUCTION

Dubuque is the oldest city in Iowa, and much has been written about the Key City. The city's namesake, Julien Dubuque, lived and mined lead in the area until his death in 1810. After the Black Hawk War was over, settlers moved to what is now Dubuque in June 1833, agreeing to abide by the terms of the peace treaty.

What began as a one-square-mile area marking Dubuque's limits was expanded several times. The city continued growing and in 1855, the Illinois Central Railroad reached Dunleith (East Dubuque), Illinois, opposite the Key City. In time, four Class A railroads operated through Dubuque. The Illinois Central controlled the Dubuque and Pacific Railroad that became the Dubuque and Sioux City Railroad.

By way of purchasing the Chicago, Clinton, Dubuque and Minnesota Railroad, which operated along the western bank of the Mississippi River, the Chicago, Milwaukee and St. Paul Railway entered Dubuque. The CCD&M was a large property and had branch lines running inland several places. In 1929, the CM&SP became the Chicago, Milwaukee, St. Paul and Pacific Railroad. The latter road's name will be referred to as the Milwaukee or the Milwaukee Road.

The Chicago, Burlington and Quincy Railroad pulled together a group of railroads—including the Chicago, Burlington and Northern Railroad—into one great railroad. The CB&N entered Dubuque over the Illinois Central Bridge while building north to the Twin Cities along the east bank of the Mississippi River. In this book, the CB&Q will be called the Burlington in most instances.

Beginning on July 29, 1885, the Chicago Great Western Railway's tracks were laid in Dubuque in a northwest direction by the Minnesota and North Western Railroad, while westerly tracks were laid in Illinois toward Dubuque. When the CGW Railway was formed in 1892 to gather various other railroads, it quickly proved to be a stiff competitor. In the early half of the 20th century, the road had many British investors, which led to much of the motive power taking on British design qualities. In the 1920s and 1930s, the CGW Railway opted for larger freight engines: from the beautiful Texas-type 2-10-4s steam locomotives that regularly pulled 70 or more freight cars through its hilly Iowa and Illinois terrain, to six to ten diesel units dragging 100-car trains over the same route. The railway will be referred to as the Chicago Great Western or the CGW in this book.

Trolley cars were not unusual in Dubuque, but these had their classy service cut short after being in service only 64 years. Dubuque also had two funicular, which consisted of two cable cars operating on three inclined common rails; the rails expanded to four at the midway point to allow the cars to pass. The older of the two is still in service in the 21st century and offers a thrilling ride. It is called the Fenelon Place Elevator or the Fourth Street Elevator and is the shortest and steepest railway in the world, with a 67.8 percent grade.

In this book, we have told the Dubuque-related stories of each railroad, trolley, and funicular through photos and captions. We hope you enjoy *Railroads of Dubuque* as much as we enjoyed putting it together.

One

The Illinois Central

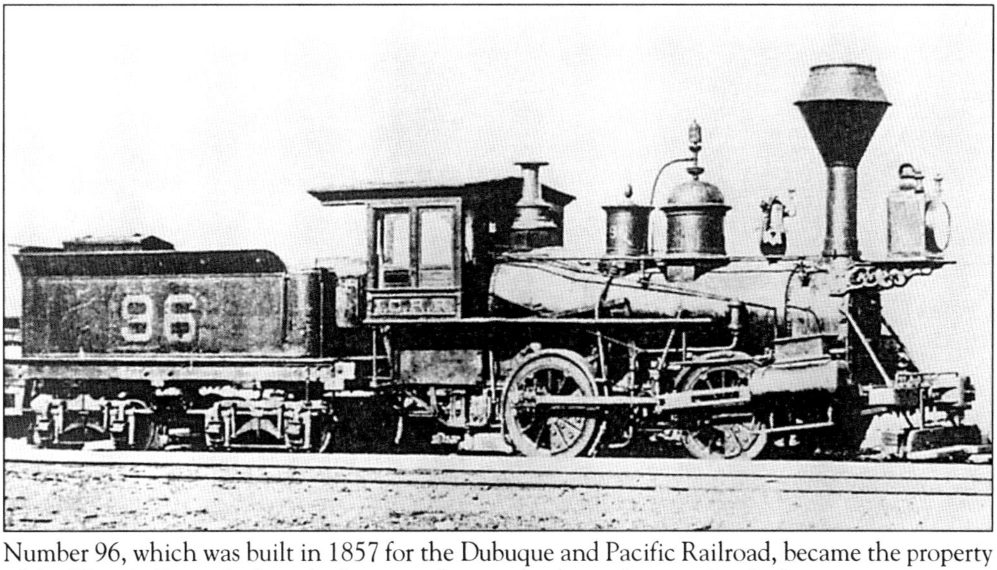

Number 96, which was built in 1857 for the Dubuque and Pacific Railroad, became the property of the Illinois Central when the latter took over the former's operation in Iowa.

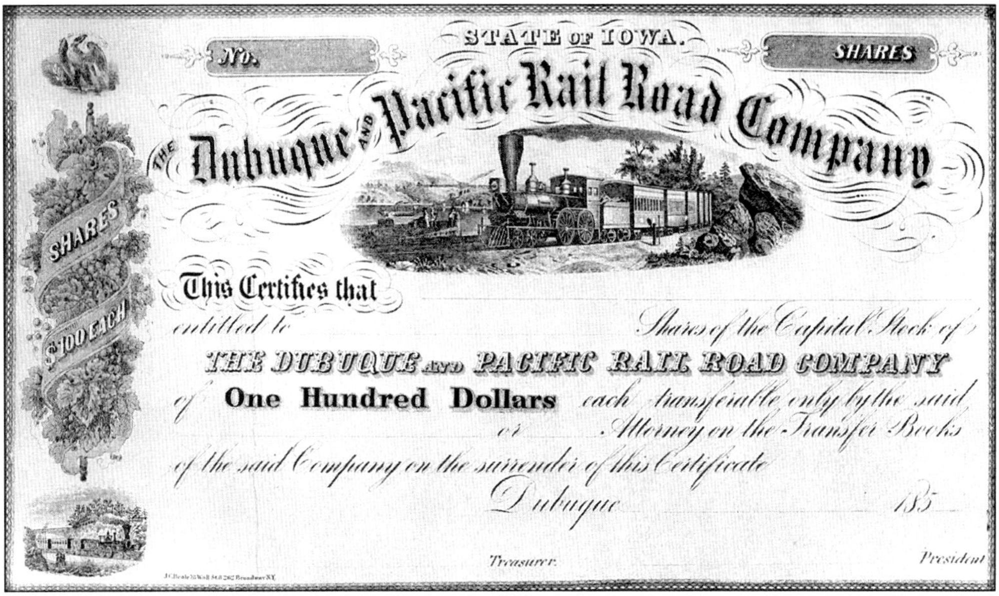

This represents an unsold share of Dubuque and Pacific Railroad stock.

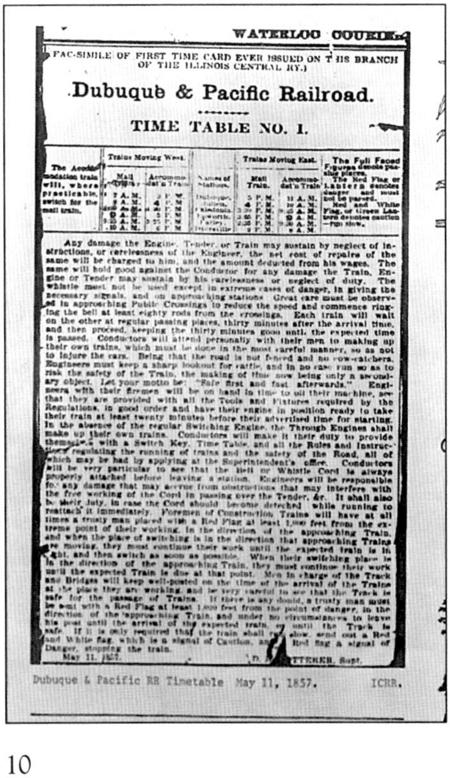

WATERLOO COURIER

(FAC-SIMILE OF FIRST TIME CARD EVER ISSUED ON THIS BRANCH OF THE ILLINOIS CENTRAL RY.)

Dubuque & Pacific Railroad.

TIME TABLE NO. 1.

The Accommodation train will, where practicable, swich for the mail train.	Trains Moving West. Mail Train.	Accommodat'n Train	Names of Stations.	Trains Moving East. Mail Train.	Accommodat'n Train	The Full Faced Figures denote passing places. The Red Flag or Lantern denotes danger and must not be passed. Red and White Flag, or Green Lantern denotes caution—run slow.
	7 A. M.	3 P. M.	Dubuque.	5 P. M.	11 A. M.	
	8 A. M.	**4** P. M.	Julien.	**4** P. M.	10 A. M.	
	[illegible] A. M.	[illegible] P. M.	Caledonia.	3.30 P. M.	[illegible] A. M.	
	9 A. M.	5 P. M.	Epworth.	[illegible] P. M.	**9** A. M.	
	9.25 A. M.	5.25 P. M.	Farley.	[illegible] P. M.	8.30 A. M.	
	10 A. M.	6 P. M.	Dyersville.	2 P. M.	8 A. M.	

Any damage the Engine, Tender, or Train may sustain by neglect of instructions, or carelessness of the Engineer, the net cost of repairs of the same will be charged to him, and the amount deducted from his wages. The same will hold good against the Conductor for any damage the Train, Engine or Tender may sustain by his carelessness or neglect of duty. The whistle must not be used except in extreme cases of danger, in giving the necessary signals, and on approaching stations. Great care must be observed in approaching Public Crossings to reduce the speed and commence ringing the bell at least eighty rods from the crossings. Each train will wait on the other at regular passing places, thirty minutes after the arrival time, and then proceed, keeping the thirty minutes good until the expected time is passed. Conductors will attend personally with their men to making up their own trains, which must be done in the most careful manner, so as not to injure the cars. Being that the road is not fenced and no cow-catchers, Engineers must keep a sharp lookout for cattle, and in no case run so as to risk the safety of the Train, the making of time now being only a secondary object. Let your motto be: "Safe first and fast afterwards." Engineers with their firemen will be on hand in time to oil their machine, see that they are provided with all the Tools and Fixtures required by the Regulations, in good order and have their engine in position ready to take their train at least twenty minutes before their advertised time for starting. In the absence of the regular Switching Engine, the Through Engines shall make up their own trains. Conductors will make it their duty to provide themselves with a Switch Key, Time Table, and all the Rules and Instructions regulating the running of trains and the safety of the Road, all of which may be had by applying at the Superintendent's office. Conductors will be very particular to see that the Bell or Whistle Cord is always properly attached before leaving a station. Engineers will be responsible for any damage that may accrue from obstructions that may interfere with the free working of the Cord in passing over the Tender, &c. It shall also be their duty, in case the Cord should become detached while running to reattach it immediately. Foremen of Construction Trains will have at all times a trusty man placed with a Red Flag at least 1,000 feet from the extreme point of their working, in the direction of the approaching Train, and when the place of switching is in the direction that approaching Trains are moving, they must continue their work until the expected train is in sight, and then swich as soon as possible. When their switching place is in the direction of the approaching Train, they must continue their work until the expected Train is due at that point. Men in charge of the Track and Bridges will keep well-posted on the time of the arrival of the Trains at the place they are working and be very careful to see that the Track is safe for the passage of Trains. If there is any doubt, a trusty man must be sent with a Red Flag at least 1,000 feet from the point of danger, in the direction of the approaching Train, and under no circumstances to leave his post until the arrival of the expected train, or until the Track is safe. If it is only required that the train shall run slow, send out a Red and White flag, which is a signal of Caution, and [illegible] Red flag a signal of Danger, stopping the train.

May 11, 1857. [illegible]TTEKER, Supt.

Dubuque & Pacific RR Timetable May 11, 1857. ICRR.

This is the only known timetable of the Dubuque and Pacific.

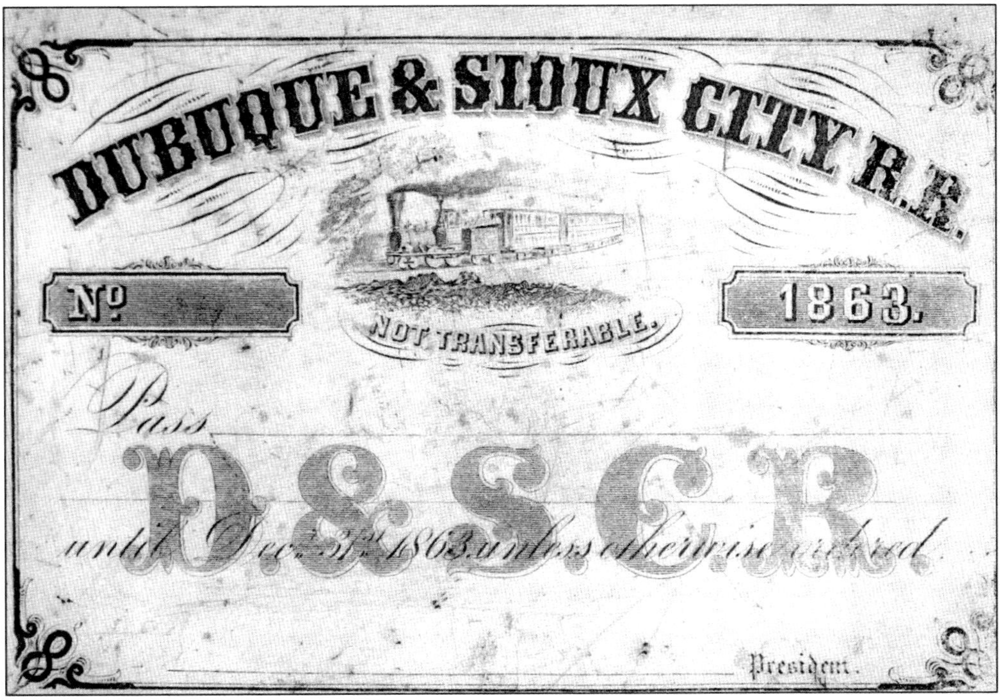

By 1863, the Dubuque and Sioux City Railroad had taken over the Dubuque and Pacific. The plate for the pass is part of the John Tigges Collection.

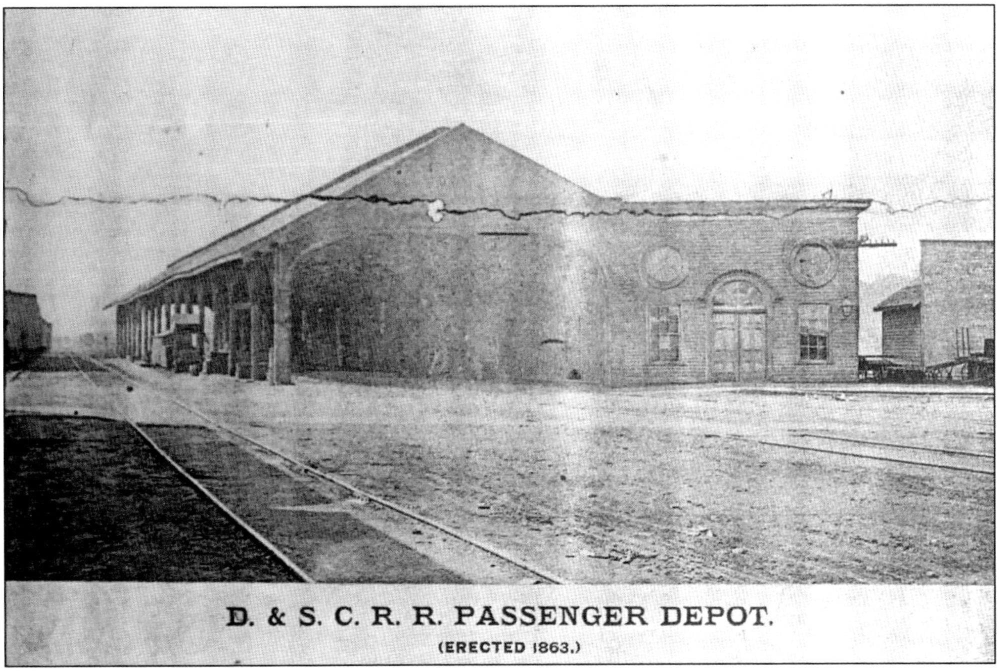

This image shows the Dubuque and Sioux City Railroad station in Dubuque, which was eventually replaced with the Illinois Central's Victorian masterpiece.

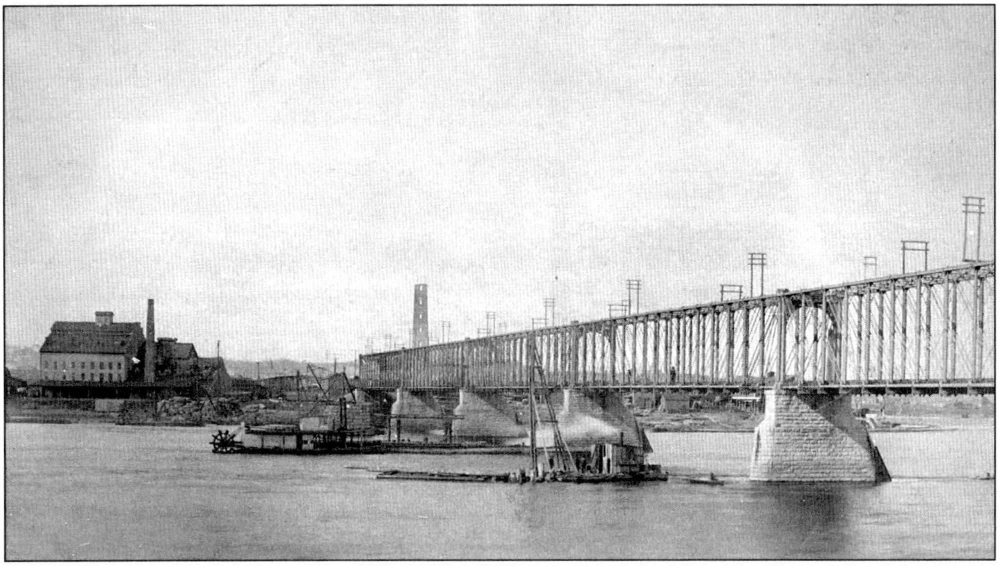

Andrew Carnegie's career was given a big boost when he sold the above cast iron bridge to the Illinois Central. The shot tower in the left center of the background still stands in the 21st century.

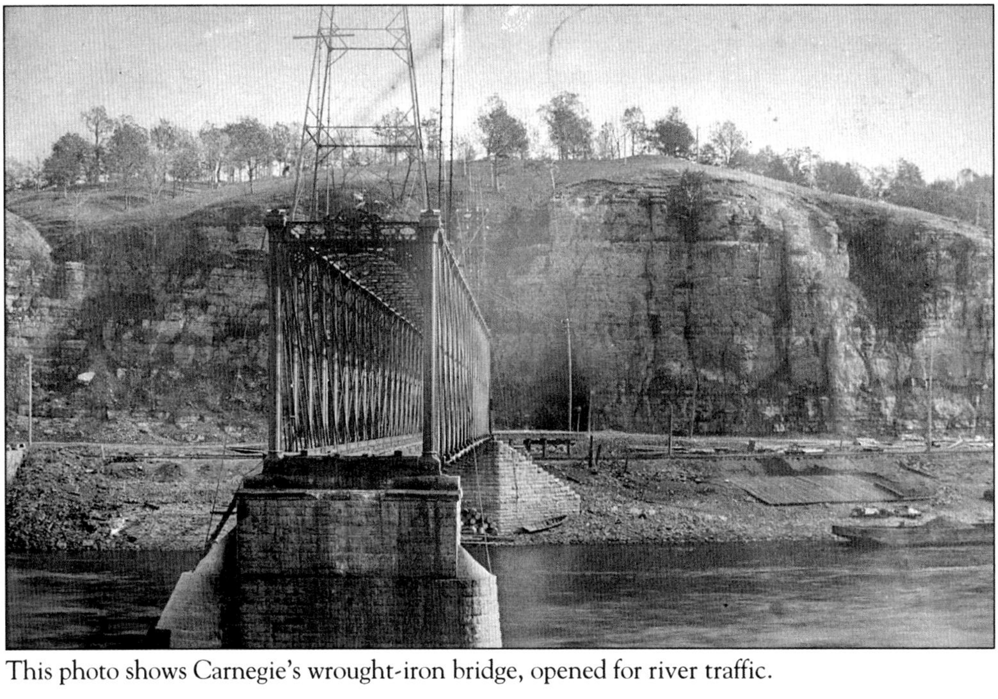

This photo shows Carnegie's wrought-iron bridge, opened for river traffic.

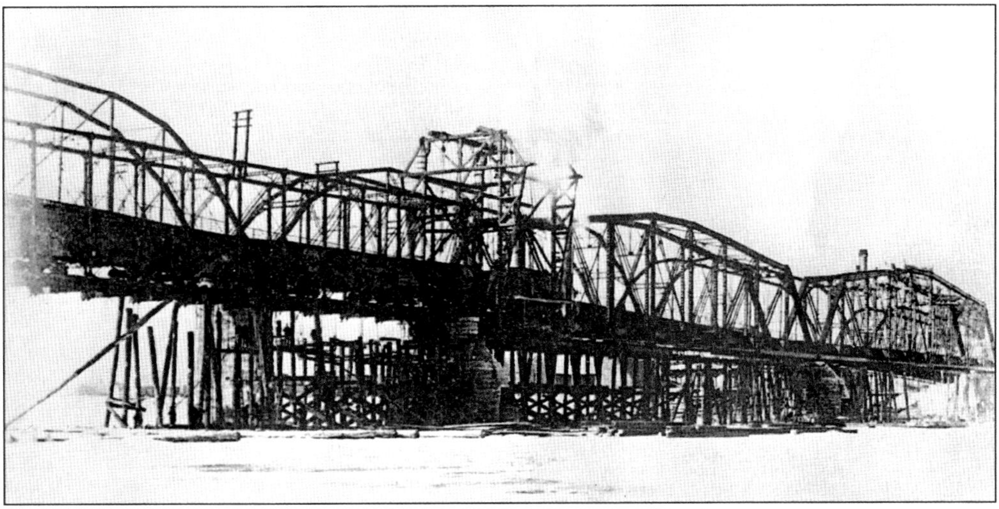

This image shows the cast iron bridge being replaced by a steel bridge.

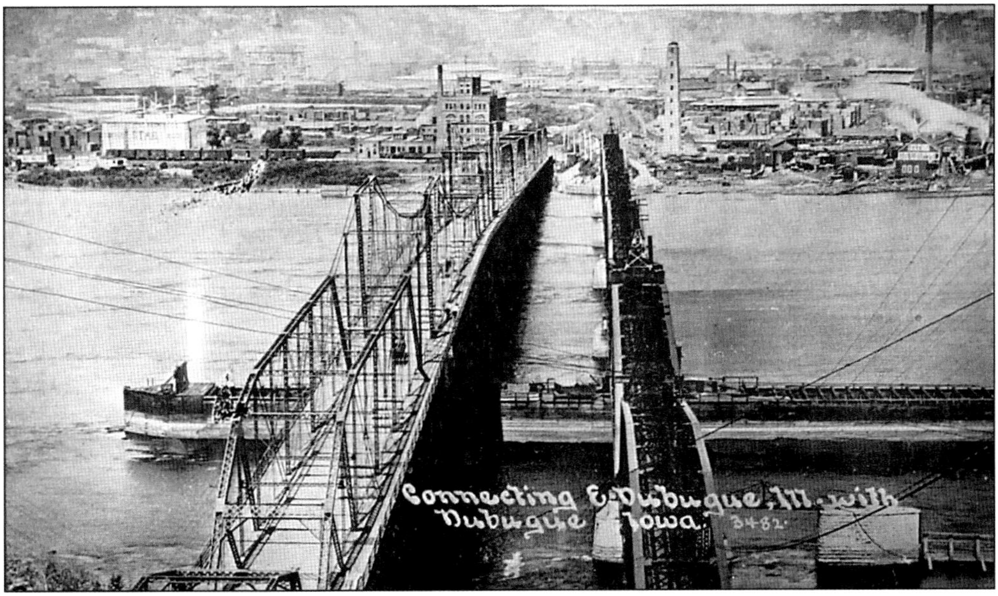

This is a view of the railroad bridge and the wagon bridge leading to Dubuque, Iowa.

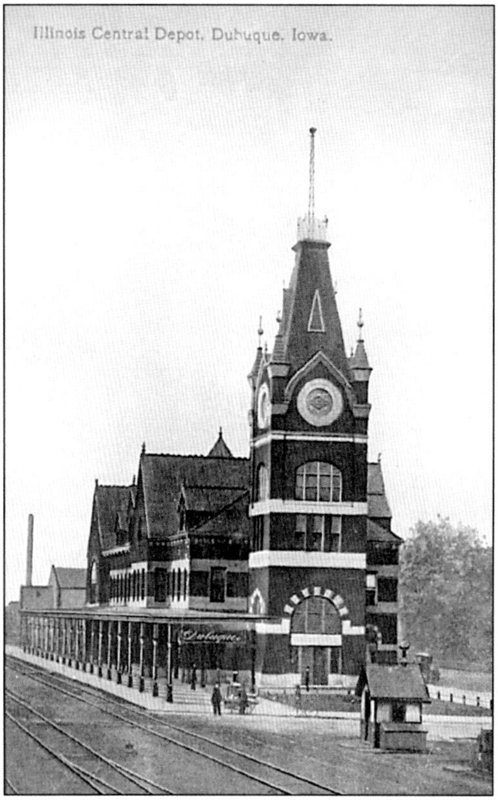

The Illinois Central's beautiful Victorian Dubuque passenger station is pictured here.

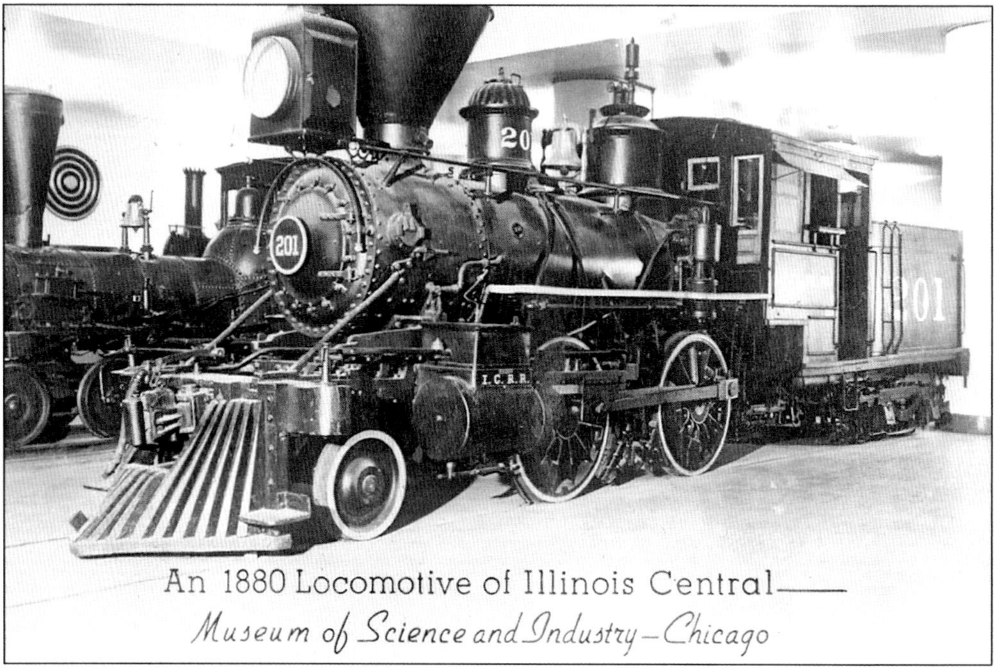

This is one type of locomotive used by the Illinois Central in 1880.

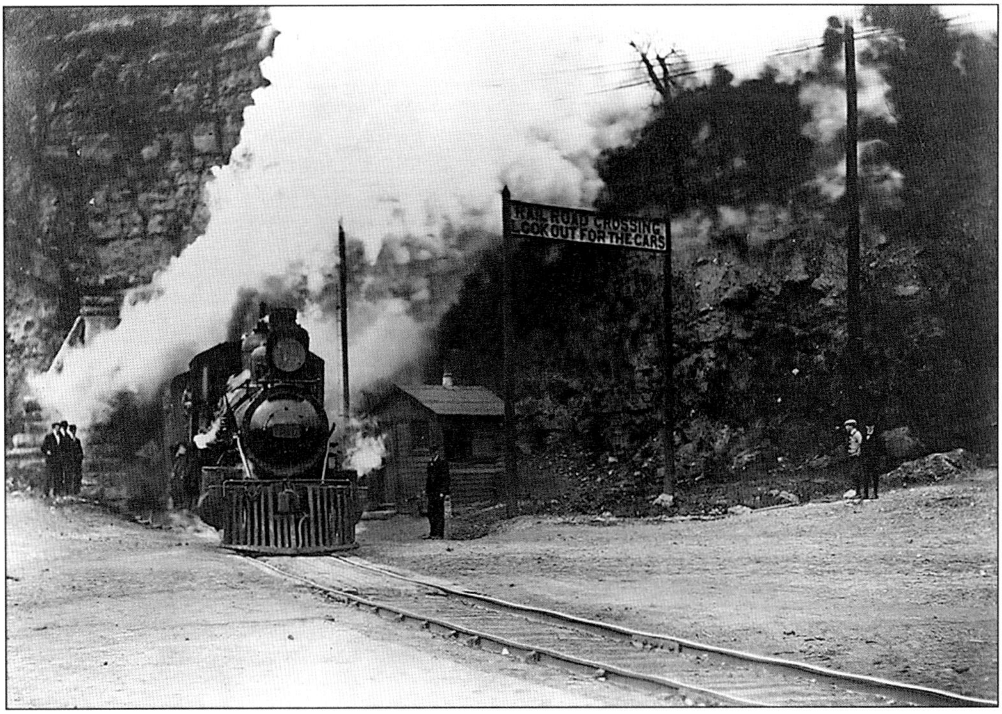

Around the turn of the 20th century, a 4-4-0 emerges from the tunnel in East Dubuque, Illinois, and crosses the road to the wagon bridge to the left.

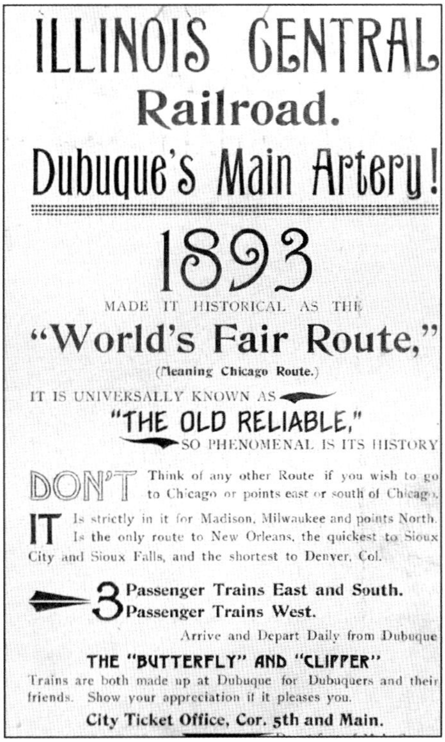

ILLINOIS CENTRAL
Railroad.
Dubuque's Main Artery!

1893
MADE IT HISTORICAL AS THE
"World's Fair Route,"
(Meaning Chicago Route.)
IT IS UNIVERSALLY KNOWN AS
"THE OLD RELIABLE,"
SO PHENOMENAL IS ITS HISTORY

DON'T Think of any other Route if you wish to go to Chicago or points east or south of Chicago.

IT Is strictly in it for Madison, Milwaukee and points North. Is the only route to New Orleans, the quickest to Sioux City and Sioux Falls, and the shortest to Denver, Col.

3 Passenger Trains East and South.
3 Passenger Trains West.
Arrive and Depart Daily from Dubuque

THE "BUTTERFLY" AND "CLIPPER"
Trains are both made up at Dubuque for Dubuquers and their friends. Show your appreciation if it pleases you.
City Ticket Office, Cor. 5th and Main.

As of 1893, Dubuquers could take the "Butterfly" east or the "Clipper" west, with return to the Key City.

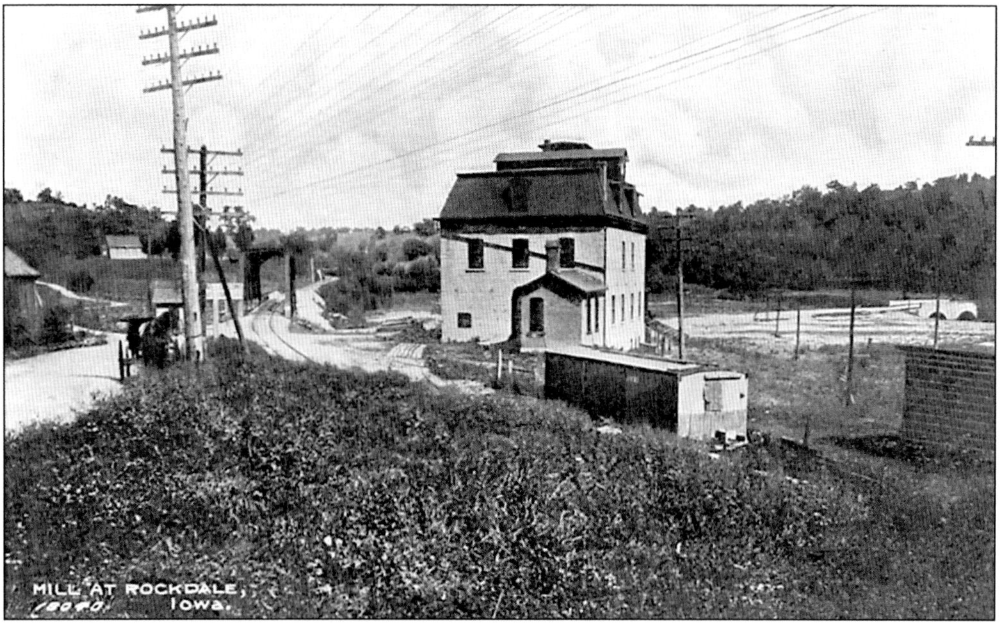

In 1907, the Illinois Central tracks followed Catfish Creek away from the Mississippi River, through Rockdale, Iowa, and continued westward.

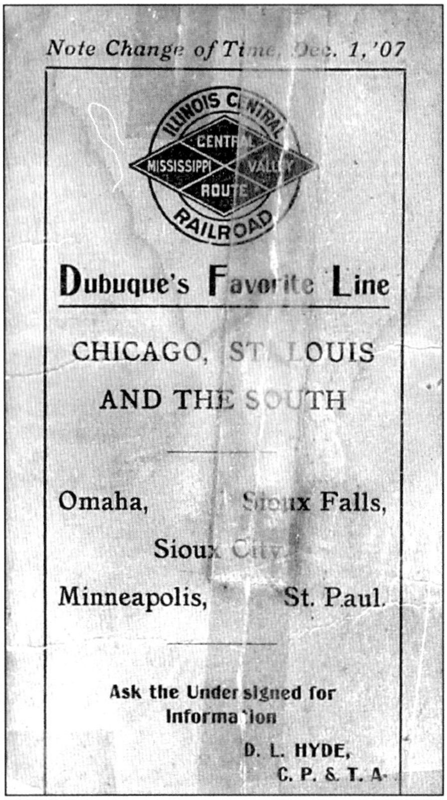

Note Change of Time, Dec. 1, '07

ILLINOIS CENTRAL RAILROAD
CENTRAL MISSISSIPPI VALLEY ROUTE

Dubuque's Favorite Line

CHICAGO, ST. LOUIS
AND THE SOUTH

Omaha, Sioux Falls,
Sioux City,
Minneapolis, St. Paul.

Ask the Undersigned for Information

D. L. HYDE,
C. P. & T. A.

This schedule from "Dubuque's Favorite Line," the Illinois Central Railroad, shows destinations from Dubuque.

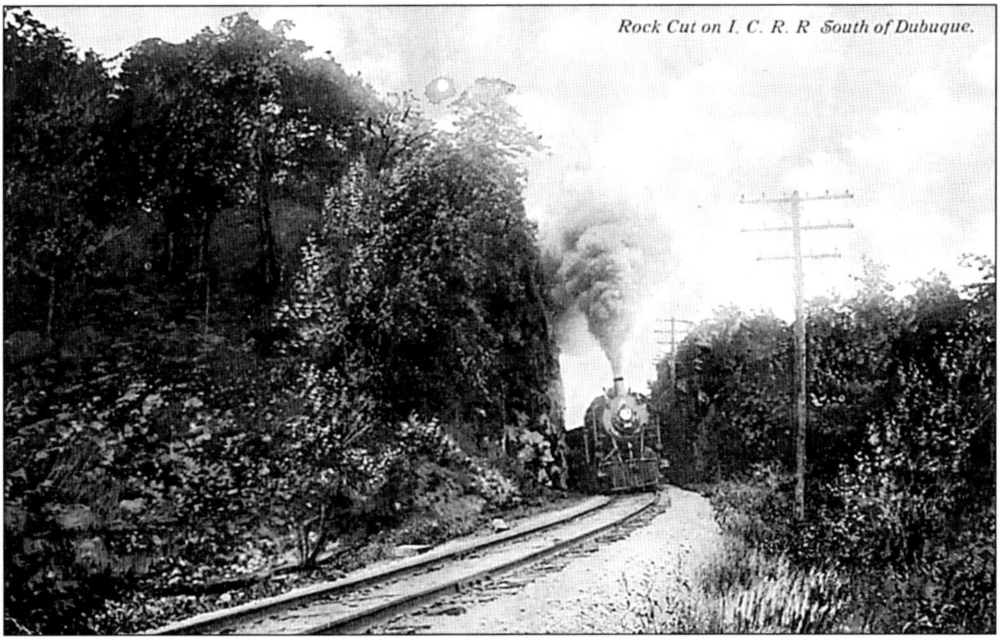

A locomotive storms through "Rock Cut," south of Dubuque, away from the Mississippi River, bound for points west.

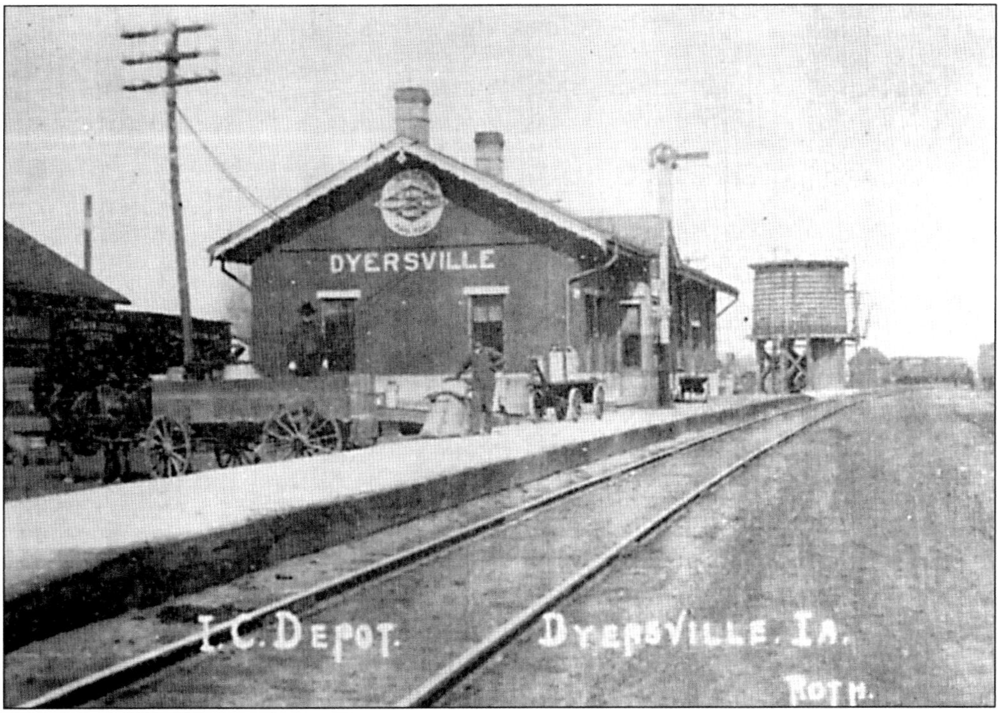

In the years it served the Illinois Central and Iowa communities, the Dyersville, Iowa, railroad station—west of Dubuque—saw many arrivals and departures.

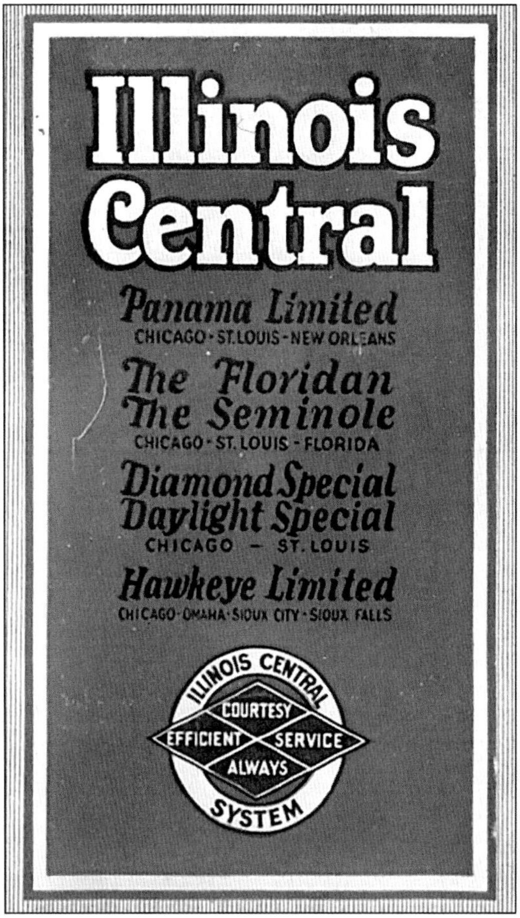

Ticket holders, like the one shown at left, held a traveler's identification as well as tickets and reservations.

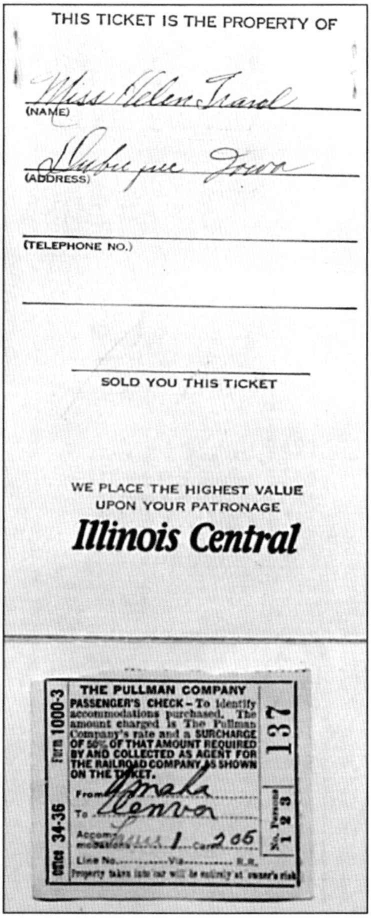

The inside of this ticket holder identifies Miss Helen Tranel as the passenger. She was assigned to a lower berth in car 205 en route to Denver from Omaha.

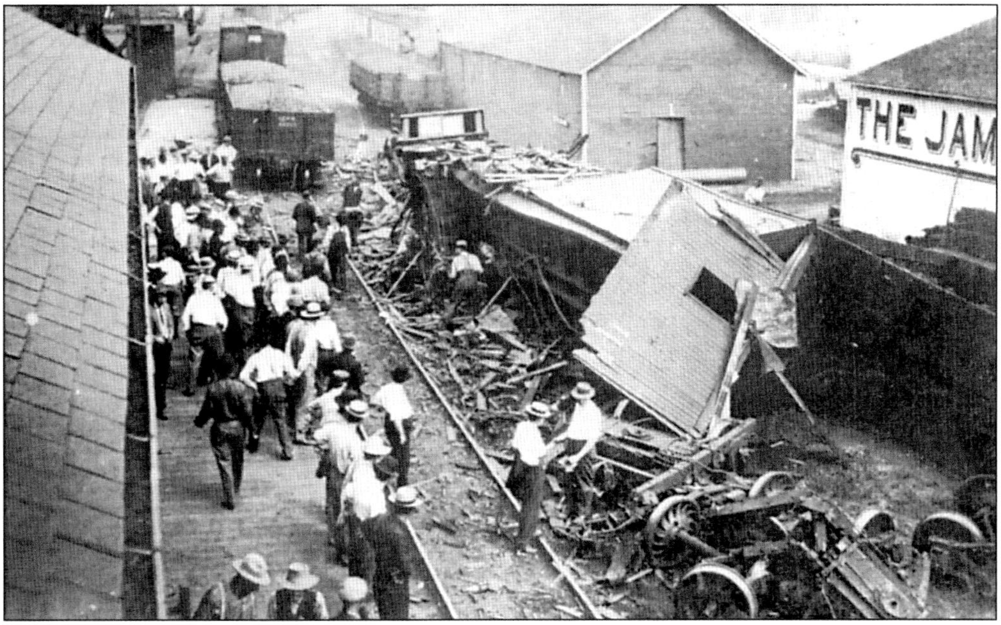

Wrecks occurred on all railroads at one time or another. The above derailment occurred in Dyersville, Iowa, near the station.

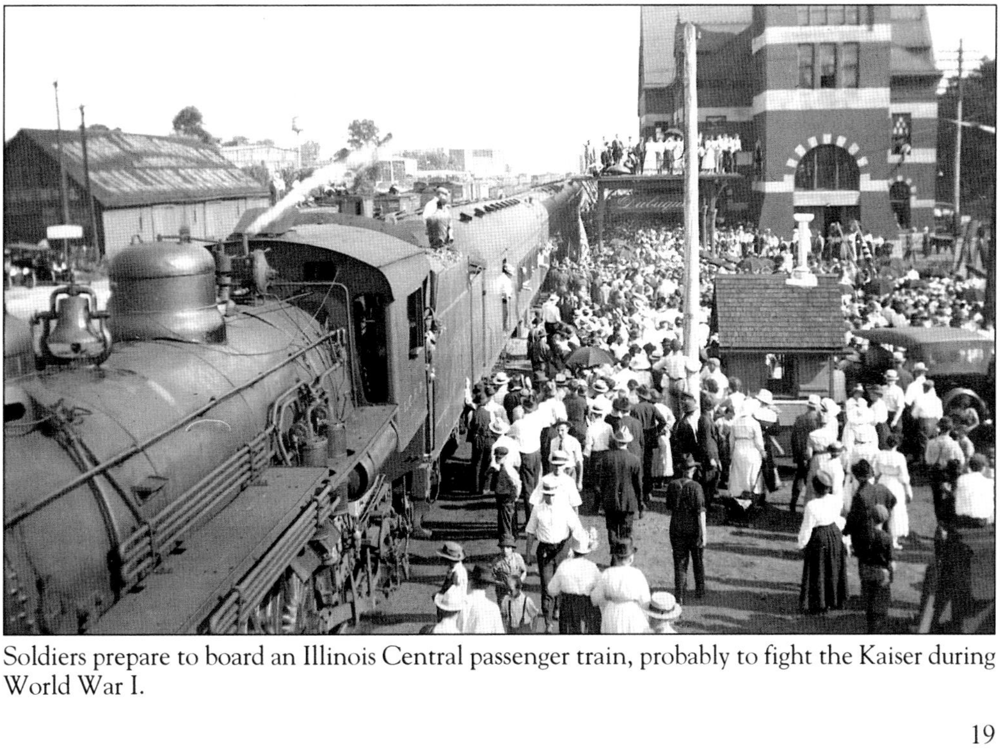

Soldiers prepare to board an Illinois Central passenger train, probably to fight the Kaiser during World War I.

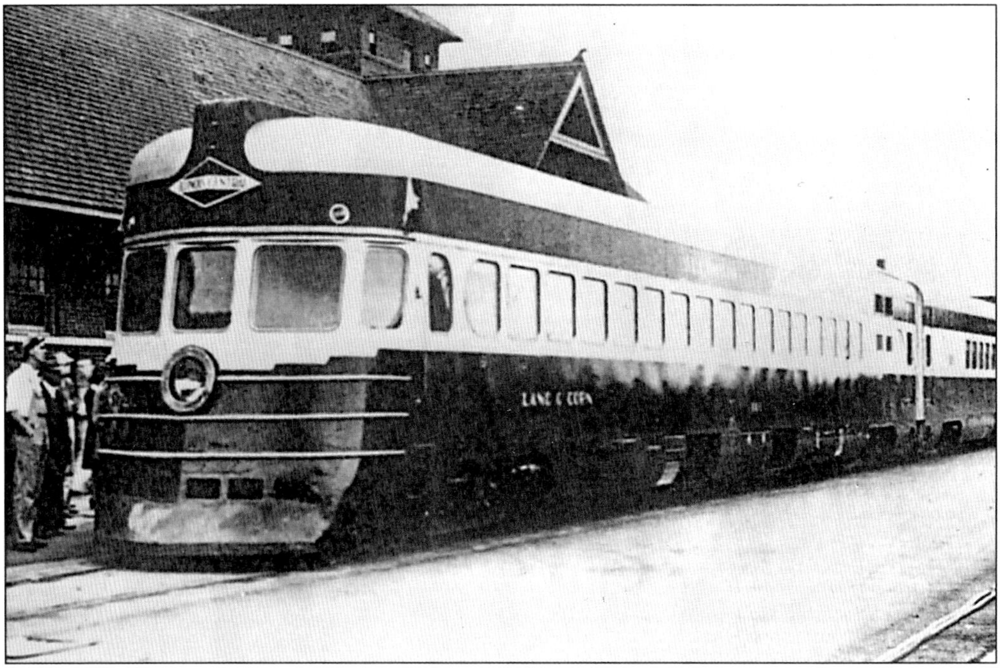

The original "Land of Corn" was a streamlined motor car and trailer.

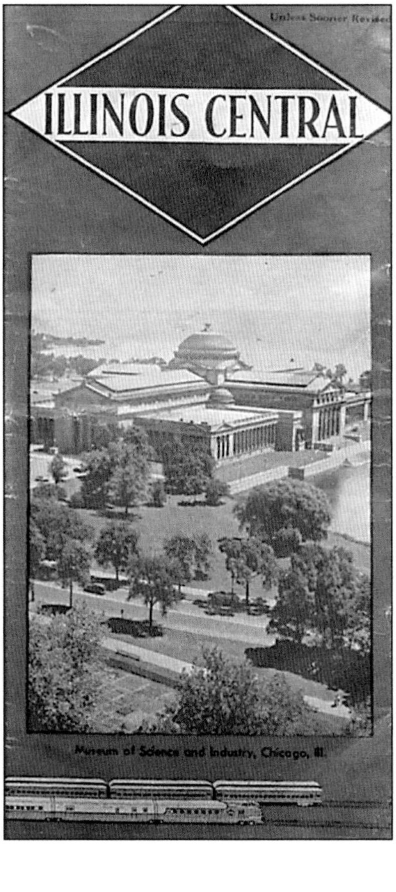

A 1946 Illinois Central timetable is shown here.

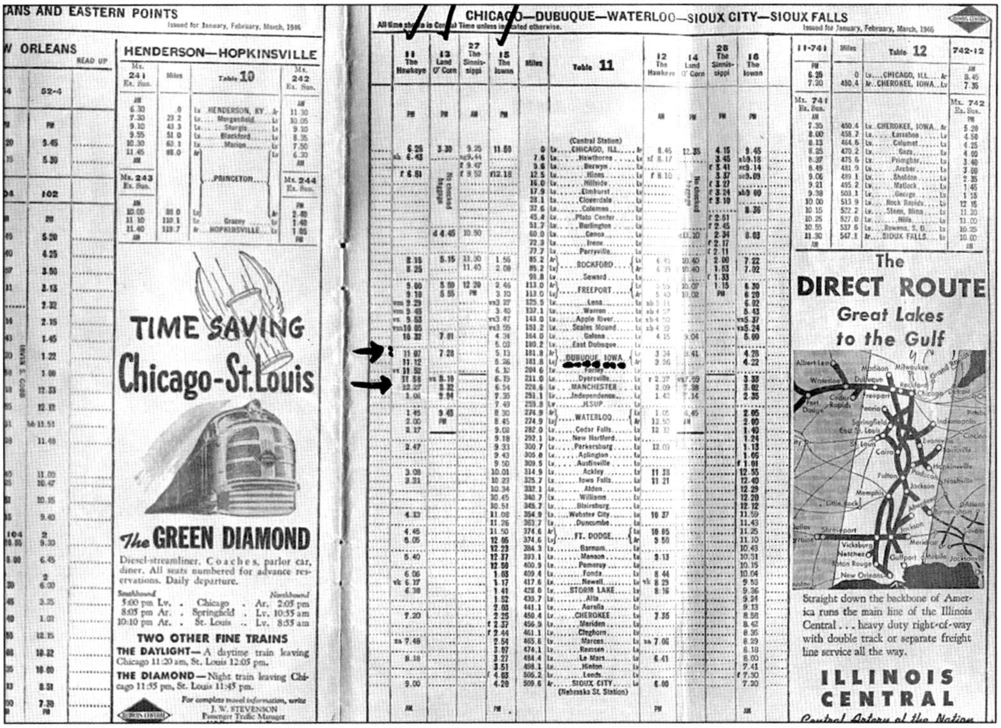

In 1946, the Illinois Central offered three options to travel, in either of two directions.

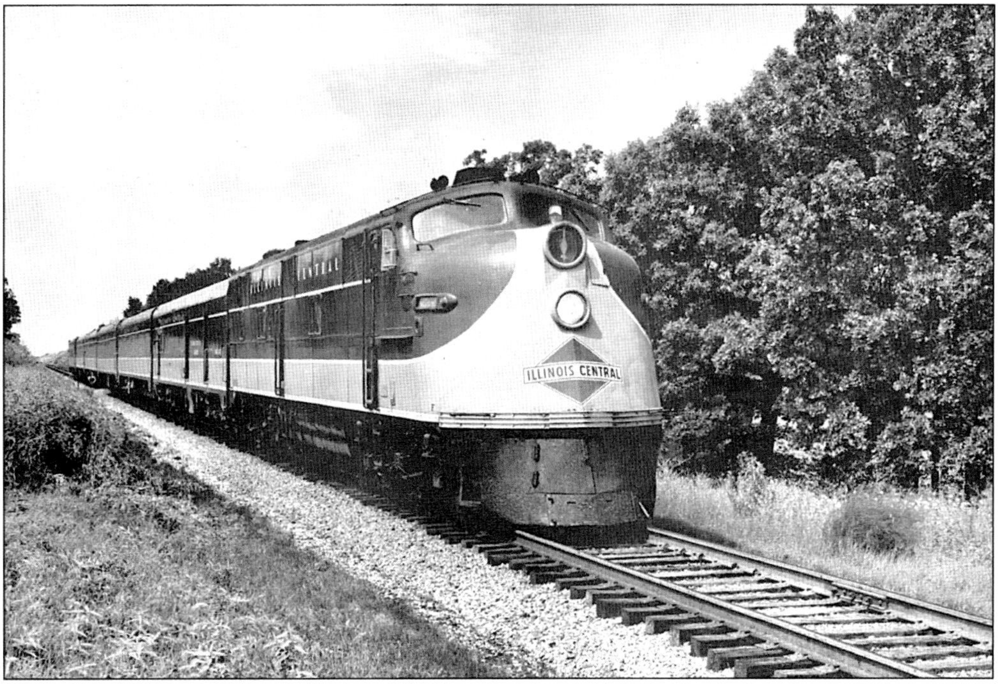

An Electromotive diesel locomotive, pulling a six-car "Land of Corn," slips through the country for which it was named.

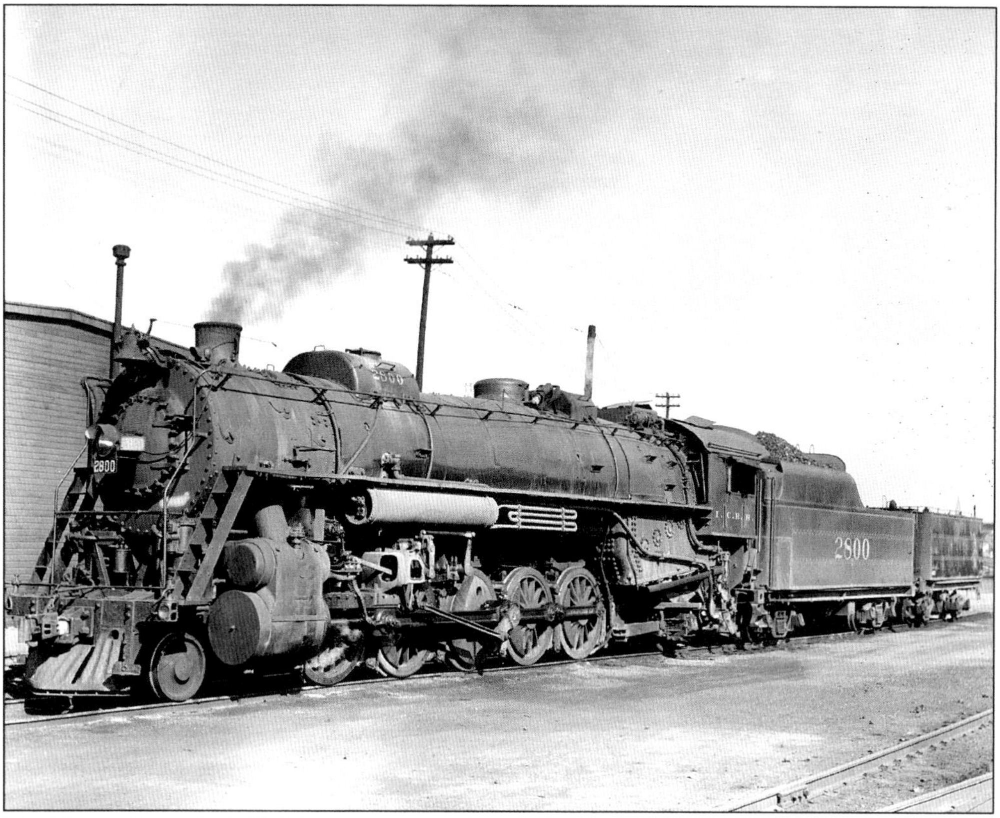

The Illinois Central's 2-10-2 locomotive number 2800 rests up next to the Dubuque roundhouse.

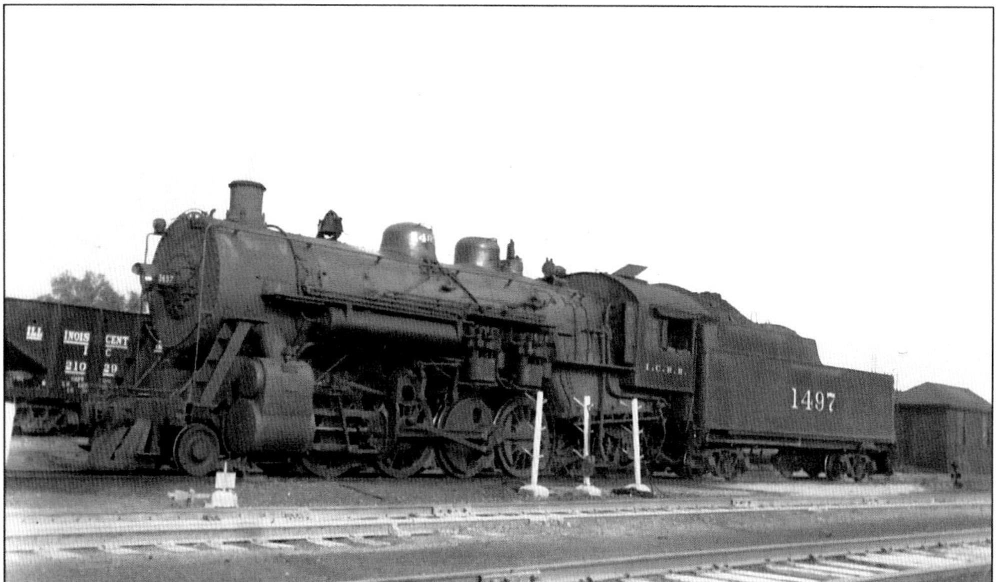

The Illinois Central continued using steam engines, such as this one, to haul freight well into the 1950s.

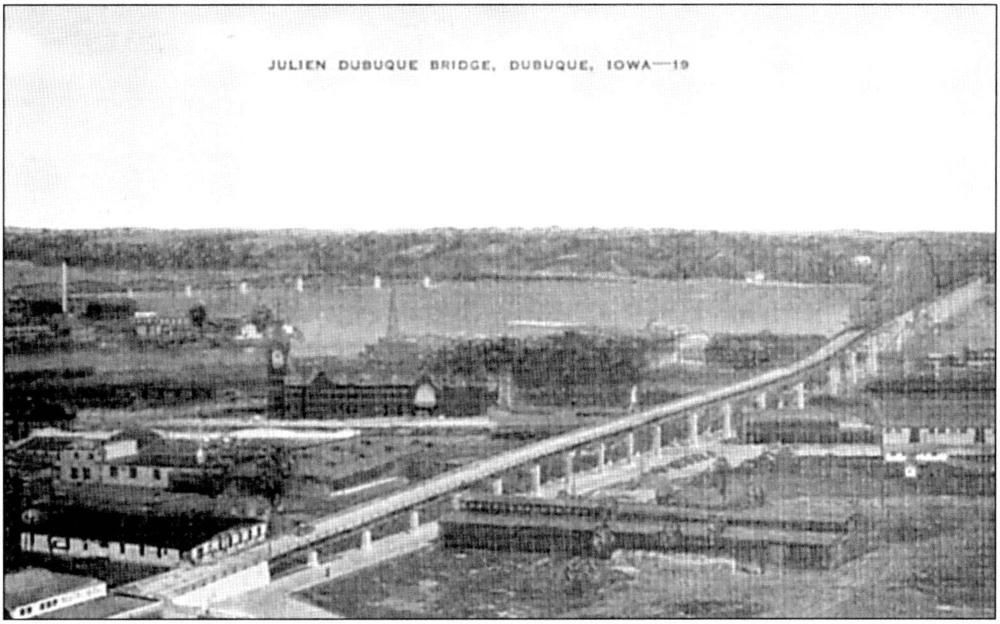

While the Illinois Central depot once dominated the landscape on Dubuque's south end, the Julien Dubuque Bridge overwhelmed the area in 1944.

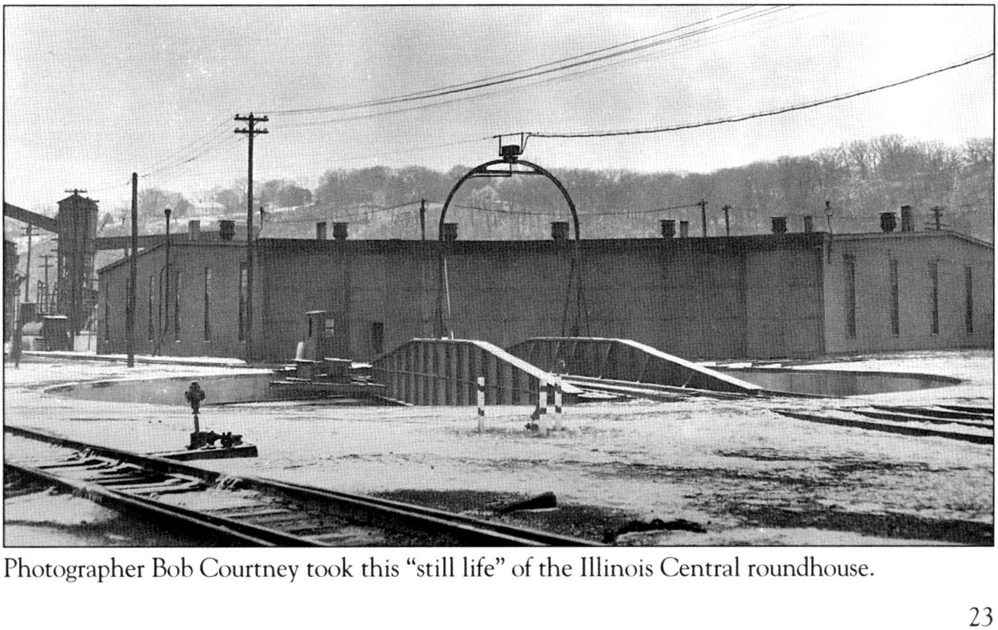

Photographer Bob Courtney took this "still life" of the Illinois Central roundhouse.

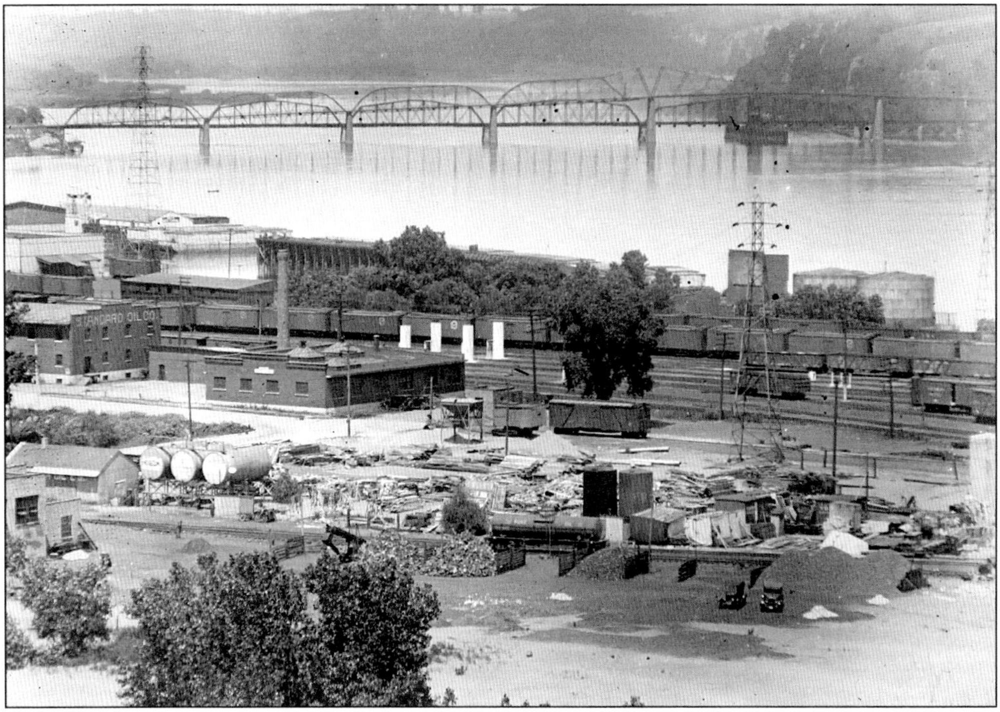

This photograph, taken just north of the Illinois Central roundhouse and yards, with a "cut" of at least 12 refrigerator cars, a few gondolas, and boxcars, was taken sometime in the late 1920s.

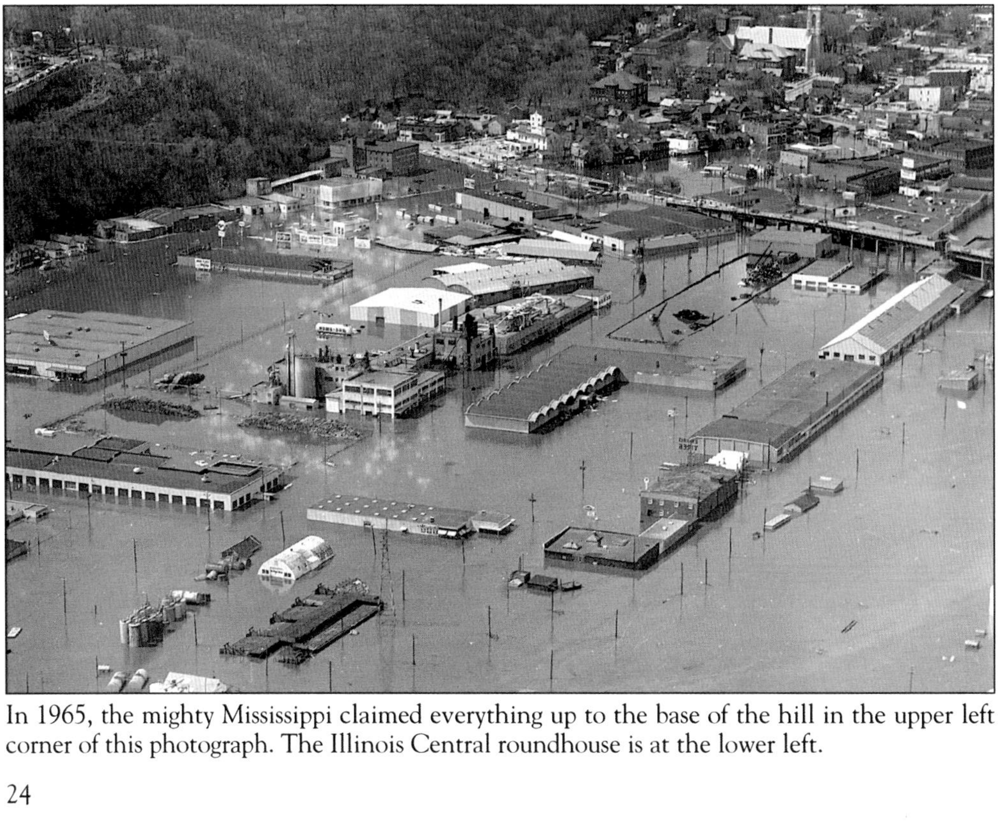

In 1965, the mighty Mississippi claimed everything up to the base of the hill in the upper left corner of this photograph. The Illinois Central roundhouse is at the lower left.

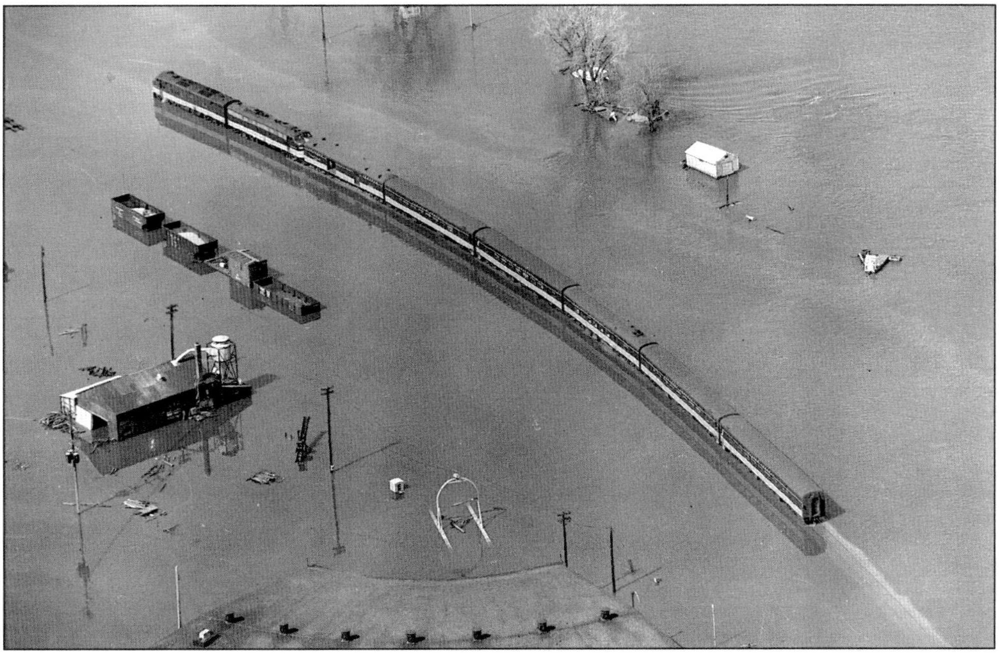

In this image, the "Land of Corn" creeps through the water at two to three miles per hour to keep the traction motors on the two diesels' axles from getting wet.

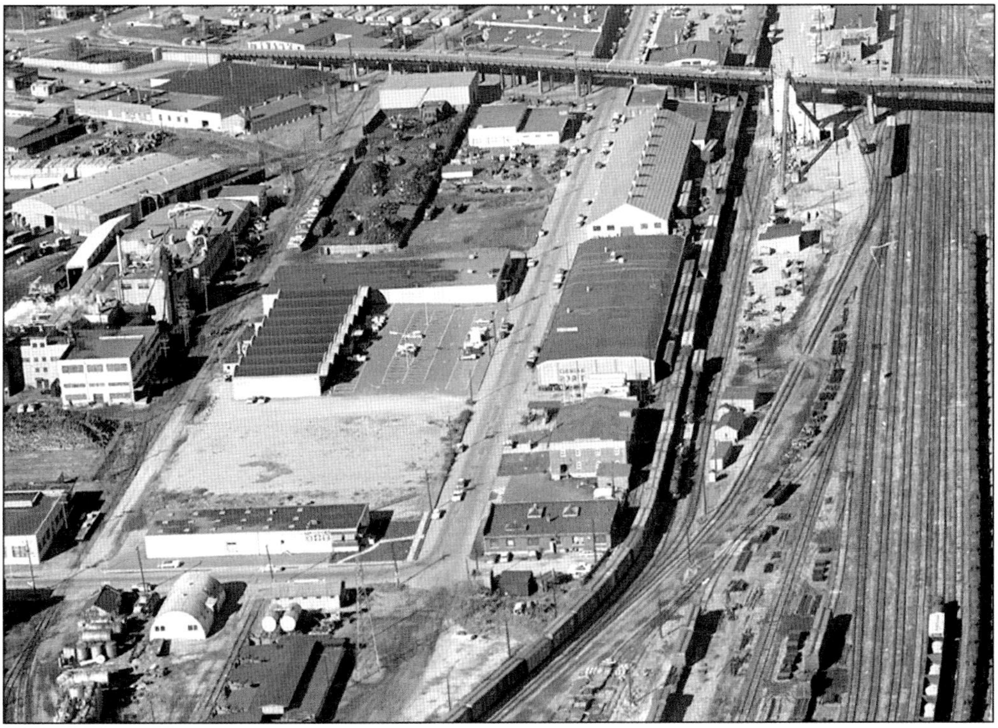

A much drier scene of the same area shows the Illinois Central yards on the right. The long string of cars extending under the bridge at the top is a Milwaukee freight train.

Amtrak's "Blackhawk" served Dubuque using the Illinois Central's one-story depot, built in 1944, and its tracks, until it was discontinued.

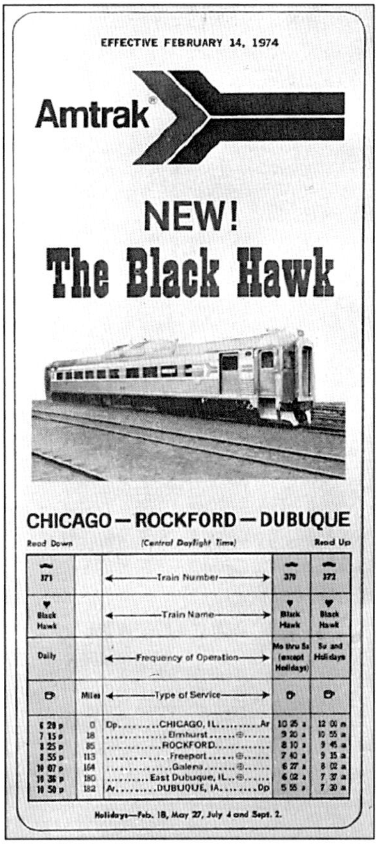

EFFECTIVE FEBRUARY 14, 1974

Amtrak®

NEW!

The Black Hawk

CHICAGO — ROCKFORD — DUBUQUE

Read Down (Central Daylight Time) Read Up

371		←Train Number→	370	372
♥ Black Hawk		←Train Name→	♥ Black Hawk	♥ Black Hawk
Daily		←Frequency of Operation→	Mo thru Sa (except Holidays)	Su and Holidays
	Miles	←Type of Service→		
6 20 p	0	Dp .... CHICAGO, IL .... Ar	10 25 a	12 00 n
7 15 p	18	.... Elmhurst ...... ⊕	9 20 a	10 55 a
8 25 p	85	.... ROCKFORD	8 10 a	9 45 a
8 55 p	113	.... Freeport ...... ⊕	7 40 a	9 15 a
10 07 p	164	.... Galena ...... ⊕	6 27 a	8 02 a
10 36 p	180	.... East Dubuque, IL .. ⊕	6 02 a	7 37 a
10 50 p	182	Ar .... DUBUQUE, IA .... Dp	5 55 a	7 30 a

Holidays—Feb. 18, May 27, July 4 and Sept. 2.

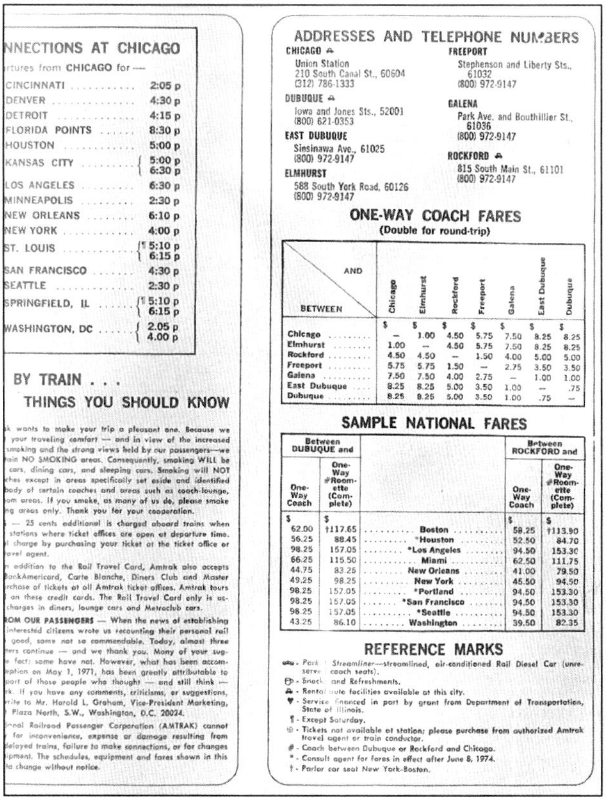

NNECTIONS AT CHICAGO

rtures from CHICAGO for —

CINCINNATI	2:05 p
DENVER	4:30 p
DETROIT	4:15 p
FLORIDA POINTS	8:30 p
HOUSTON	5:00 p
KANSAS CITY	5:00 p 6:30 p
LOS ANGELES	6:30 p
MINNEAPOLIS	2:30 p
NEW ORLEANS	6:10 p
NEW YORK	4:00 p
ST. LOUIS	¶ 5:10 p 6:15 p
SAN FRANCISCO	4:30 p
SEATTLE	2:30 p
SPRINGFIELD, IL	¶ 5:10 p 6:15 p
WASHINGTON, DC	2.05 p 4.00 p

BY TRAIN . . .

THINGS YOU SHOULD KNOW

k wants to make your trip a pleasant one. Because we your traveling comfort — and in view of the increased smoking and the strong views held by our passengers—we tain NO SMOKING areas. Consequently, smoking WILL be cars, dining cars, and sleeping cars. Smoking will NOT ches except in areas specifically set aside and identified body of certain coaches and areas such as coach-lounge, om areas. If you smoke, as many of us do, please smoke ng areas only. Thank you for your cooperation.

— 25 cents additional is charged aboard trains when stations where ticket offices are open at departure time. l charge by purchasing your ticket at the ticket office or ravel agent.

n addition to the Rail Travel Card, Amtrak also accepts BankAmericard, Carte Blanche, Diners Club and Master rchase of tickets at all Amtrak ticket offices. Amtrak tours on these credit cards. The Rail Travel Card only is ac- charges in diners, lounge cars and Metroclub cars.

ROM OUR PASSENGERS — When the news of establishing interested citizens wrote us recounting their personal rail good, some not so commendable. Today, almost three ters continue — and we thank you. Many of your sug- e fact; some have not. However, what has been accom- eption on May 1, 1971, has been greatly attributable to port of those people who thought — and still think — rk. If you have any comments, criticisms, or suggestions, rite to Mr. Harold L. Graham, Vice-President Marketing, Plaza North, S.W., Washington, D.C. 20024.

ional Railroad Passenger Corporation (AMTRAK) cannot for inconvenience, expense or damage resulting from delayed trains, failure to make connections, or for changes ipment. The schedules, equipment and fares shown in this to change without notice.

ADDRESSES AND TELEPHONE NUMBERS

CHICAGO
Union Station
210 South Canal St., 60604
(312) 786-1333

DUBUQUE
Iowa and Jones Sts., 52001
(800) 621-0353

EAST DUBUQUE
Sinsinawa Ave., 61025
(800) 972-9147

ELMHURST
588 South York Road, 60126
(800) 972-9147

FREEPORT
Stephenson and Liberty Sts., 61032
(800) 972-9147

GALENA
Park Ave. and Bouthillier St., 61036
(800) 972-9147

ROCKFORD
815 South Main St., 61101
(800) 972-9147

ONE-WAY COACH FARES
(Double for round-trip)

BETWEEN \ AND	Chicago	Elmhurst	Rockford	Freeport	Galena	East Dubuque	Dubuque
	$	$	$	$	$	$	$
Chicago	—	1.00	4.50	5.75	7.50	8.25	8.25
Elmhurst	1.00	—	4.50	5.75	7.50	8.25	8.25
Rockford	4.50	4.50	—	1.50	4.00	5.00	5.00
Freeport	5.75	5.75	1.50	—	2.75	3.50	3.50
Galena	7.50	7.50	4.00	2.75	—	1.00	1.00
East Dubuque	8.25	8.25	5.00	3.50	1.00	—	.75
Dubuque	8.25	8.25	5.00	3.50	1.00	.75	—

SAMPLE NATIONAL FARES

Between DUBUQUE and			Between ROCKFORD and	
One-Way Coach	One-Way #Roomette (Complete)		One-Way Coach	One-Way #Roomette (Complete)
$	$		$	$
62.00	†117.65	Boston	58.25	†113.90
56.25	88.45	*Houston	52.50	84.70
98.25	157.05	*Los Angeles	94.50	153.30
66.25	115.50	Miami	62.50	111.75
44.75	83.25	New Orleans	41.00	79.50
49.25	98.25	New York	45.50	94.50
98.25	157.05	*Portland	94.50	153.30
98.25	157.05	*San Francisco	94.50	153.30
98.25	157.05	*Seattle	94.50	153.30
43.25	86.10	Washington	39.50	82.35

REFERENCE MARKS

- Park Streamliner—streamlined, air-conditioned Rail Diesel Car (unreserved coach seats).
- Snack and Refreshments.
- Rental auto facilities available at this city.
- ♥ - Service financed in part by grant from Department of Transportation, State of Illinois.
- ¶ - Except Saturday.
- ⊕ - Tickets not available at station; please purchase from authorized Amtrak travel agent or train conductor.
- # - Coach between Dubuque or Rockford and Chicago.
- * - Consult agent for fares in effect after June 8, 1974.
- † - Parlor car seat New York-Boston.

Amtrak's fares were quite reasonable in 1974, when compared to today's rates. The train left Dubuque in the morning and returned the same night

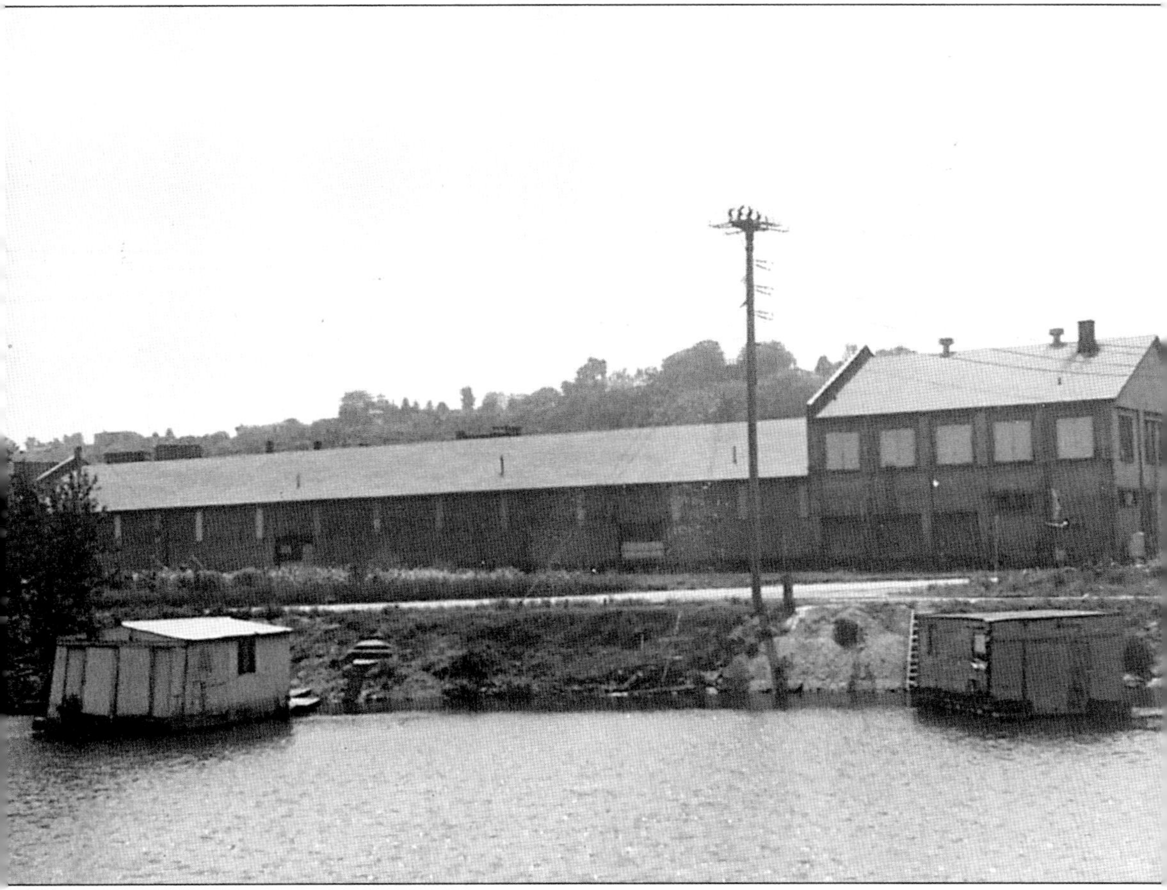

This photograph shows the Illinois Central Railroad's freight house before it was razed to make way for Dubuque's new waterfront and railroad tracks.

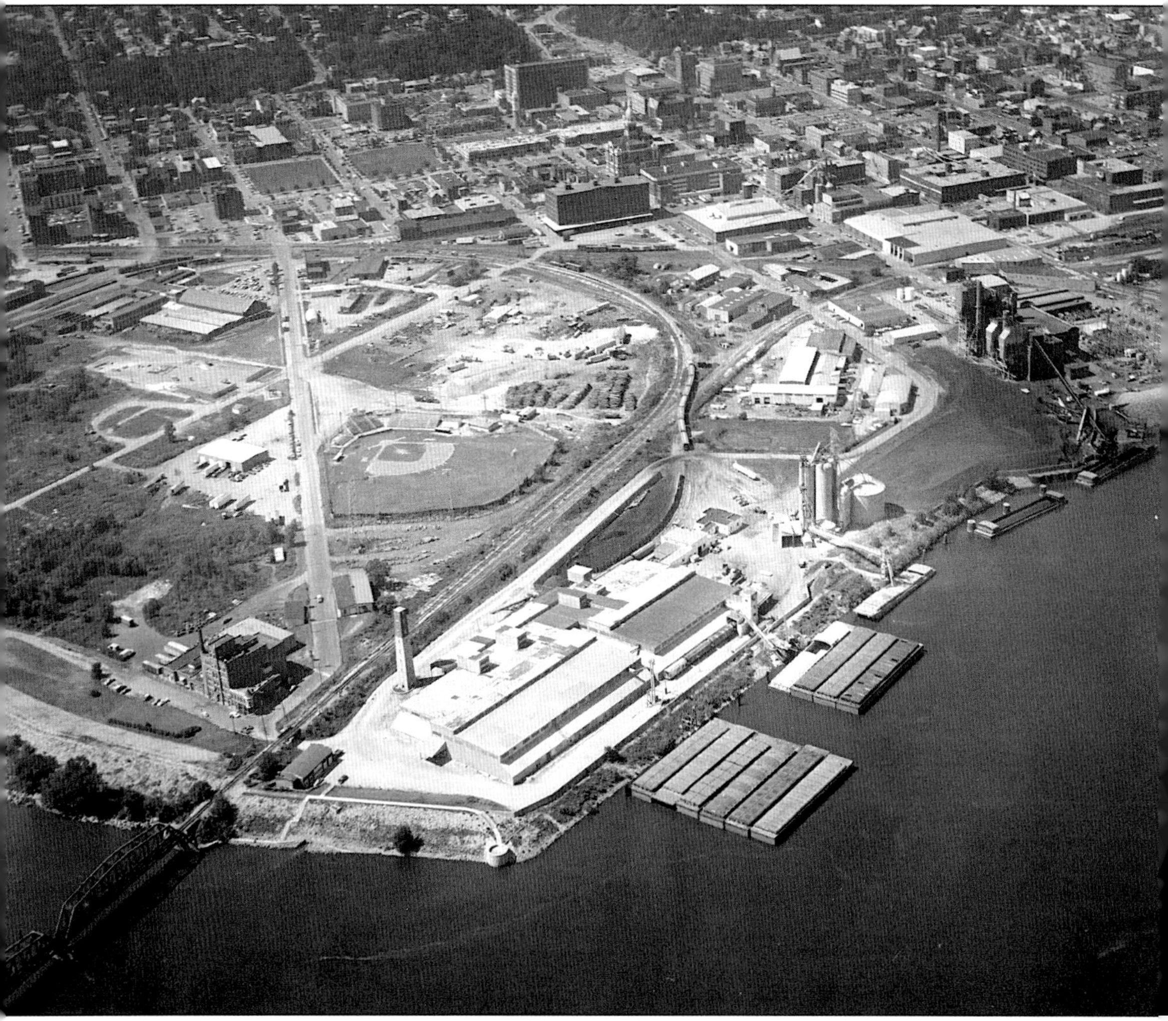

A 1978 panoramic photograph shows the Illinois Central Railroad Bridge at lower left. The shot tower, across Fourth Street from the Dubuque Star Brewery, points to the John Petrakis Ballpark.

Two

THE MILWAUKEE ROAD

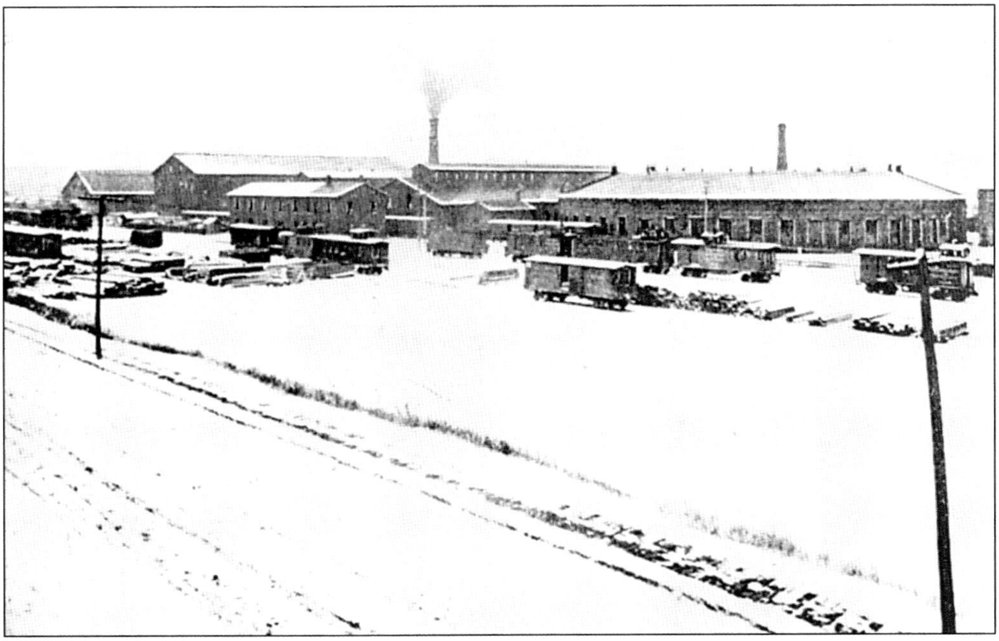

Snow covers the ground in this photo of the Chicago, Milwaukee & St. Paul Railway yards, roundhouse, and shops in Dubuque.

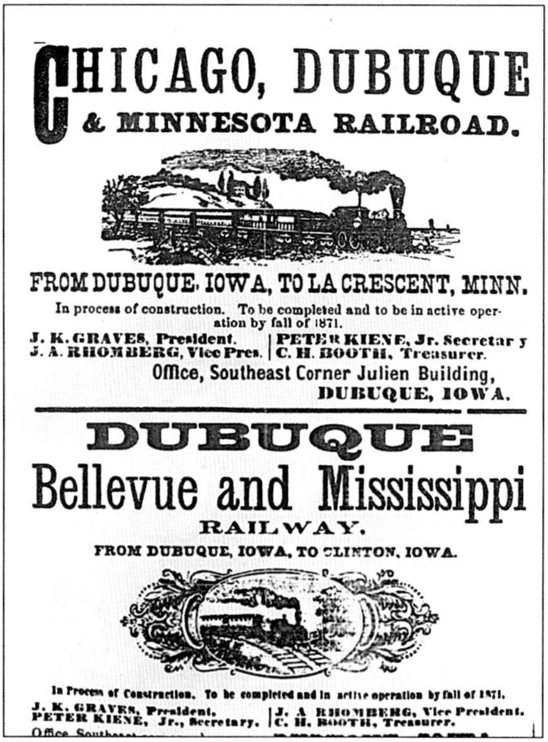

These two railroads consolidated to become the Chicago, Clinton, Dubuque and Minnesota Railroad, headed by James F. Joy. In 1880, the Milwaukee acquired the "Rail Road," which headquartered in Dubuque.

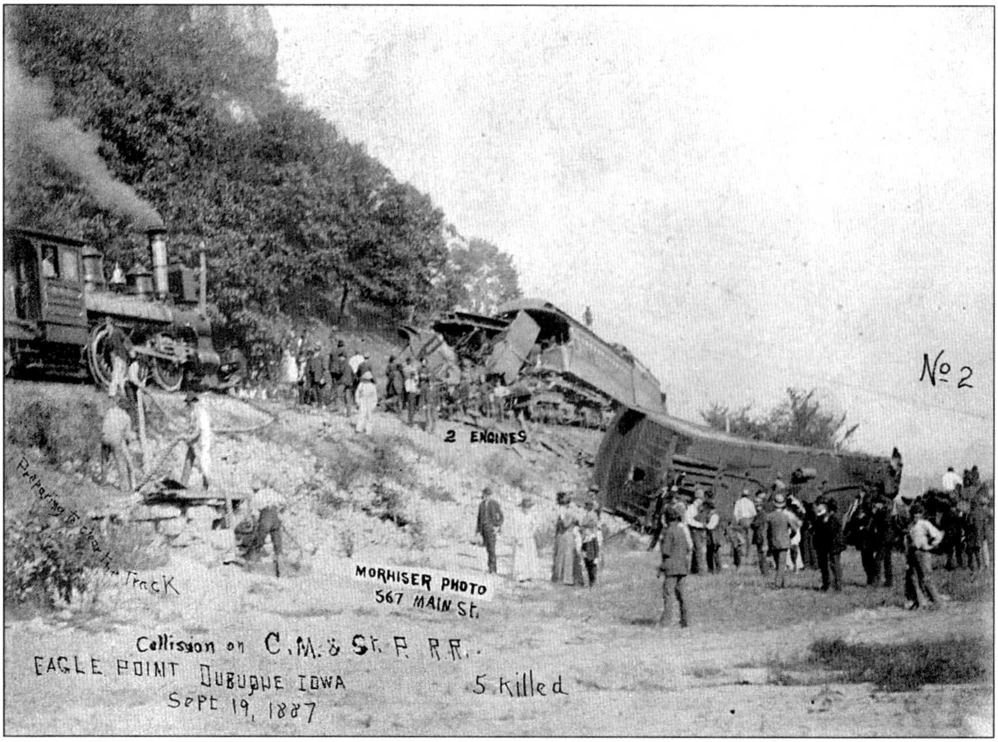

On September 19, 1887, two Chicago, Milwaukee & St. Paul Railway trains collided head-on, north of Dubuque beneath Eagle Point Bluff. Five people were killed.

In 1893, the Milwaukee Road operated in seven states and traversed over 6,100 miles of tracks.

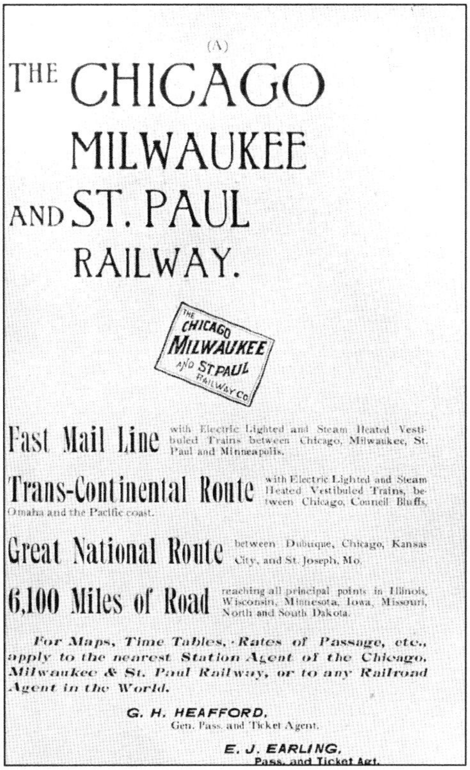
(A)

THE CHICAGO MILWAUKEE AND ST. PAUL RAILWAY.

Fast Mail Line with Electric Lighted and Steam Heated Vestibuled Trains between Chicago, Milwaukee, St. Paul and Minneapolis.

Trans-Continental Route with Electric Lighted and Steam Heated Vestibuled Trains, between Chicago, Council Bluffs, Omaha and the Pacific coast.

Great National Route between Dubuque, Chicago, Kansas City, and St. Joseph, Mo.

6,100 Miles of Road reaching all principal points in Illinois, Wisconsin, Minnesota, Iowa, Missouri, North and South Dakota.

For Maps, Time Tables, Rates of Passage, etc., apply to the nearest Station Agent of the Chicago, Milwaukee & St. Paul Railway, or to any Railroad Agent in the World.

G. H. HEAFFORD,
Gen. Pass. and Ticket Agent.

E. J. EARLING,
Pass. and Ticket Agt.

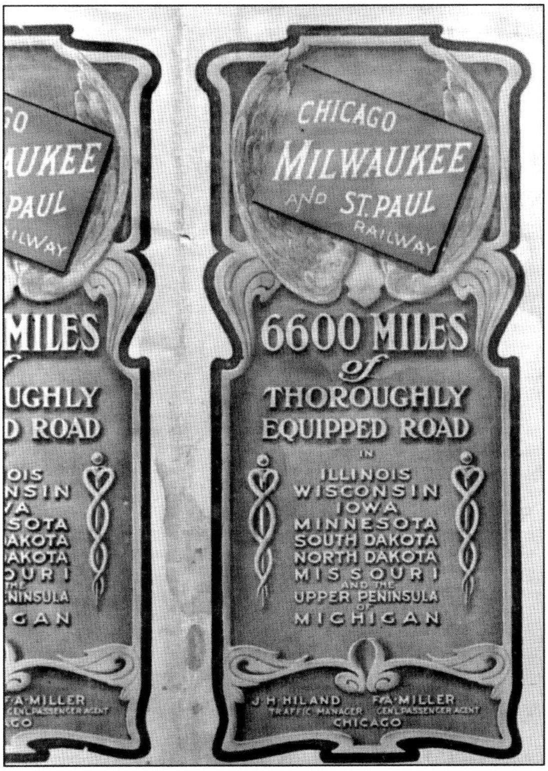

The 1902 time tables for the Chicago, Milwaukee & St. Paul Railway are shown here.

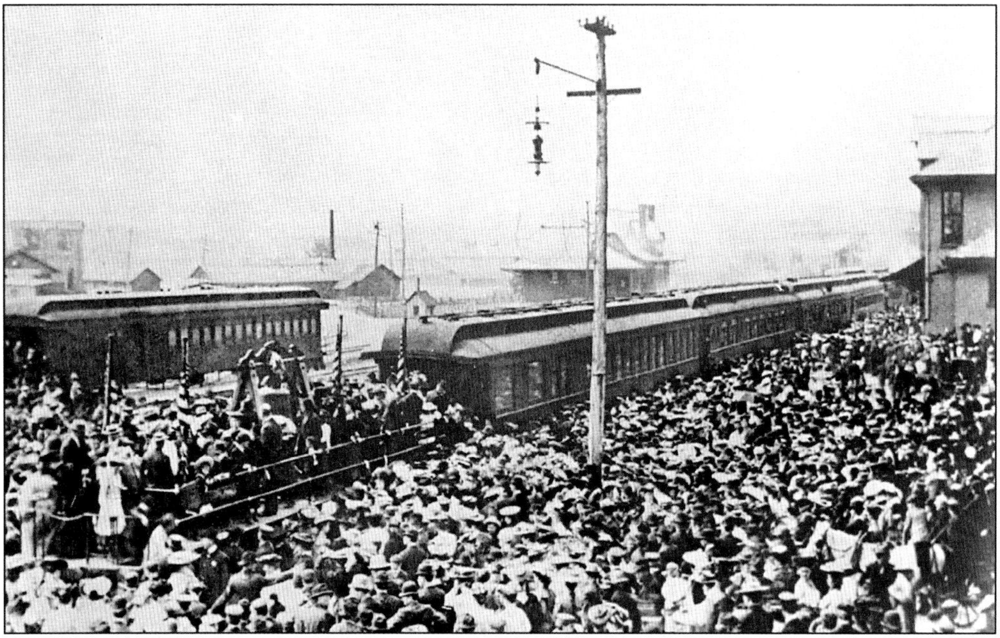

This is a 1904 photograph of the Liberty Bell as it stopped in Dubuque at the Milwaukee Road station en route to the St. Louis World's Fair.

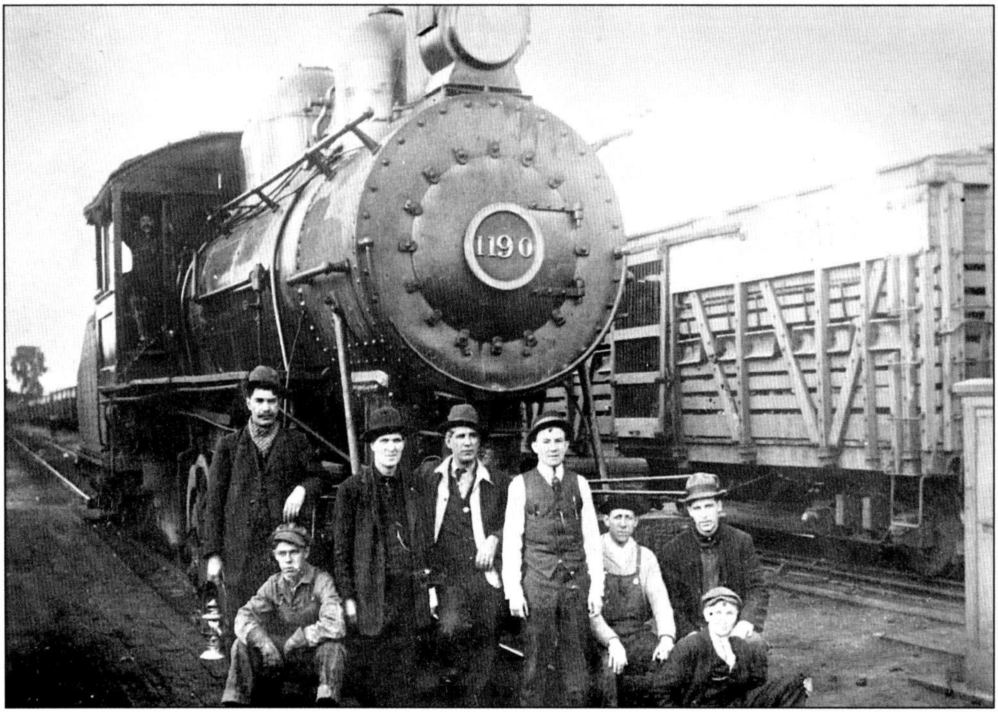

Switch engine number 1190 poses with her crew and some other employees in the Milwaukee Road yards around 1918.

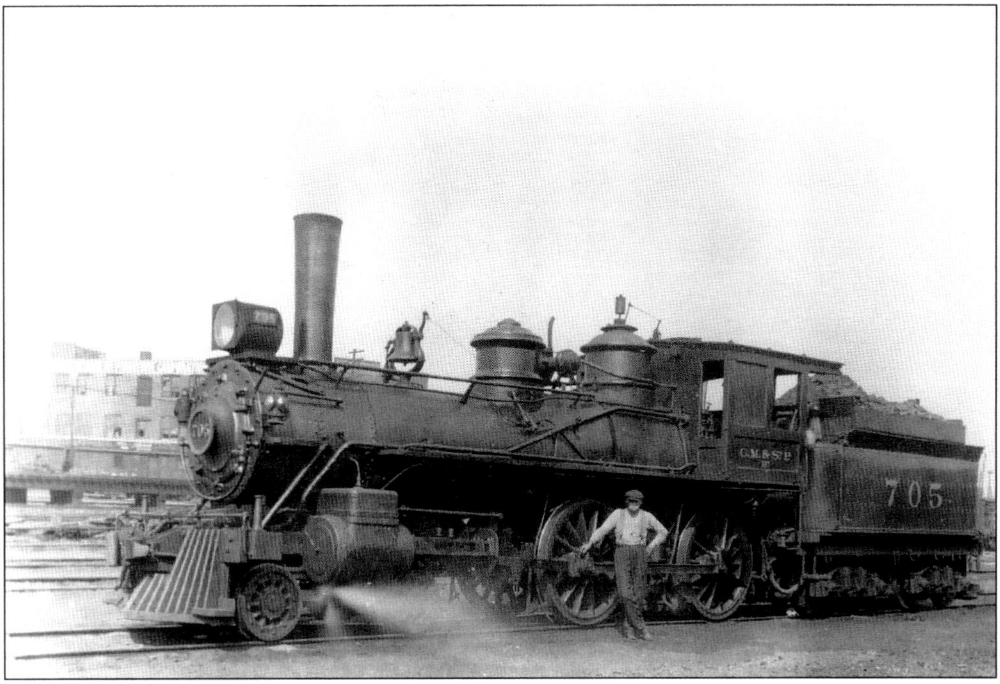

In this 1915 photograph, number 705's fireman casually poses next to the drivers while the engineer looks out to see what is going on.

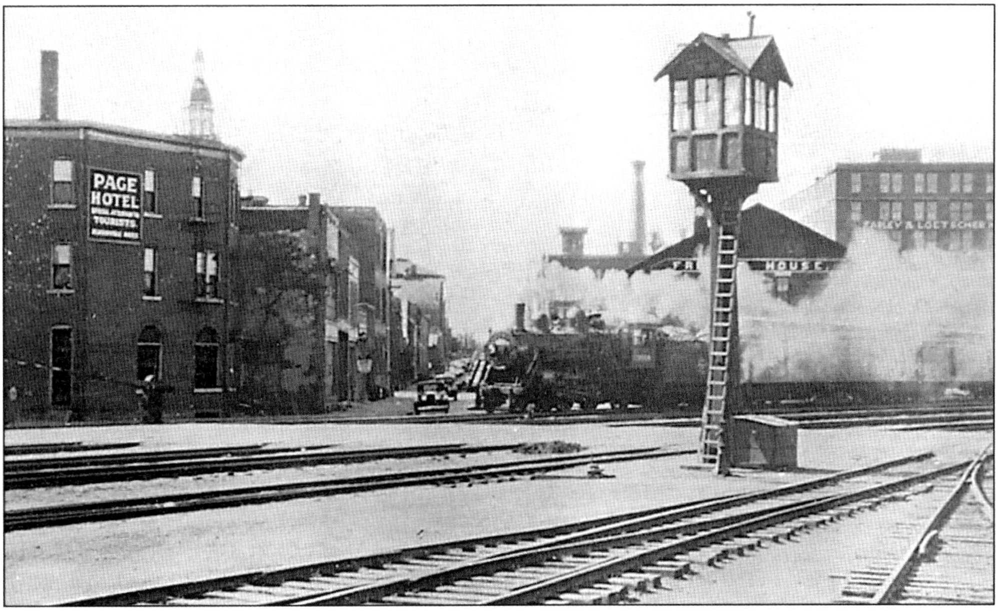

A 4-4-2 passenger engine approaches the Dubuque depot in downtown Dubuque after passing through the yards in this 1920s image.

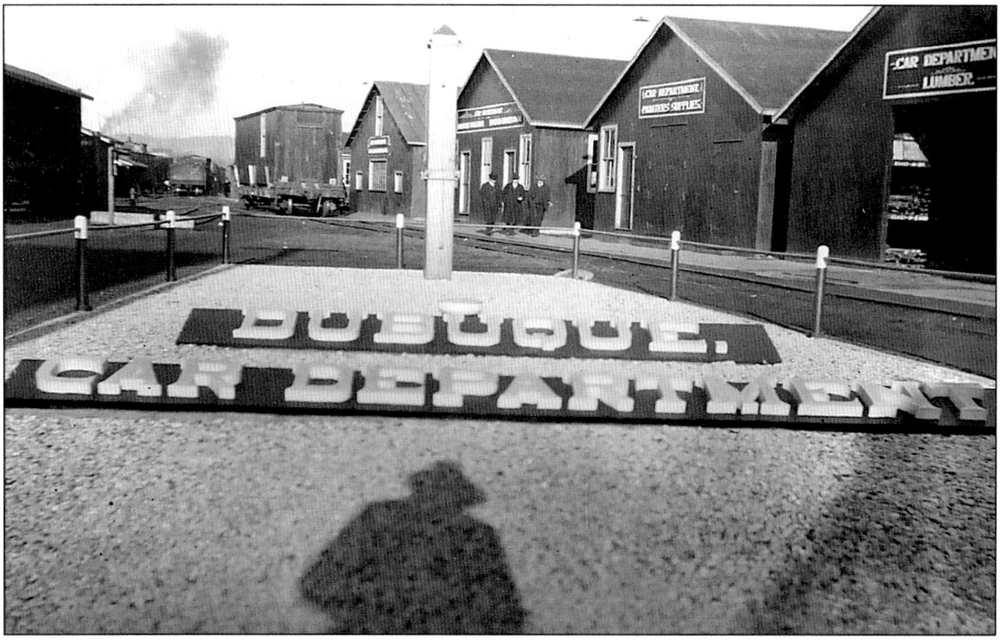

This is a view of the Dubuque Car Department stores area that provided most of the material to erect passenger cars, cabooses, and freight cars around the turn of the 20th century.

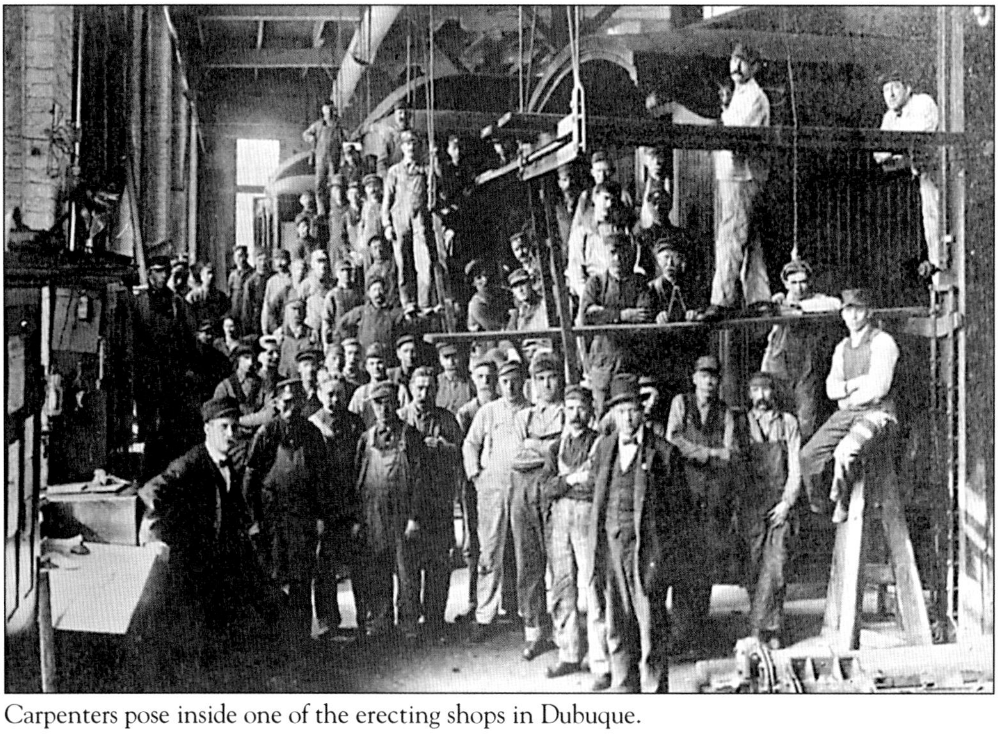

Carpenters pose inside one of the erecting shops in Dubuque.

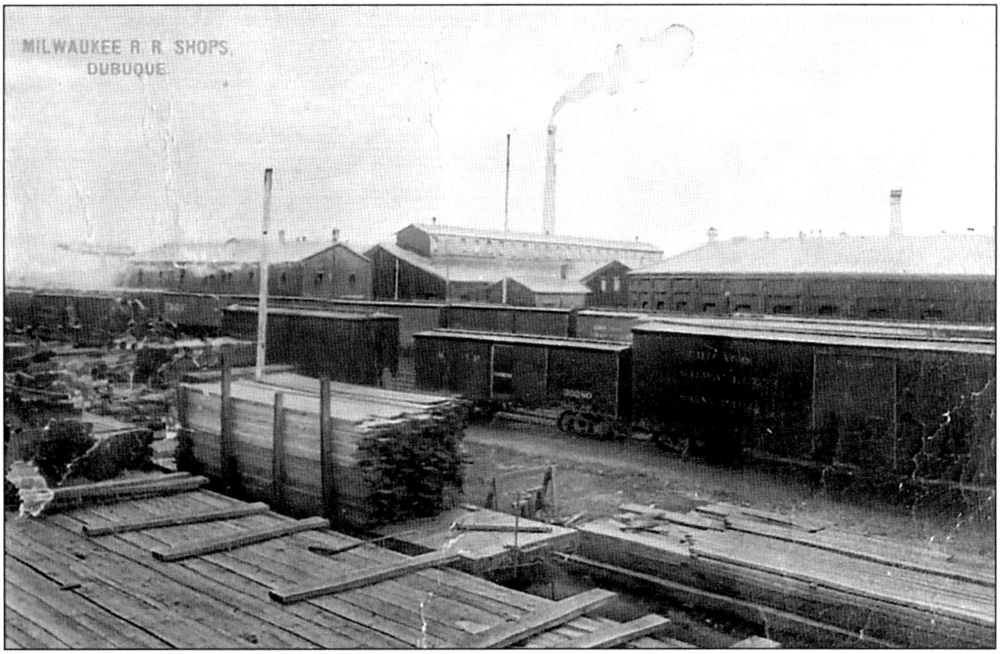

The Dubuque yards, shops, and roundhouse are pictured during the summer.

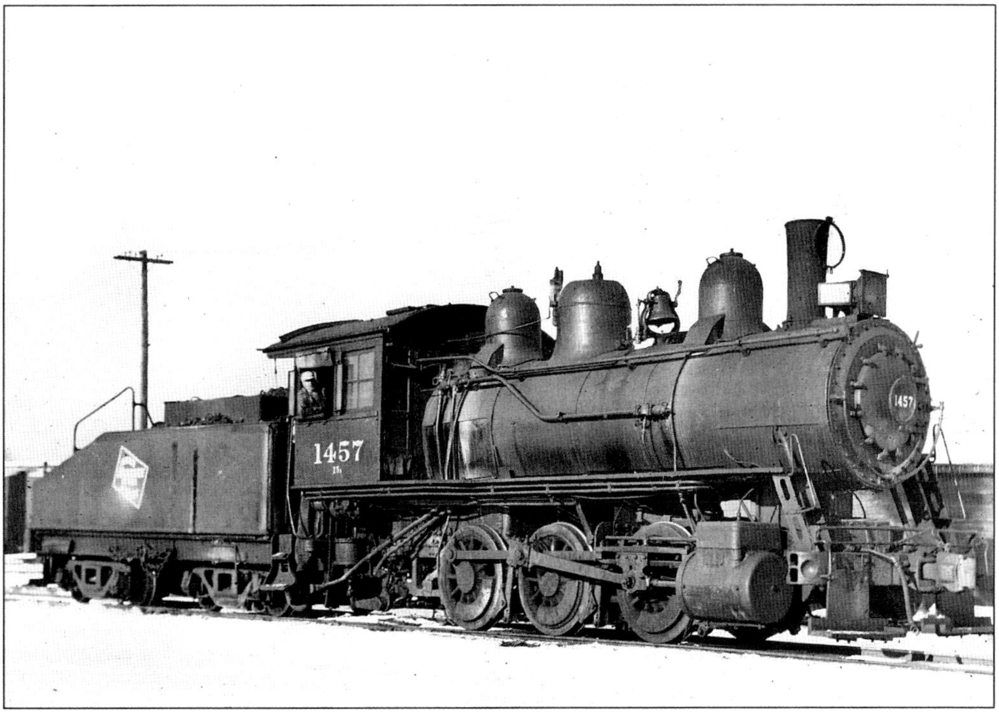

A switch engine pauses to have its portrait taken at the Milwaukee Road yards.

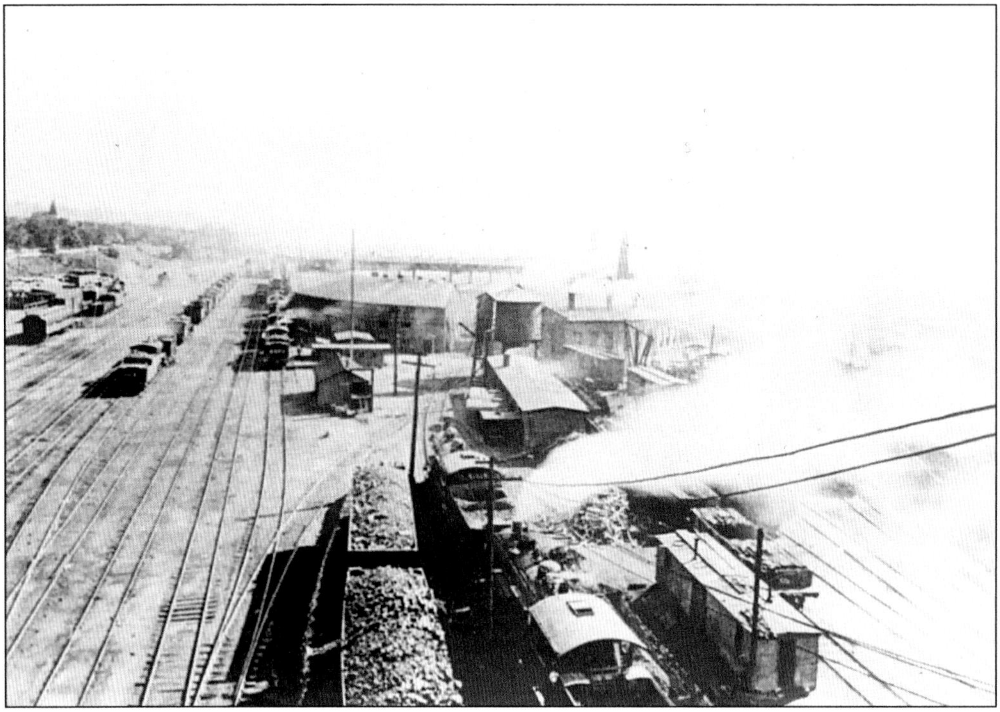

This photograph shows the Milwaukee Roads yards when steam was king.

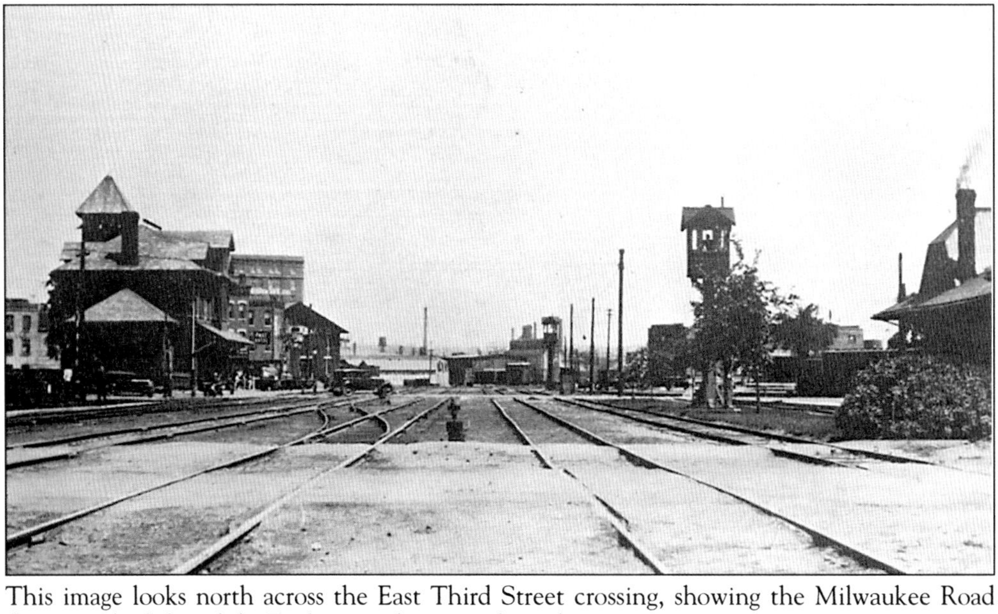

This image looks north across the East Third Street crossing, showing the Milwaukee Road depot on the left and the Burlington depot on the right.

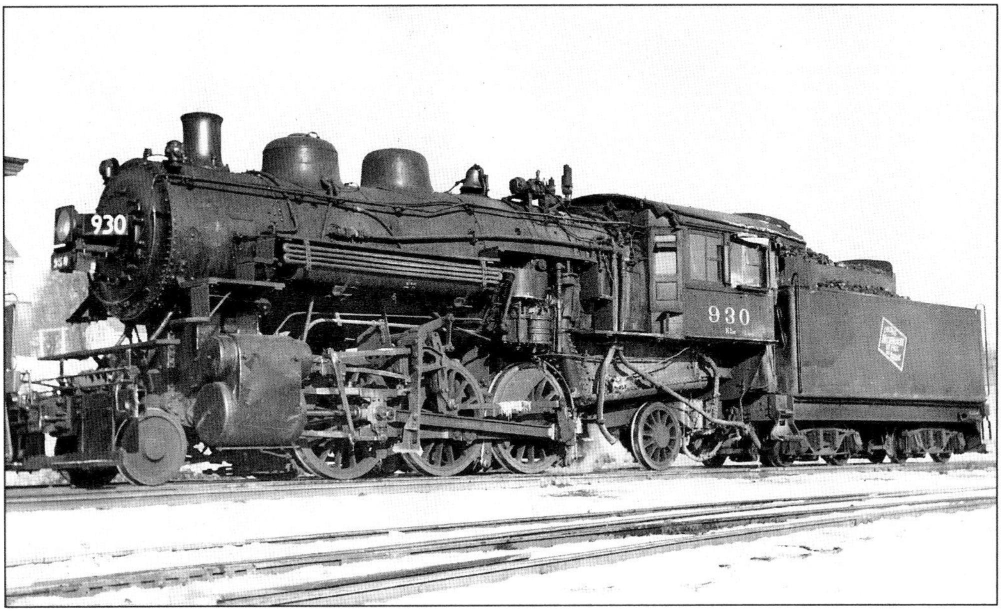

Number 930 is pictured switching cars in the Dubuque yards.

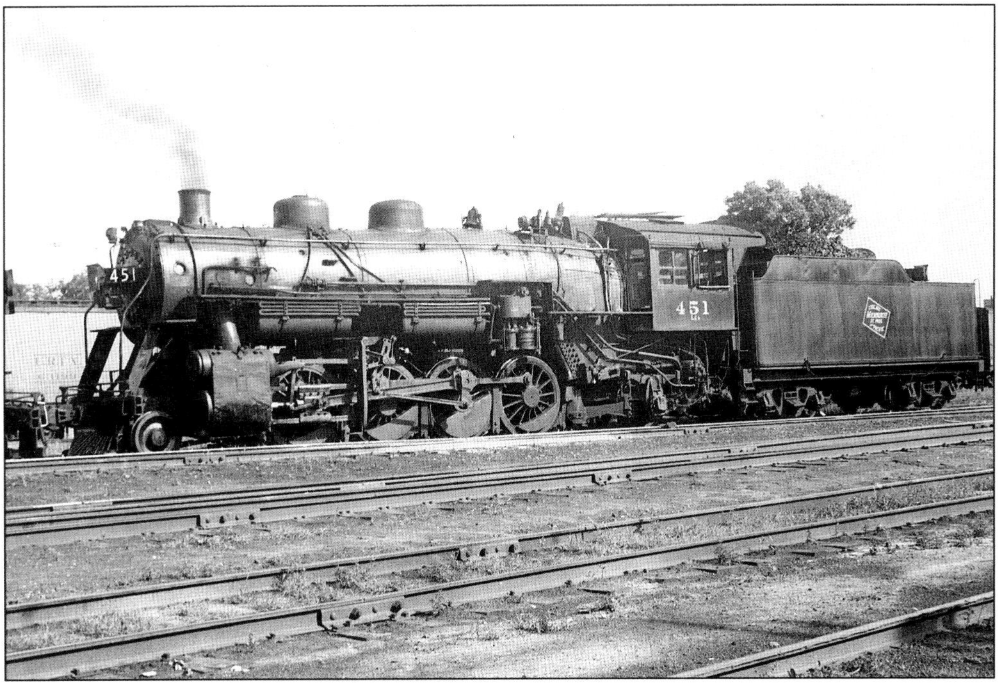

Number 452, pictured here, was built by the Baldwin Locomotive Works in 1923 and was scrapped in 1954.

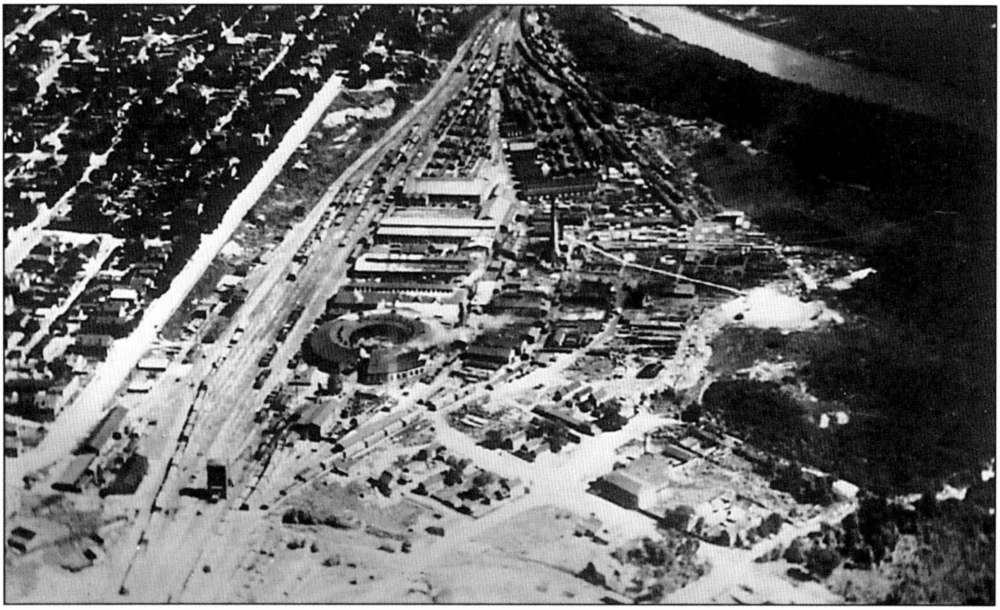

Dubuque's Milwaukee Road roundhouse, shops, and yards are pictured *c.* 1920.

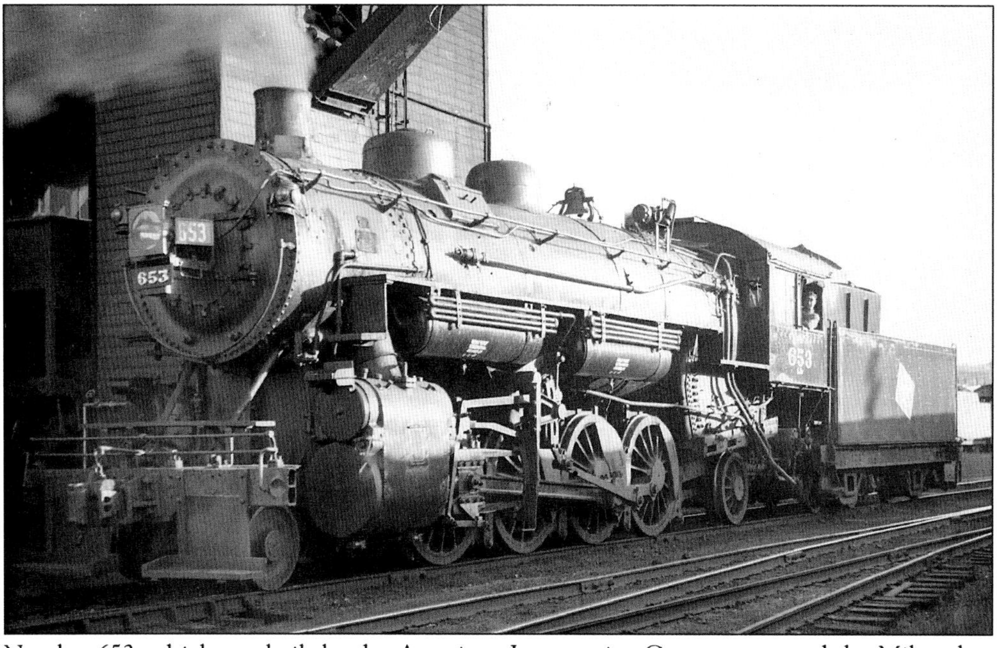

Number 653, which was built by the American Locomotive Company, served the Milwaukee Road for 42 years.

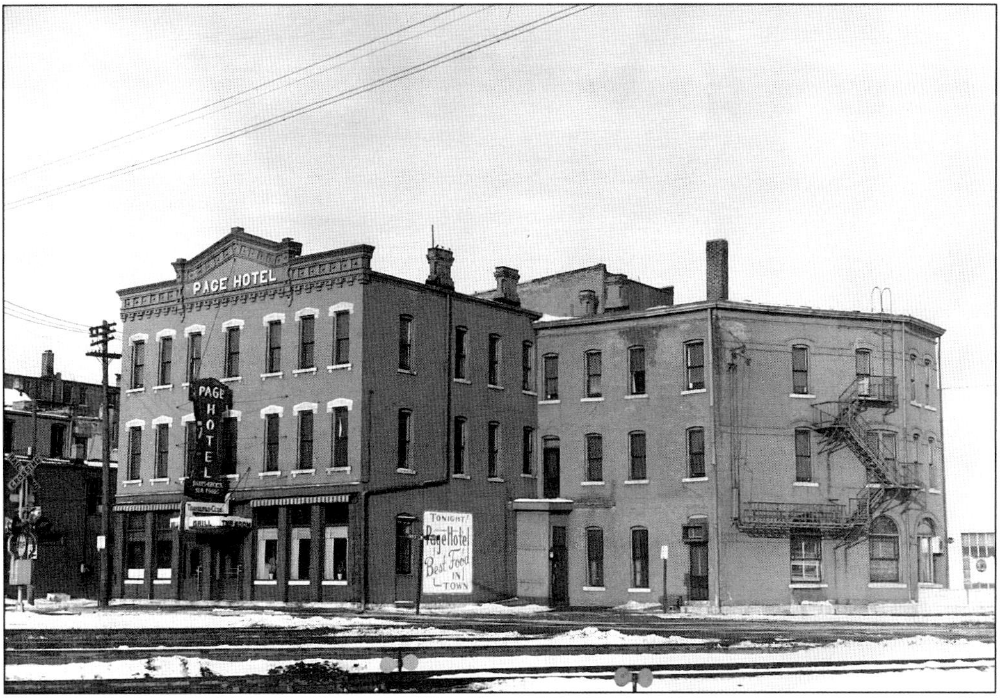

The Page Hotel's restaurant was popular with Dubuquers and rail passengers who got off the trains in Dubuque. The Milwaukee Depot was less than one block away across Fourth Street.

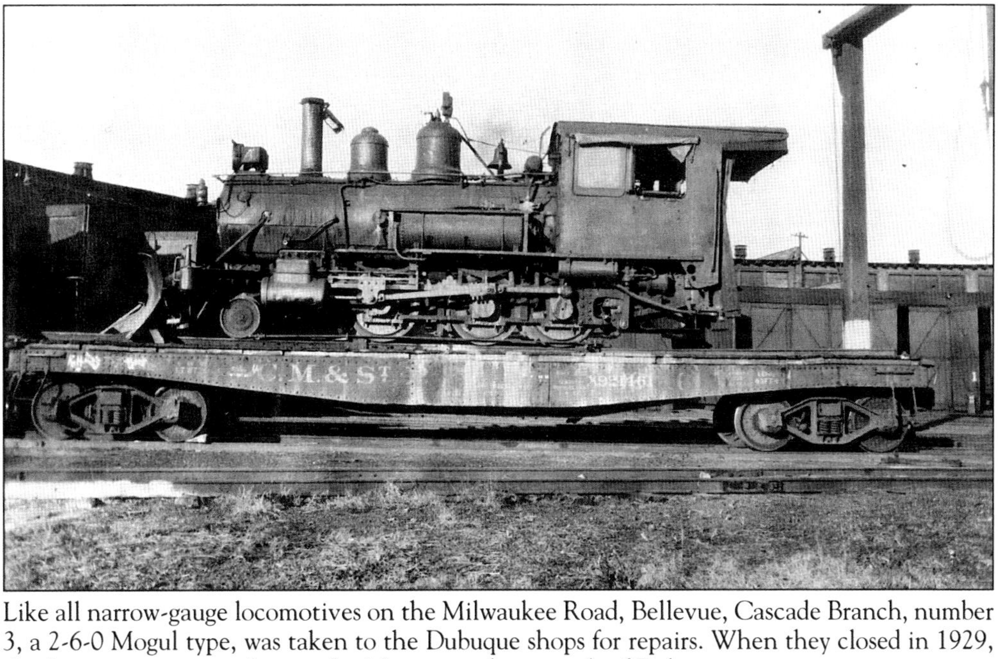

Like all narrow-gauge locomotives on the Milwaukee Road, Bellevue, Cascade Branch, number 3, a 2-6-0 Mogul type, was taken to the Dubuque shops for repairs. When they closed in 1929, the diminutives were taken to the Marquette shop, north of Dubuque.

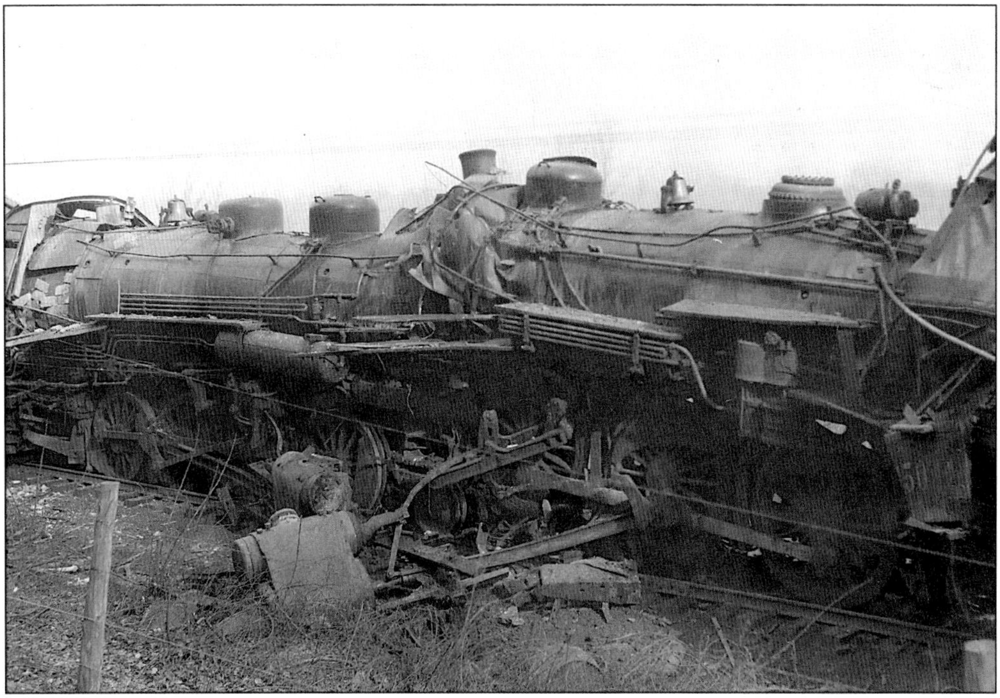

Another "cornfield meeting" between a passenger train and a freight train occurred on March 6, 1938.

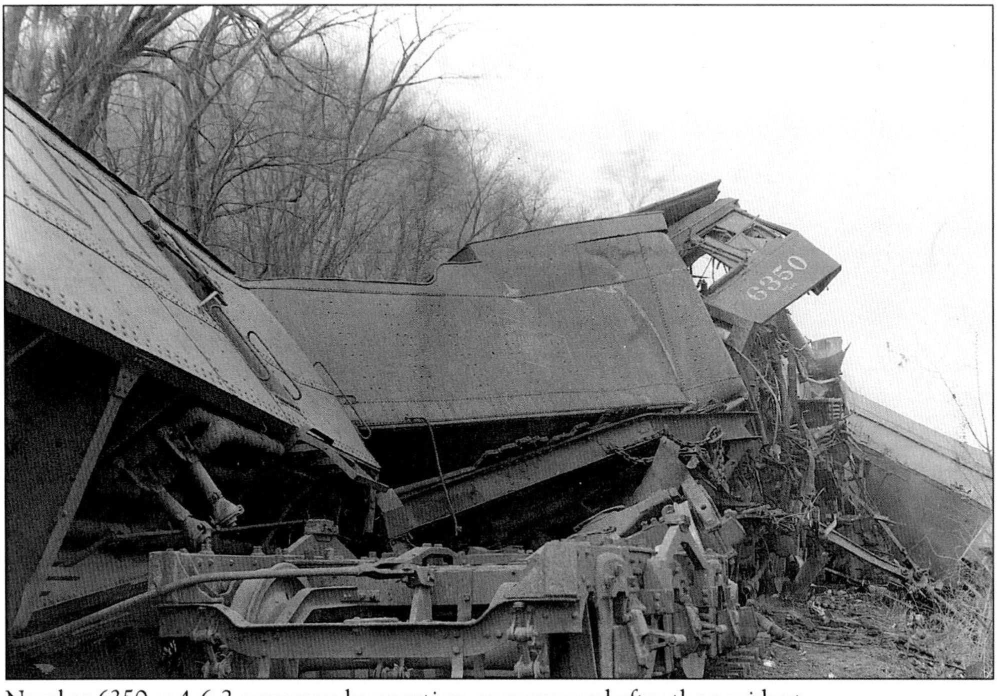

Number 6350, a 4-6-2 passenger locomotive, was scrapped after the accident.

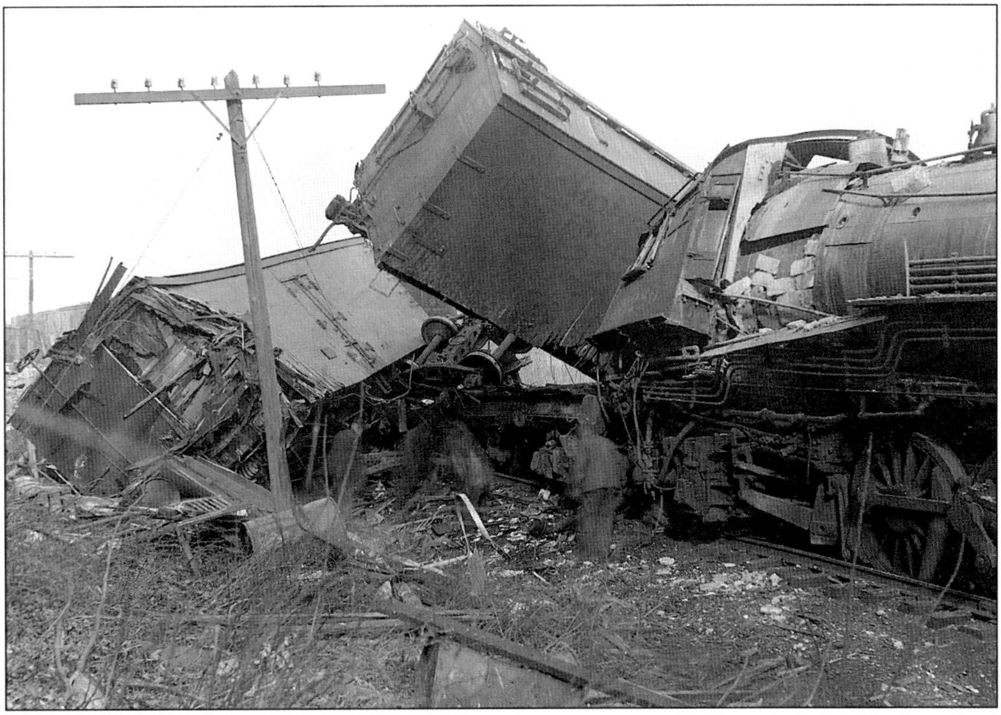

The freight locomotive involved in the accident, number 8280, a 2-8-2 Mikado wheel arrangement, was scrapped the following year.

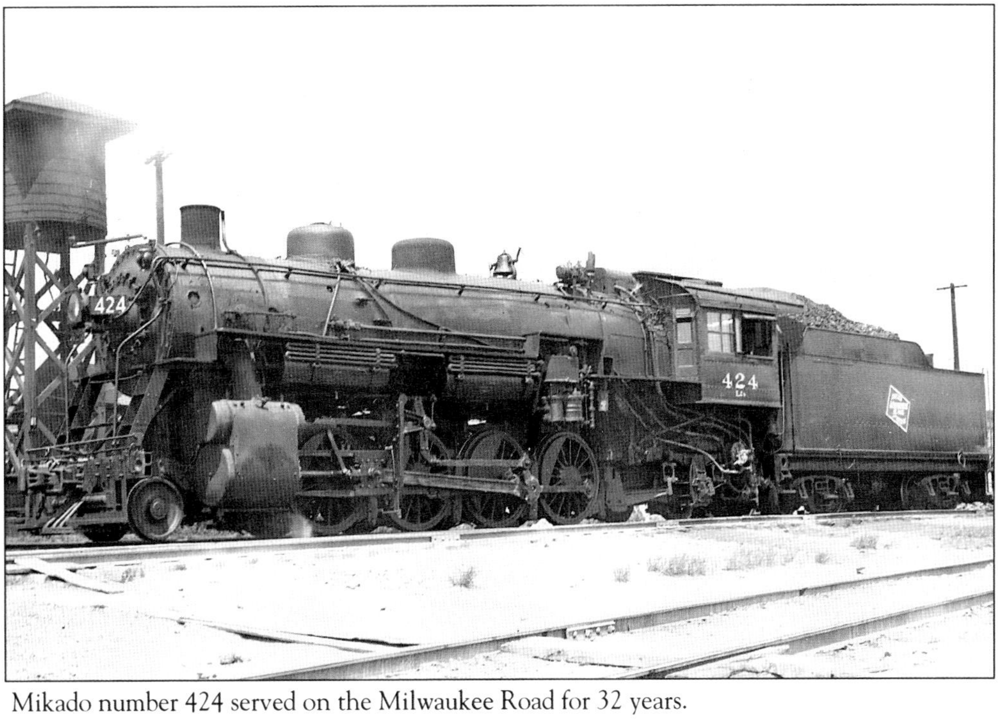

Mikado number 424 served on the Milwaukee Road for 32 years.

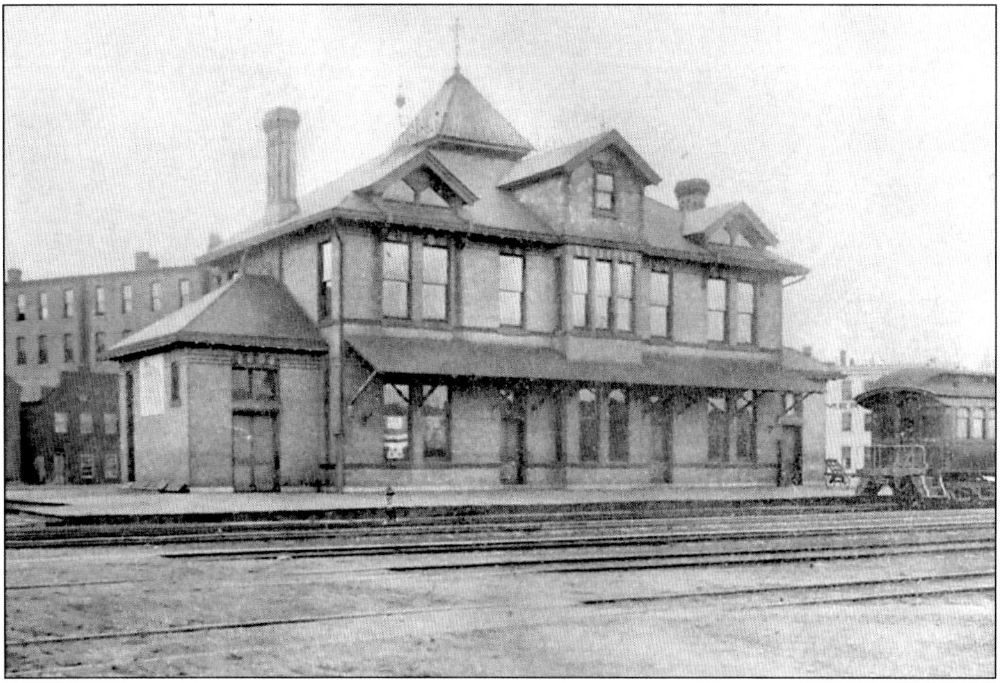

The Chicago, Dubuque and Minnesota Rail Road and the Dubuque, Bellevue and Mississippi Railway built this depot in Dubuque prior to the Chicago, Milwaukee and St. Paul Railway's acquisition of the two aforementioned companies.

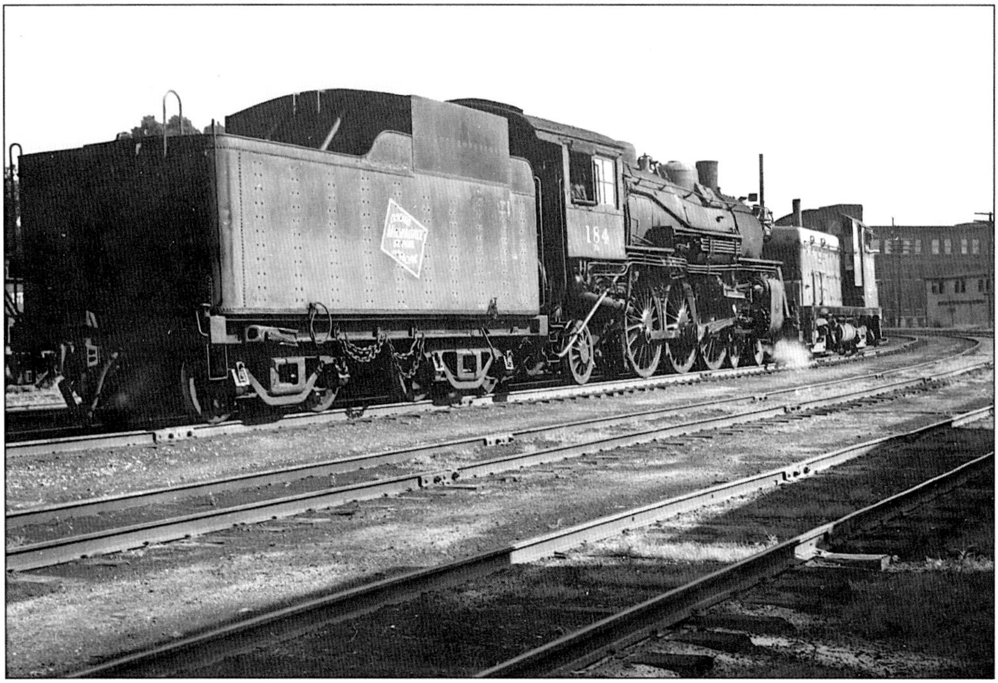

With the steam engine and the diesel switch engine so close, it makes one wonder what they were saying to each other. The diesel was painted in Hiawatha colors—orange and gray separated by a maroon stripe.

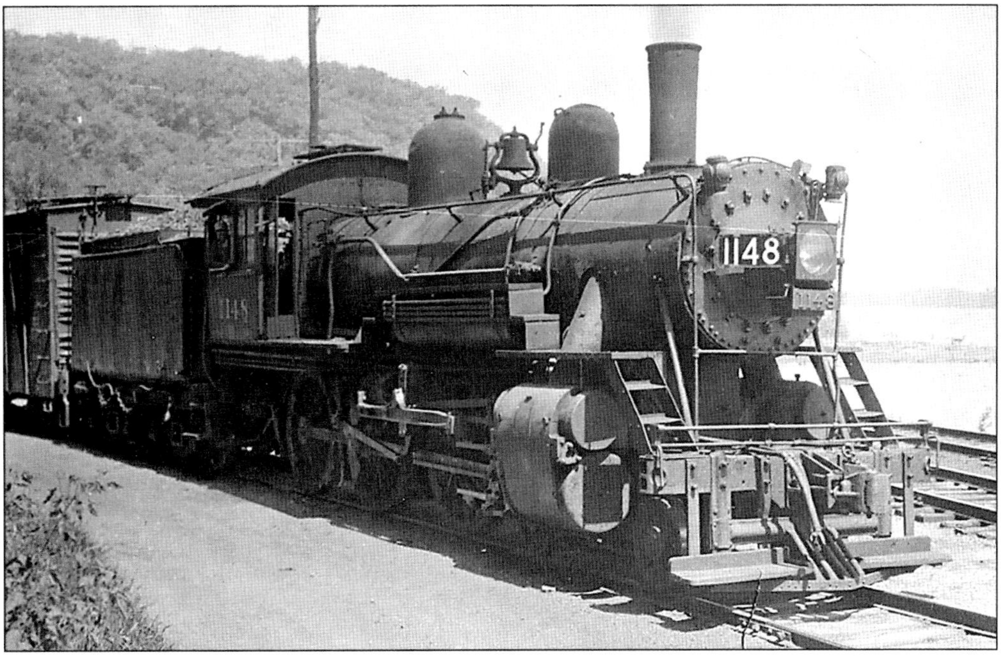

In this image from the 1930s, ten-wheeler number 1148 arrives at Waukon Junction north of Dubuque.

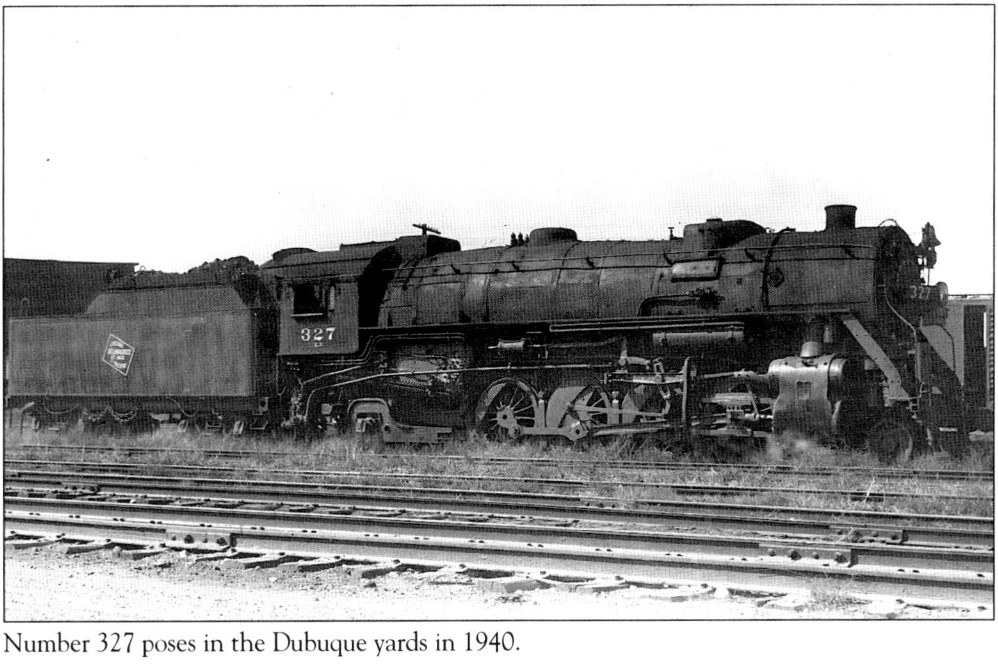

Number 327 poses in the Dubuque yards in 1940.

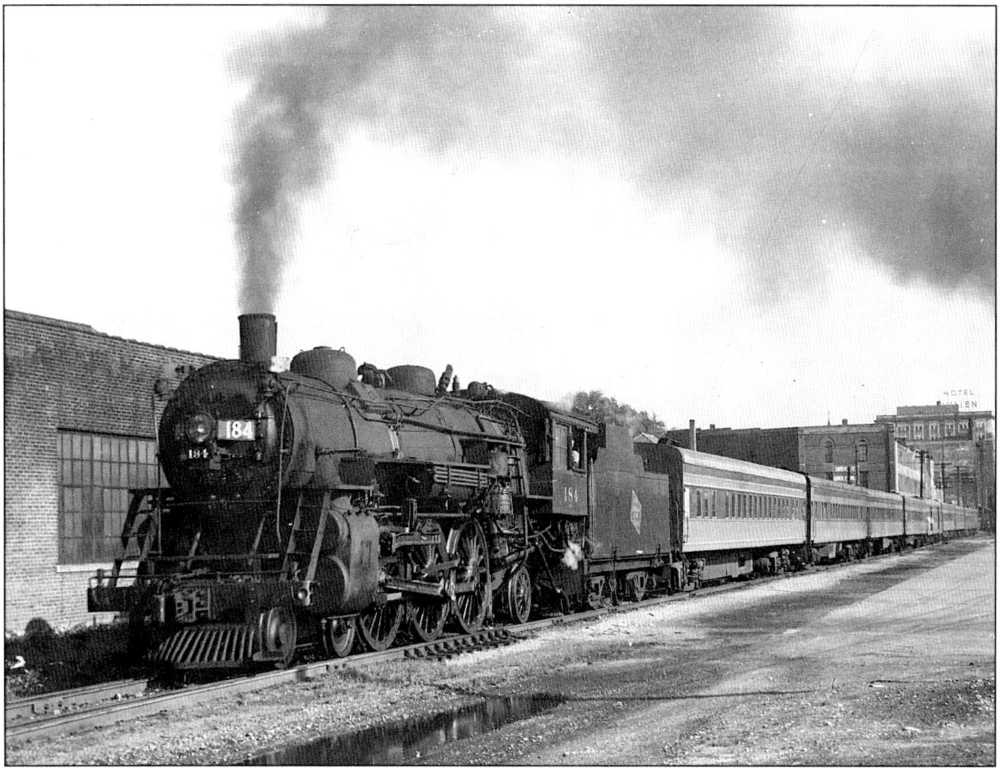

Number 184 takes a trainload of baseball fans from Dubuque to Chicago.

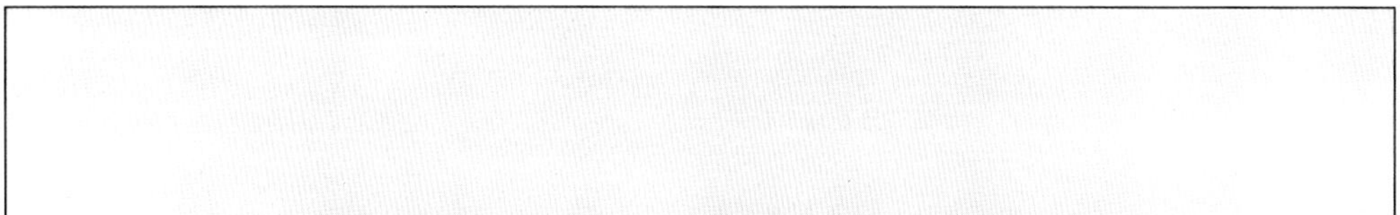

The Chicago, Milwaukee, St. Paul & Pacific Railroad's freight house in Dubuque is pictured.

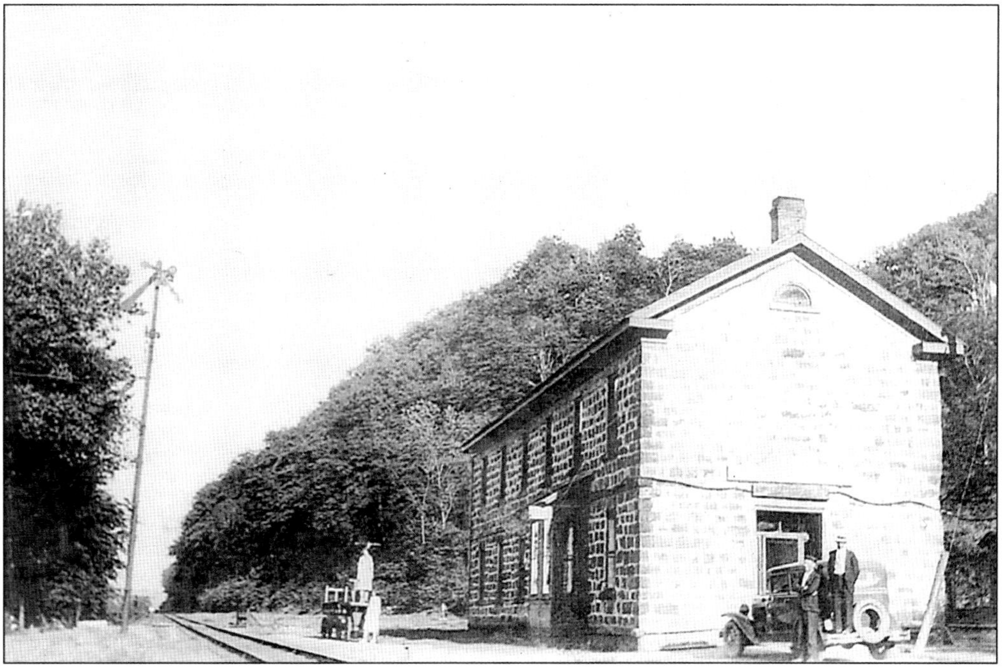

Specht's Ferry Station housed the station agent's family on the second floor. A handful of families lived close to this picturesque spot a few miles north of Dubuque.

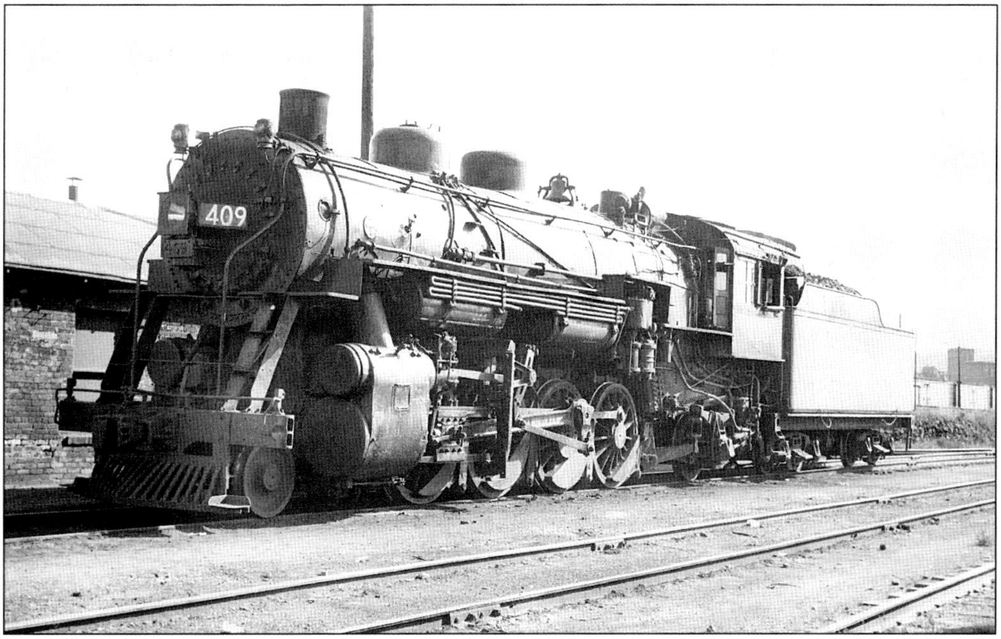

Freight hauler number 409 rests up next to the sand drying house during a hot afternoon in the 1940s in Dubuque.

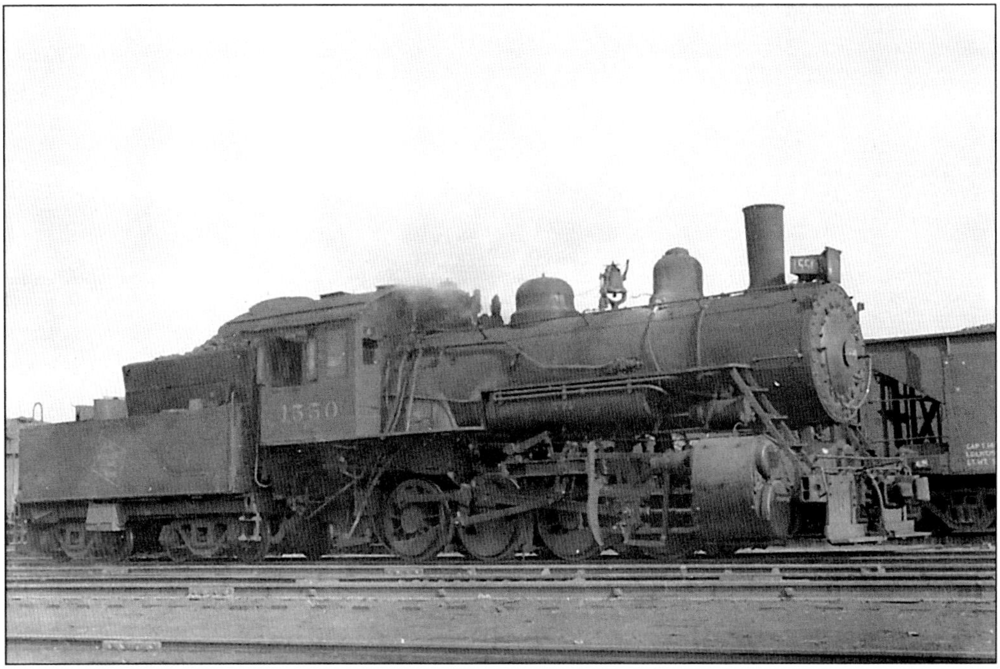

Eight-wheeler switch engine number 1550 was assigned to Dubuque for several years.

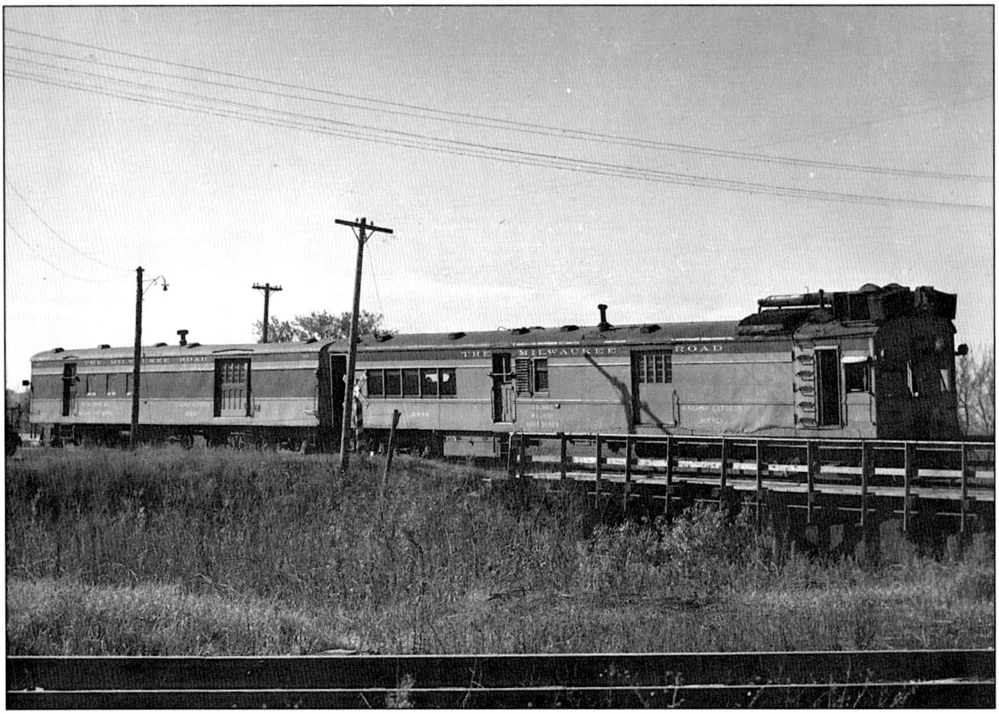

Gas-electric motors served the Dubuque-to-Green Island "Dinky" and pulled one coach.

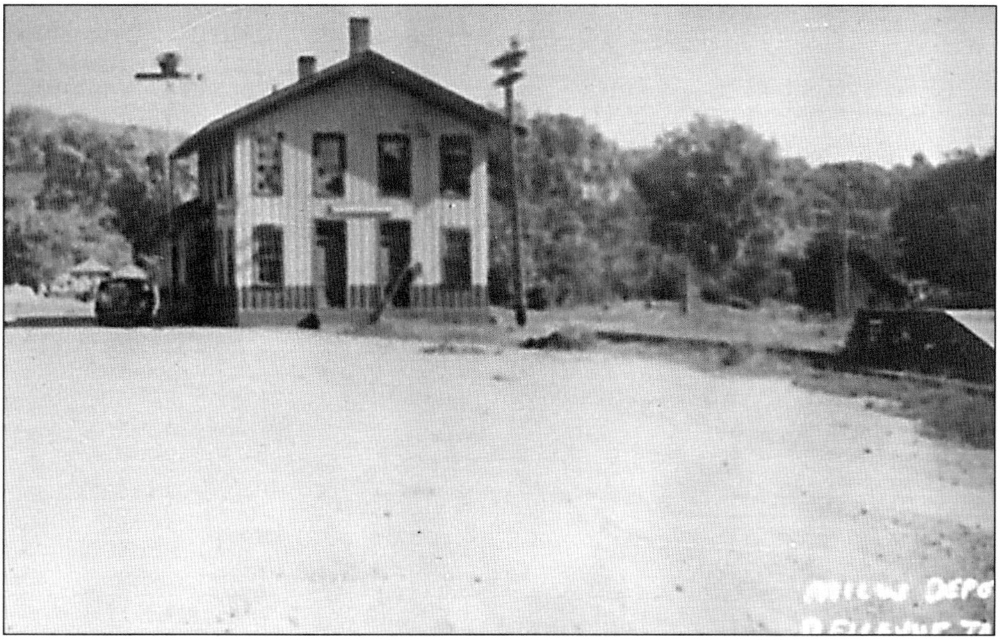

The Bellevue, Iowa, station south of Dubuque was served by the "Dinky" and other passenger trains over the years.

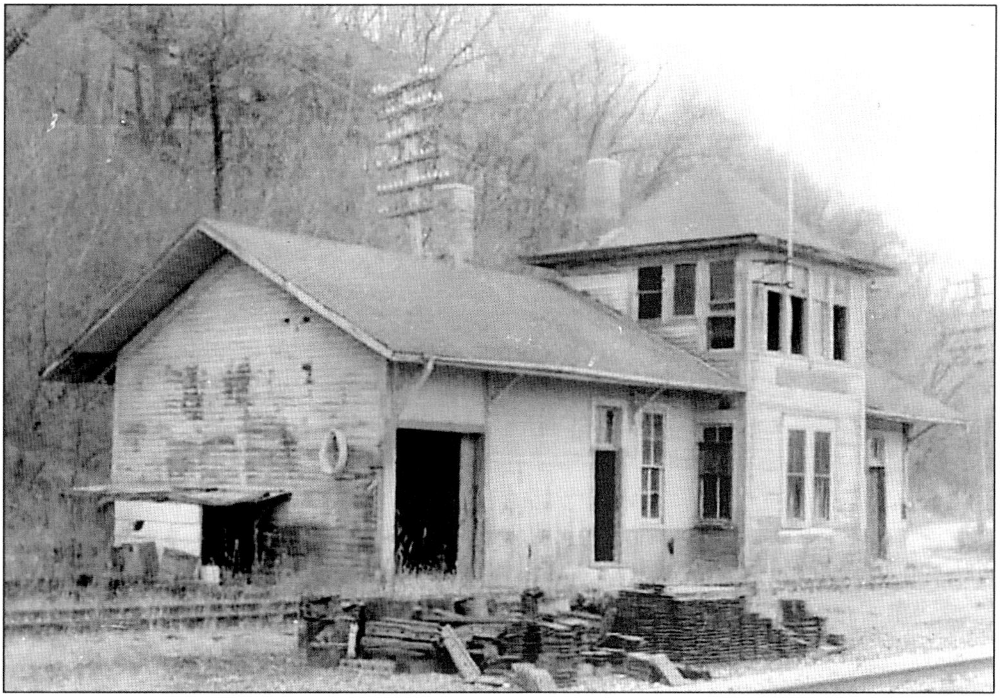

Green Island's Milwaukee Road depot has seen better days—days when it saw two Hiawathas, two Arrows, and other passenger trains daily.

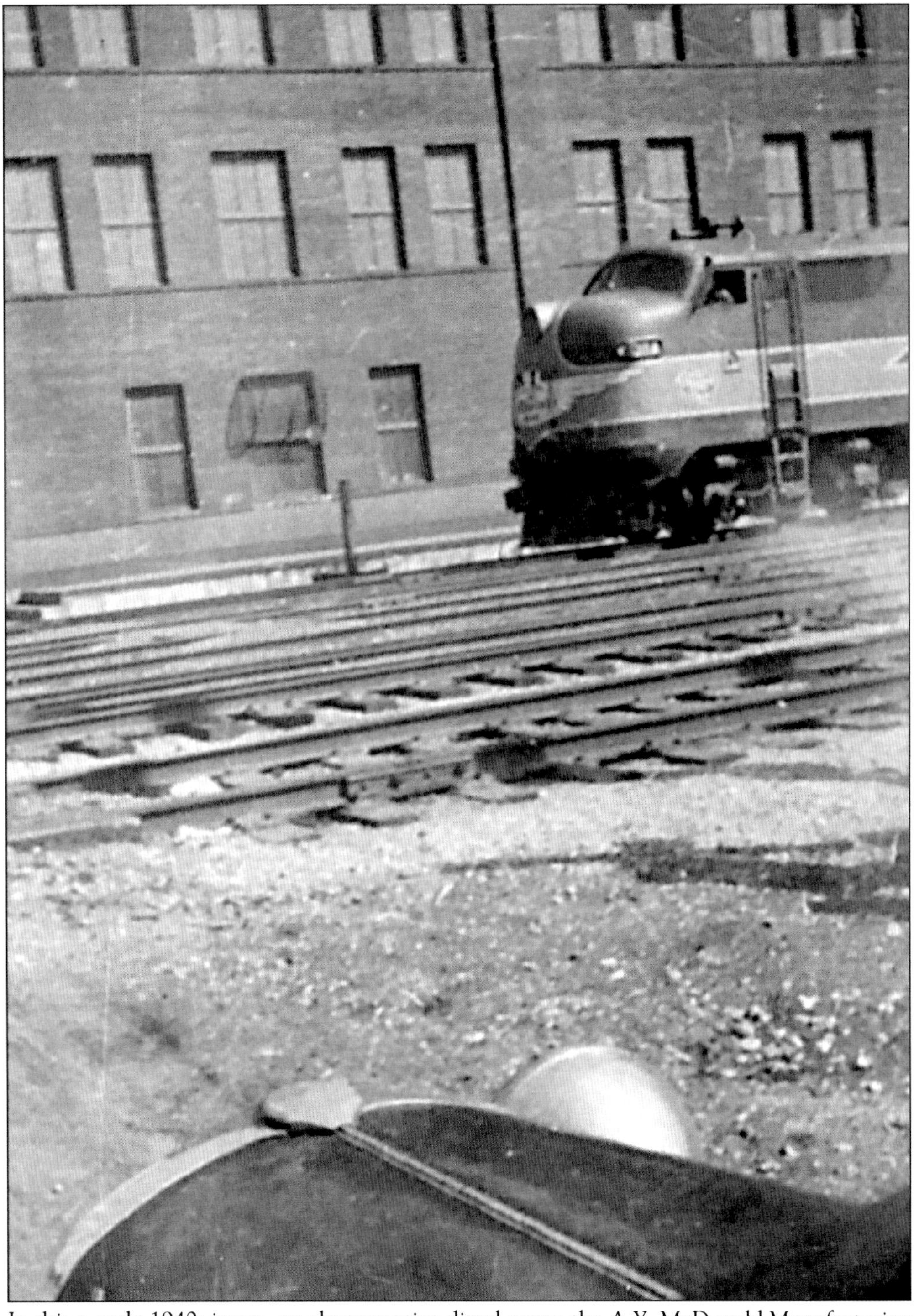

In this c. early-1940s image, an electromotive diesel passes the A.Y. McDonald Manufacturing Company in Dubuque.

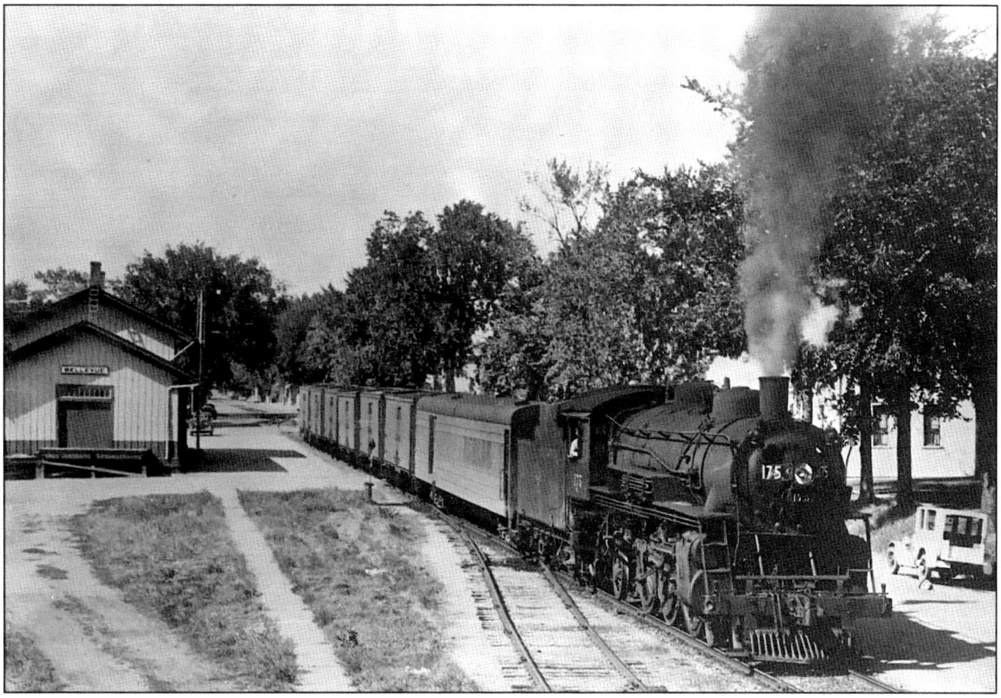

If the train pictured above was on time, this photograph was taken at 2:47 p.m. on a summer afternoon in Bellevue. It was scheduled to meet the westbound Hiawatha at 3:36 p.m. in Green Island.

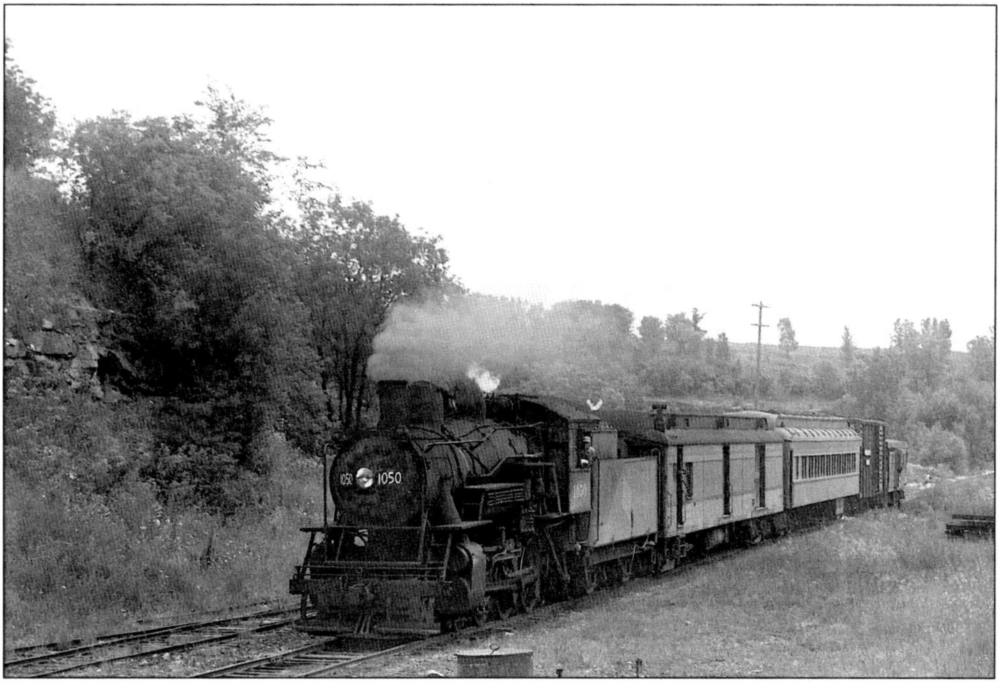

In this photograph, a mixed train chugs along on the Waukon Branch. This was typical of branch line trains on the Milwaukee.

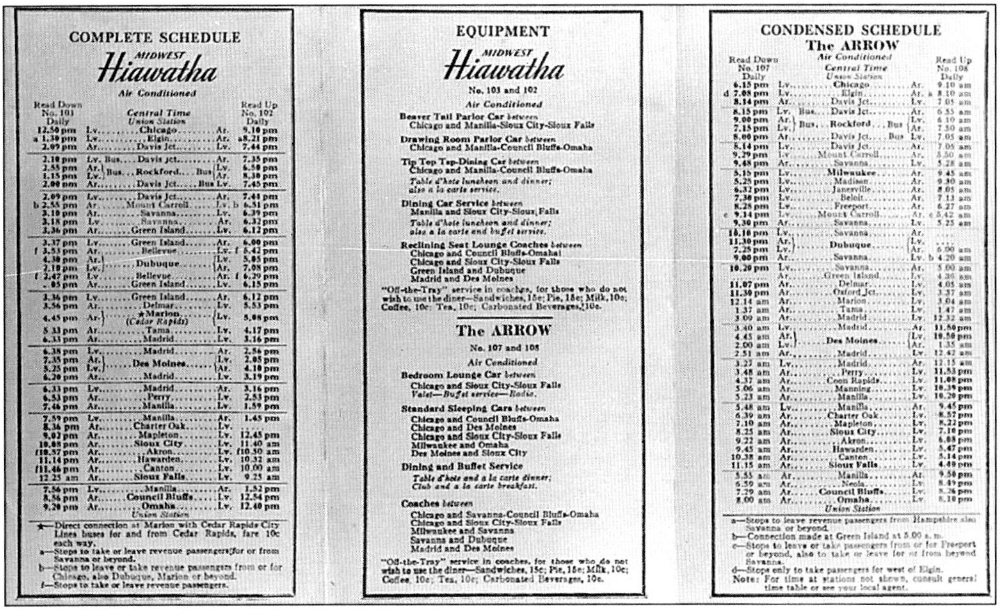

COMPLETE SCHEDULE

MIDWEST *Hiawatha*

Air Conditioned

Read Down No. 101 Daily		Central Time Union Station		Read Up No. 102 Daily
12.50 pm	Lv.	Chicago	Ar.	9.10 pm
a 1.30 pm	Lv.	Elgin	Ar.	a8.21 pm
2.09 pm	Ar.	Davis Jct.	Lv.	7.44 pm
2.10 pm	Lv. Bus	Davis Jct.	Ar.	7.35 pm
2.55 pm	Ar.	Bus...Rockford...Bus	Lv.	6.50 pm
1.15 pm	Lv.		Ar.	8.30 pm
2.00 pm	Ar.	Davis Jct....Bus	Lv.	7.45 pm
2.09 pm	Lv.	Davis Jct.	Ar.	7.44 pm
b 2.55 pm	Ar.	Mount Carroll	Lv. b	6.51 pm
3.10 pm	Ar.	Savanna	Lv.	6.39 pm
3.18 pm	Lv.	Savanna	Ar.	6.32 pm
3.36 pm	Ar.	Green Island	Lv.	6.12 pm
3.37 pm	Lv.	Green Island	Ar.	6.00 pm
f 3.53 pm	Ar.	Bellevue	Lv. f	5.42 pm
4.30 pm	Ar.	Dubuque	Lv.	5.05 pm
2.10 pm	Lv.		Ar.	7.08 pm
f 2.47 pm	Lv.	Bellevue	Ar. f	6.29 pm
.05 pm	Ar.	Green Island	Lv.	6.15 pm
3.36 pm	Lv.	Green Island	Ar.	6.12 pm
3.56 pm	Ar.	Delmar	Lv.	5.53 pm
4.45 pm	Ar.	★Marion (*Cedar Rapids*)	Lv.	5.08 pm
5.33 pm	Ar.	Tama	Lv.	4.17 pm
6.33 pm	Ar.	Madrid	Lv.	3.16 pm
6.38 pm	Lv.	Madrid	Ar.	2.56 pm
7.35 pm	Ar.	Des Moines	Lv.	2.05 pm
5.25 pm	Lv.		Ar.	4.10 pm
6.20 pm	Ar.	Madrid	Lv.	3.19 pm
6.33 pm	Lv.	Madrid	Ar.	3.16 pm
6.53 pm	Ar.	Perry	Lv.	2.53 pm
7.46 pm	Ar.	Manilla	Lv.	1.59 pm
7.59 pm	Lv.	Manilla	Ar.	1.45 pm
8.36 pm	Ar.	Charter Oak	Lv.	.....
9.02 pm	Ar.	Mapleton	Lv.	12.45 pm
10.08 pm	Ar.	Sioux City	Lv.	11.40 am
f10.57 pm	Ar.	Akron	Lv.	f10.50 am
11.14 pm	Ar.	Hawarden	Lv.	10.32 am
f11.46 pm	Ar.	Canton	Lv.	10.00 am
12.25 am	Ar.	Sioux Falls	Lv.	9.25 am
7.56 pm	Lv.	Manilla	Ar.	1.52 pm
8.56 pm	Ar.	Council Bluffs	Lv.	12.54 pm
9.20 pm	Ar.	Omaha *Union Station*	Lv.	12.40 pm

★—Direct connection at Marion with Cedar Rapids City Lines buses for and from Cedar Rapids, fare 10c each way.
a—Stops to take or leave revenue passengers for or from Savanna or beyond.
b—Stops to leave or take revenue passengers from or for Chicago, also Dubuque, Marion or beyond.
f—Stops to take or leave revenue passengers.

EQUIPMENT

MIDWEST *Hiawatha*

No. 103 and 102

Air Conditioned

Beaver Tail Parlor Car *between*
Chicago and Manilla-Sioux City-Sioux Falls

Drawing Room Parlor Car *between*
Chicago and Manilla-Council Bluffs-Omaha

Tip Top Tap-Dining Car *between*
Chicago and Manilla-Council Bluffs-Omaha
Table d'hote luncheon and dinner; also a la carte service.

Dining Car Service *between*
Manilla and Sioux City-Sioux Falls
Table d'hote luncheon and dinner; also a la carte and buffet service.

Reclining Seat Lounge Coaches *between*
Chicago and Council Bluffs-Omaha
Chicago and Sioux City-Sioux Falls
Green Island and Dubuque
Madrid and Des Moines

"Off-the-Tray" service in coaches, for those who do not wish to use the diner—Sandwiches, 15c; Pie, 15c; Milk, 10c; Coffee, 10c; Tea, 10c; Carbonated Beverages, 10c.

The ARROW

No. 107 and 108

Air Conditioned

Bedroom Lounge Car *between*
Chicago and Sioux City-Sioux Falls
Valet—Buffet service—Radio.

Standard Sleeping Cars *between*
Chicago and Council Bluffs-Omaha
Chicago and Des Moines
Chicago and Sioux City-Sioux Falls
Milwaukee and Omaha
Des Moines and Sioux City

Dining and Buffet Service
Table d'hote and a la carte dinner; Club and a la carte breakfast.

Coaches *between*
Chicago and Savanna-Council Bluffs-Omaha
Chicago and Sioux City-Sioux Falls
Milwaukee and Savanna
Savanna and Dubuque
Madrid and Des Moines

"Off-the-Tray" service in coaches, for those who do not wish to use the diner—Sandwiches, 15c; Pie, 15c; Milk, 10c; Coffee, 10c; Tea, 10c; Carbonated Beverages, 10c.

CONDENSED SCHEDULE

The ARROW

Air Conditioned

Read Down No. 107 Daily		Central Time Union Station		Read Up No. 108 Daily
6.15 pm	Lv.	Chicago	Ar.	9.10 am
d 7.08 pm	Lv.	Elgin	Ar. a	8.10 am
8.14 pm	Ar.	Davis Jct.	Lv.	7.05 am
8.15 pm	Lv. Bus	Davis Jct.	Ar.	6.55 am
9.00 pm	Ar.	Bus...Rockford...Bus	Lv.	6.10 am
7.15 pm	Lv.		Ar.	7.50 am
8.00 pm	Ar.	Davis Jct....Bus	Lv.	7.05 am
8.14 pm	Lv.	Davis Jct.	Ar.	7.05 am
9.29 pm	Lv.	Mount Carroll	Ar.	5.50 am
9.48 pm	Ar.	Savanna	Lv.	5.28 am
5.15 pm	Lv.	Milwaukee	Ar.	9.45 am
5.25 pm	Lv.	Madison	Ar.	9.30 am
6.32 pm	Lv.	Janesville	Ar.	8.05 am
7.30 pm	Lv.	Beloit	Ar.	7.13 am
8.28 pm	Lv.	Freeport	Ar.	6.27 am
e 9.14 pm	Lv.	Mount Carroll	Ar. e	5.42 am
9.30 pm	Ar.	Savanna	Lv.	5.25 am
10.10 pm	Lv.	Savanna	Ar.	....
11.30 pm	Ar.	Dubuque	Lv.	....
7.25 pm	Lv.		Ar.	6.00 am
9.00 pm	Ar.	Savanna	Lv. b	4.20 am
10.20 pm	Lv.	Savanna	Ar.	5.00 am
....	Ar.	Green Island	Lv.	4.36 am
11.07 pm	Ar.	Delmar	Lv.	4.05 am
11.30 pm	Ar.	Oxford Jct.	Lv.	3.37 am
12.14 am	Ar.	Marion	Lv.	3.04 am
1.37 am	Ar.	Tama	Lv.	1.47 am
3.09 am	Ar.	Madrid	Lv.	12.32 am
3.40 am	Lv.	Madrid	Ar.	11.50 pm
4.45 am	Ar.	Des Moines	Lv.	10.50 pm
2.00 am	Lv.		Ar.	1.35 am
2.51 am	Ar.	Madrid	Lv.	12.42 am
3.27 am	Lv.	Madrid	Ar.	12.15 am
3.48 am	Ar.	Perry	Lv.	11.53 pm
4.37 am	Ar.	Coon Rapids	Lv.	11.08 pm
5.06 am	Ar.	Manning	Lv.	10.39 pm
5.23 am	Ar.	Manilla	Lv.	10.20 pm
5.48 am	Lv.	Manilla	Ar.	9.45 pm
6.39 am	Ar.	Charter Oak	Lv.	8.57 pm
7.10 am	Ar.	Mapleton	Lv.	8.22 pm
8.25 am	Ar.	Sioux City	Lv.	7.10 pm
9.22 am	Ar.	Akron	Lv.	6.08 pm
9.45 am	Ar.	Hawarden	Lv.	5.47 pm
10.38 am	Ar.	Canton	Lv.	5.14 pm
11.15 am	Ar.	Sioux Falls	Lv.	4.40 pm
5.55 am	Ar.	Manilla	Ar.	9.50 pm
6.59 am	Ar.	Neola	Lv.	8.49 pm
7.29 am	Ar.	Council Bluffs	Lv.	8.26 pm
8.00 am	Ar.	Omaha *Union Station*	Lv.	8.10 pm

a—Stops to leave revenue passengers from Hampshire also Savanna or beyond.
b—Connection made at Green Island at 5.00 a.m.
e—Stops to leave or take passengers from or for Freeport or beyond, also to take or leave for or from beyond Savanna.
d—Stops only to take passengers for west of Elgin.
Note: For time at stations not shown, consult general time table or see your local agent.

A timetable for the Midwest Hiawatha and the Arrow is shown here.

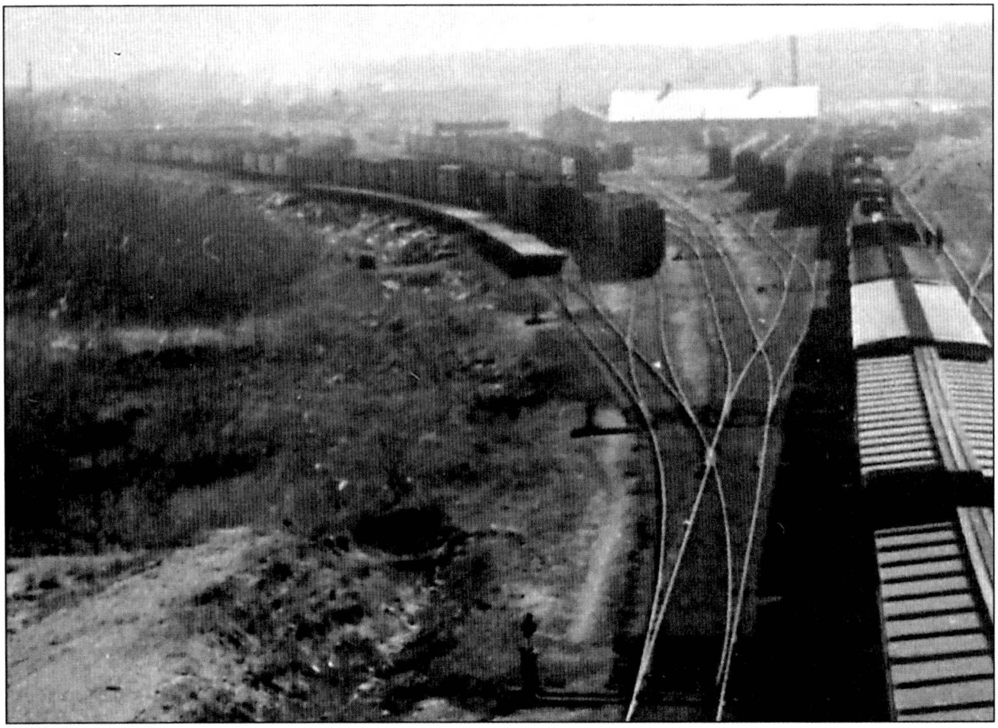

This image provides a southwesterly view of the Chicago, Milwaukee, St. Paul & Pacific Railroad yards in Dubuque from the Fengler Street overpass.

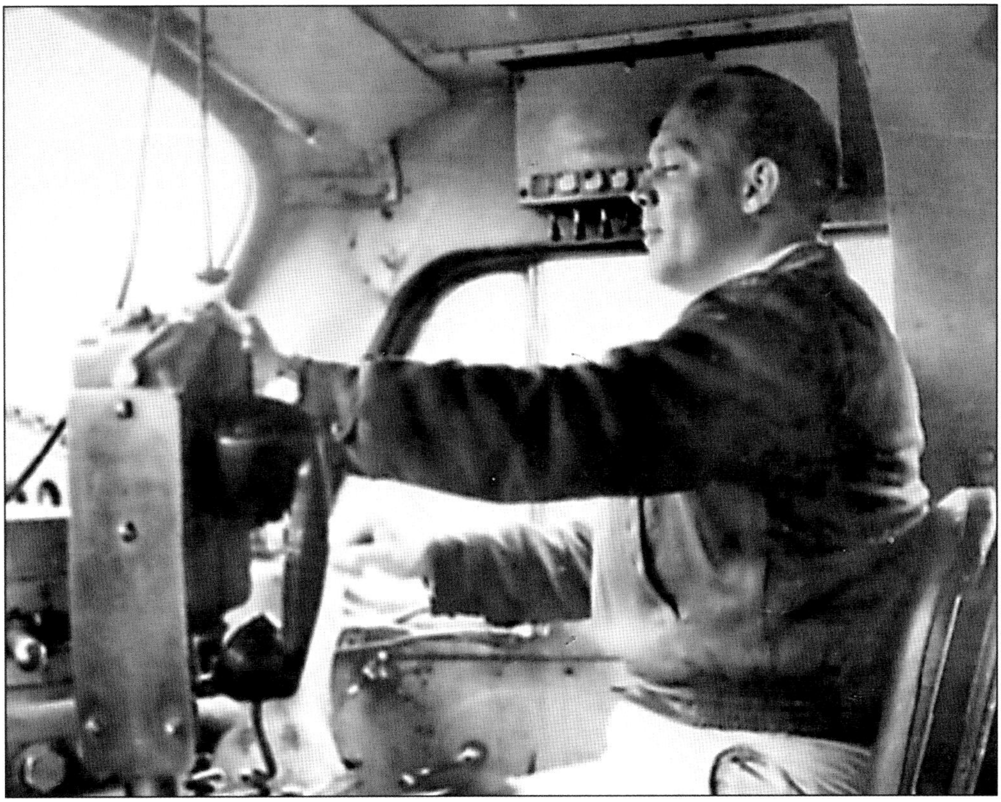

What would a rail buff give to be sitting at the throttle of a Milwaukee Road F-7 unit diesel?

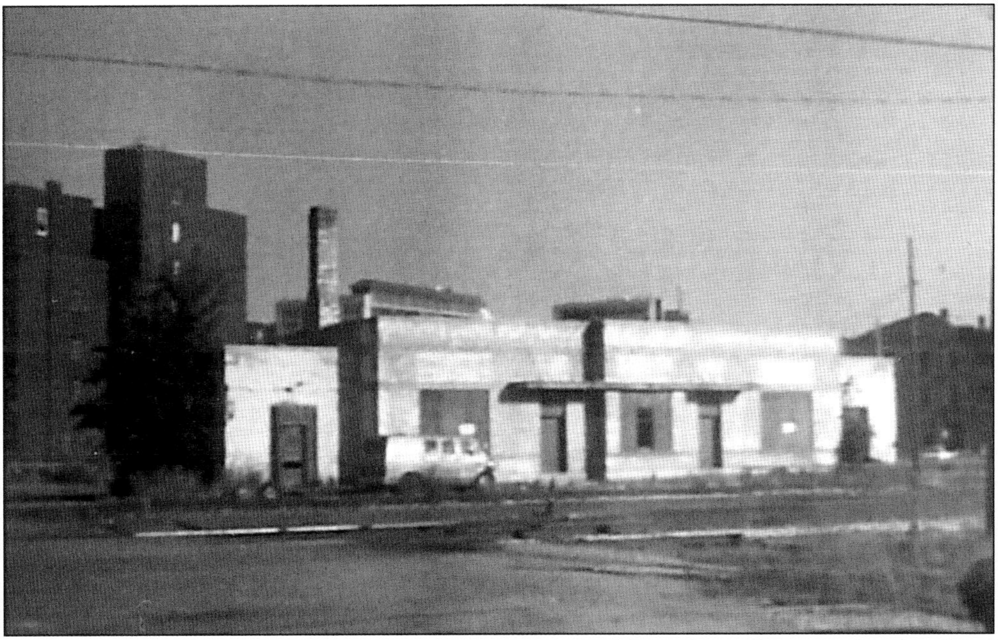

In the early 1940s, the second story and roof were removed from the Dubuque Milwaukee Road depot. This was done to modernize the road when the Midwest Hiawatha began serving the area.

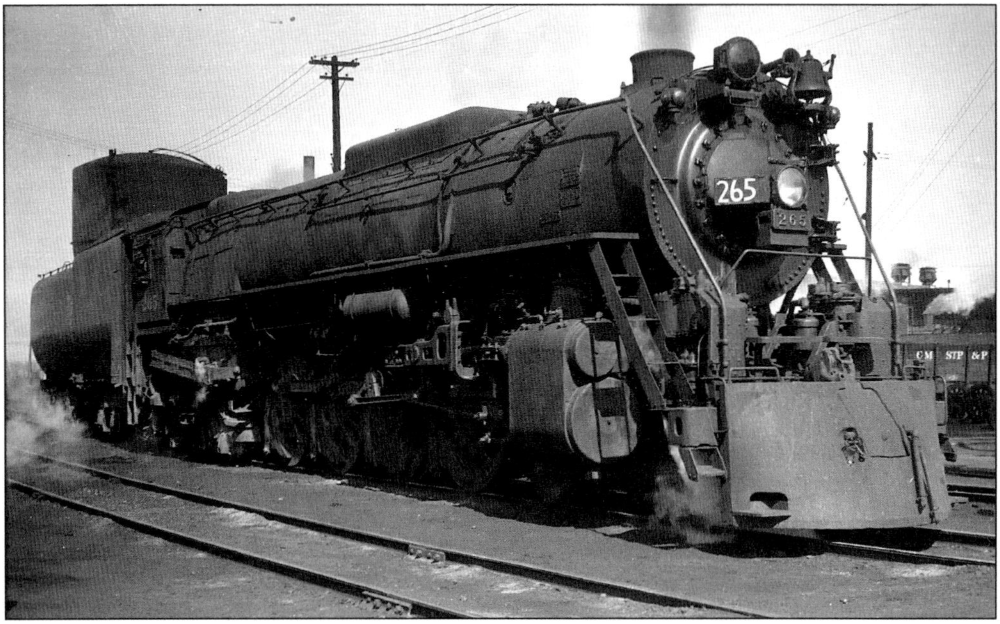

Pictured here is an S-3, 4-8-4 Northern-type locomotive. Number 265 is preserved at the Illinois Railway Museum in Union, Illinois.

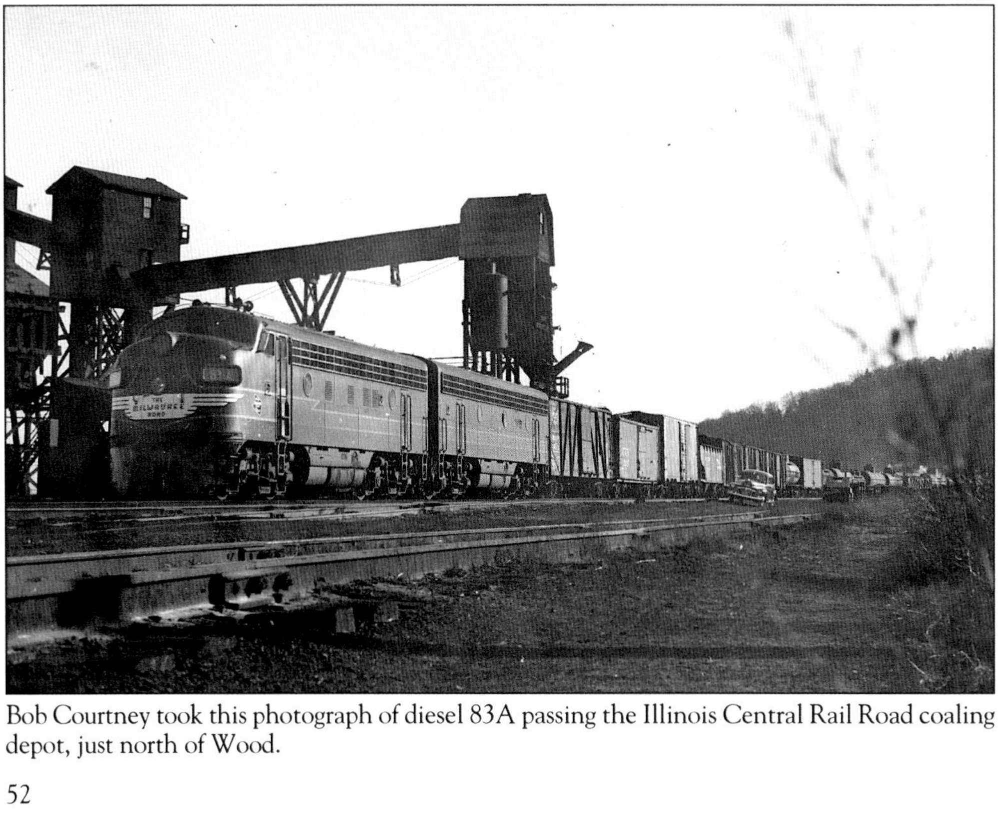

Bob Courtney took this photograph of diesel 83A passing the Illinois Central Rail Road coaling depot, just north of Wood.

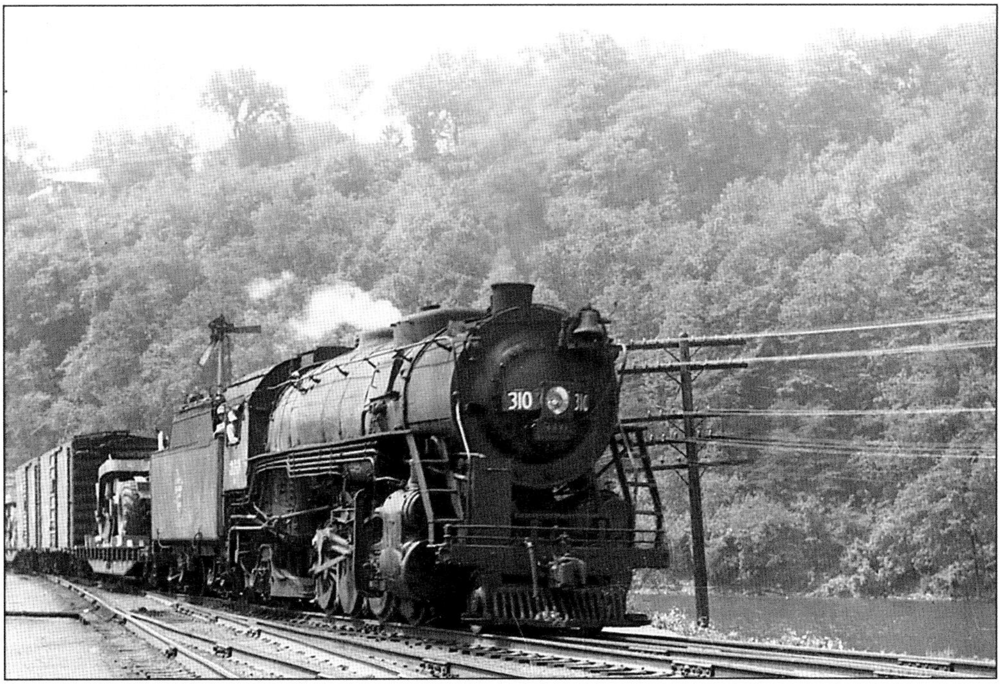

Number 310, a 2-8-2 Mikado type, puffs past Wood on its way north to Dubuque.

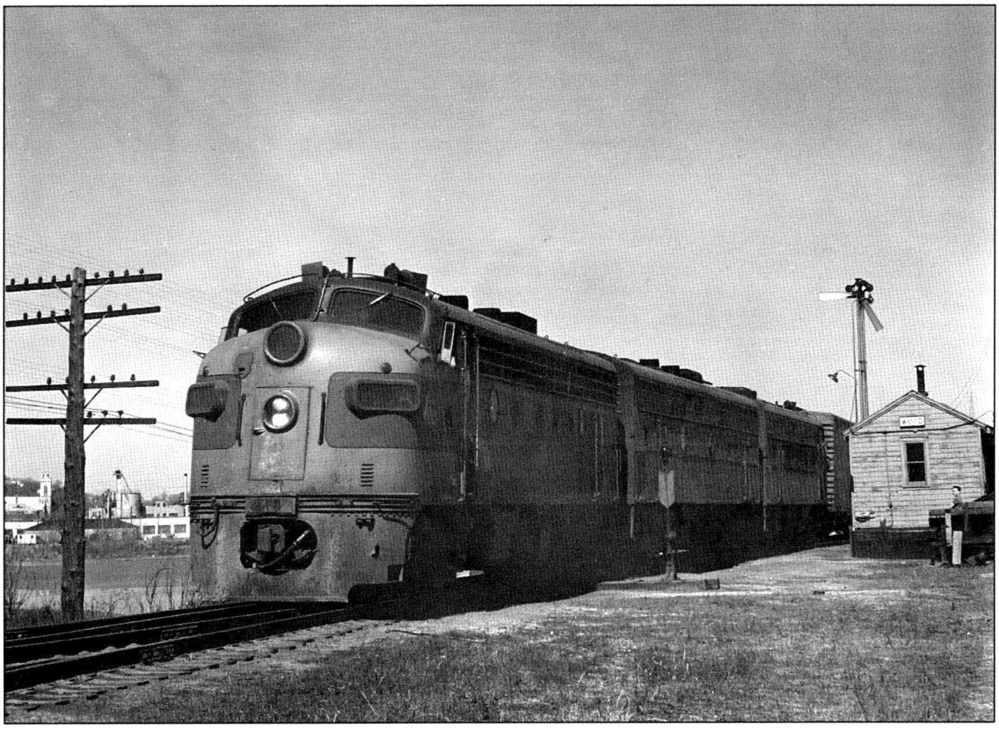

A southbound three-unit Milwaukee Road diesel drags its freight train through Wood, just south of Dubuque.

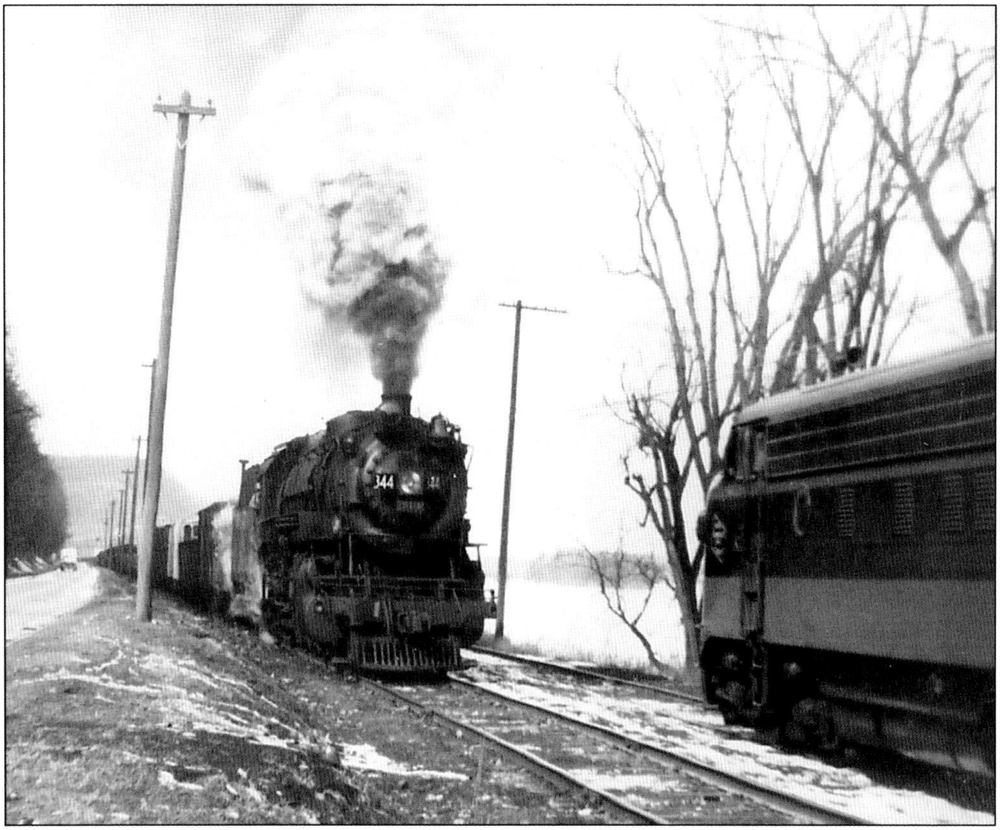

In this image from the early 1950s, Dubuque-bound number 344 eases past its eventual replacement south of Marquette. By 1956, all steam was gone from the Milwaukee.

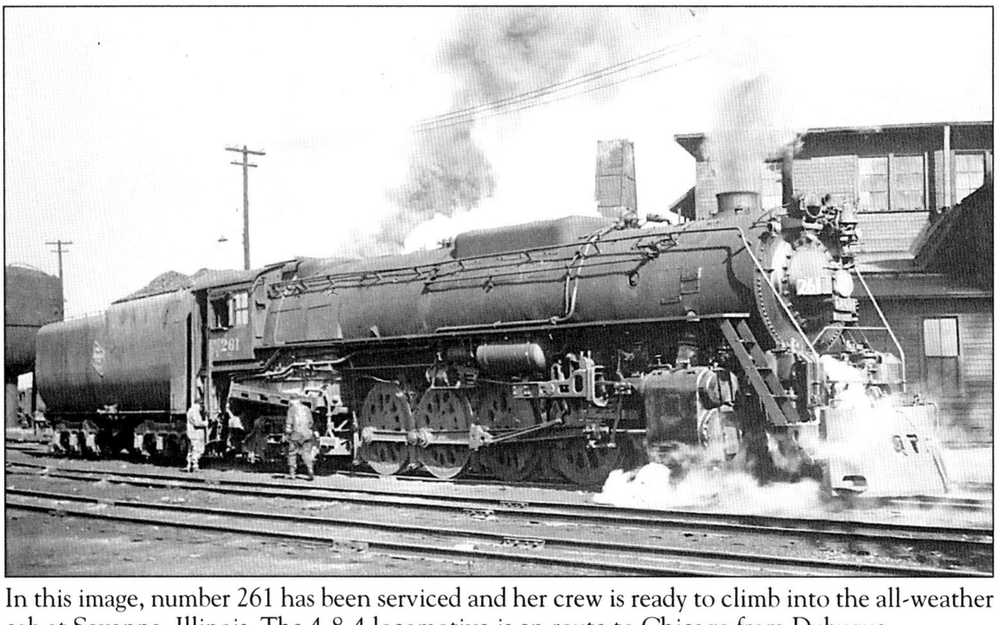

In this image, number 261 has been serviced and her crew is ready to climb into the all-weather cab at Savanna, Illinois. The 4-8-4 locomotive is en route to Chicago from Dubuque.

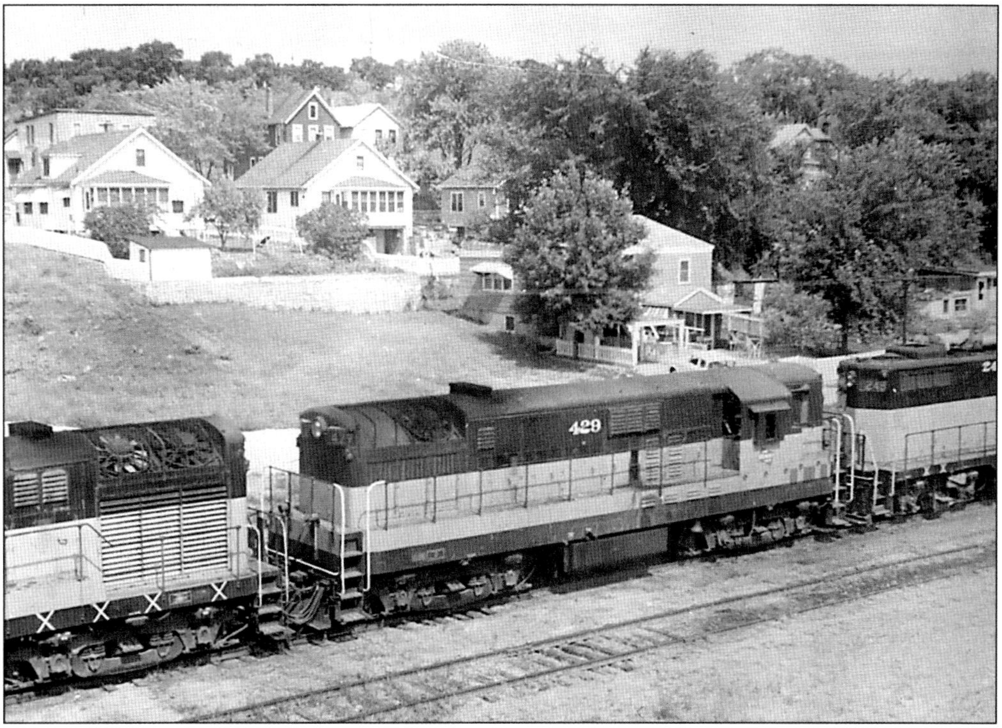

Two Fairbank Morse Chicago, Milwaukee, St. Paul & Pacific Rail Road diesel units and an Electro-motive GP9 diesel enter northbound at the Dubuque yards.

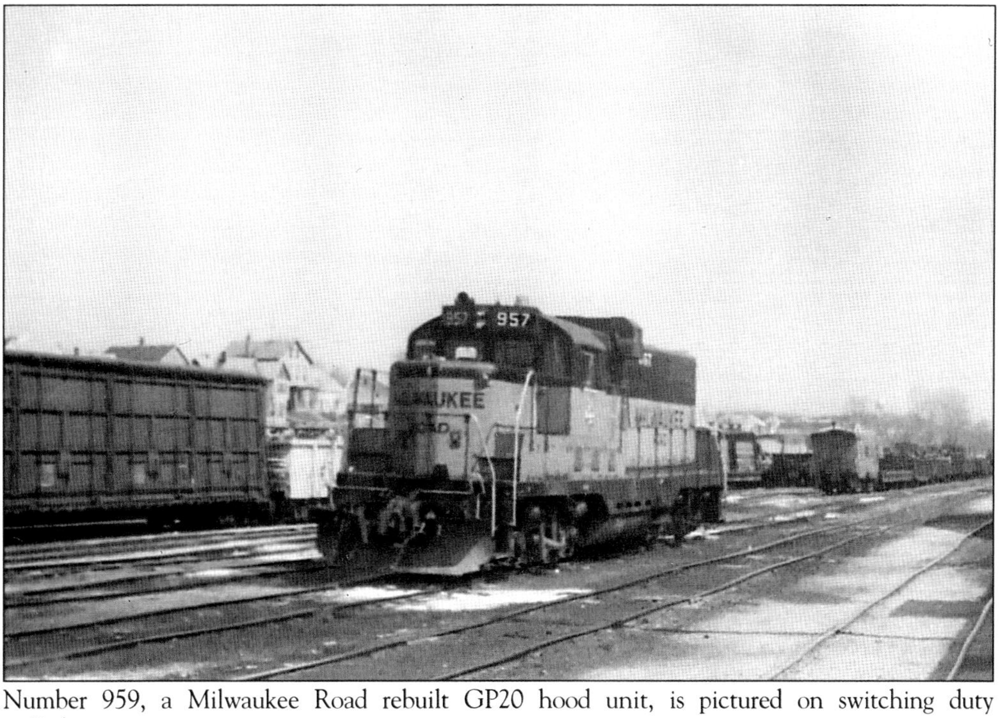

Number 959, a Milwaukee Road rebuilt GP20 hood unit, is pictured on switching duty in Dubuque.

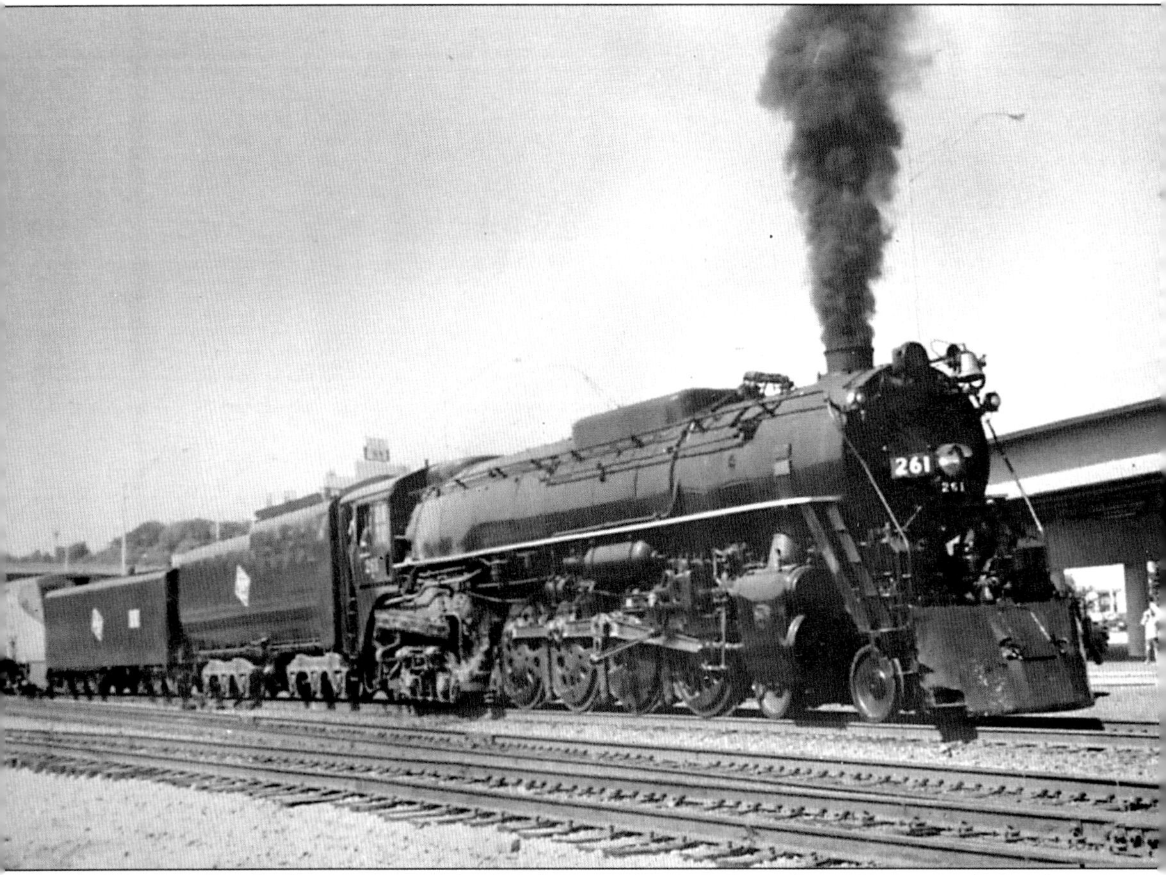

Number 261, built in 1944, was displayed at a museum in Green Bay, Wisconsin, before being restored to working condition. It has flawless service for well over 10 years. She is pictured in Dubuque in 2004, on the point of "The Grand Excursion" train.

Three

The Burlington

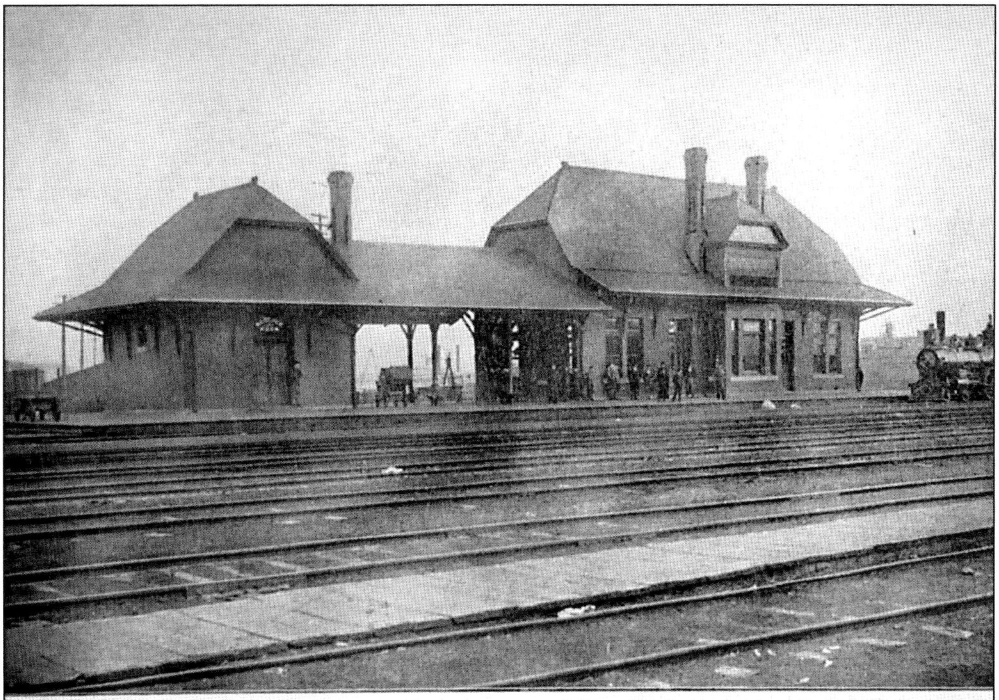
C. B. & N. R. R. COMPANY DEPOT.

The Chicago, Burlington and Northern Rail Road's Dubuque depot was built in 1881.

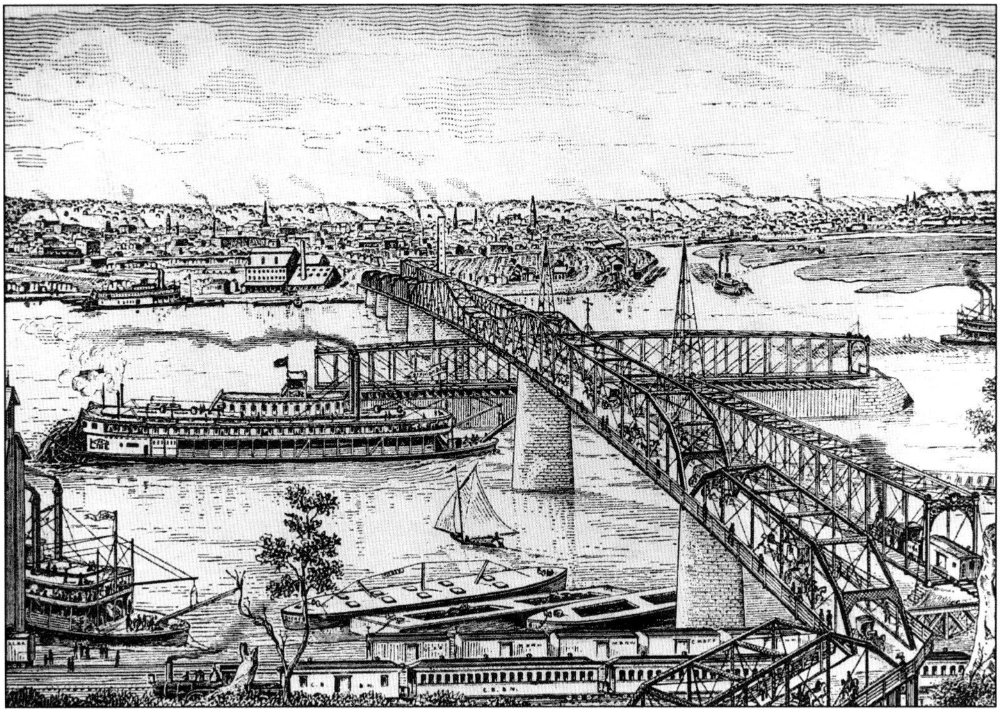

The Dubuque wagon bridge and the Illinois Central cast iron bridge are pictured here. The passenger train in the foreground is lettered for the Chicago, Burlington and Northern.

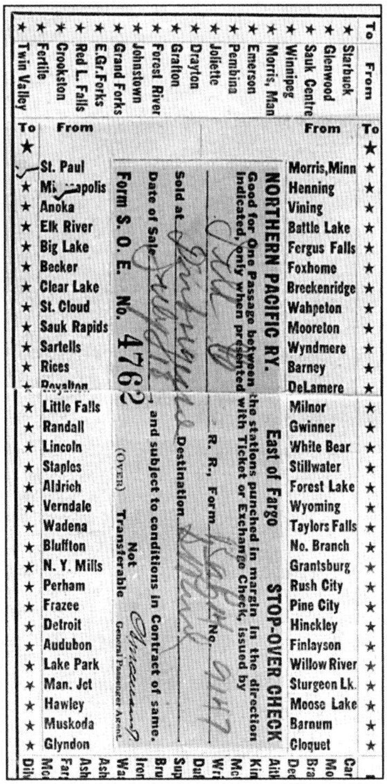

This is a ticket for the Northern Pacific Railroad, which had running rights on the Burlington from Chicago to the Twin Cities.

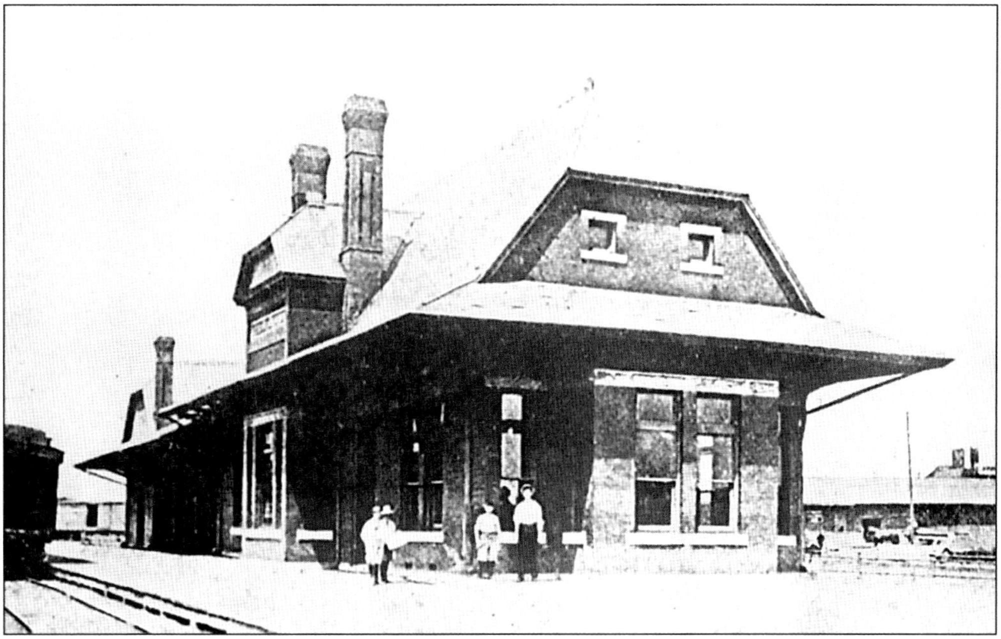

This image shows the south side of the Chicago, Burlington and Northern depot in Dubuque.

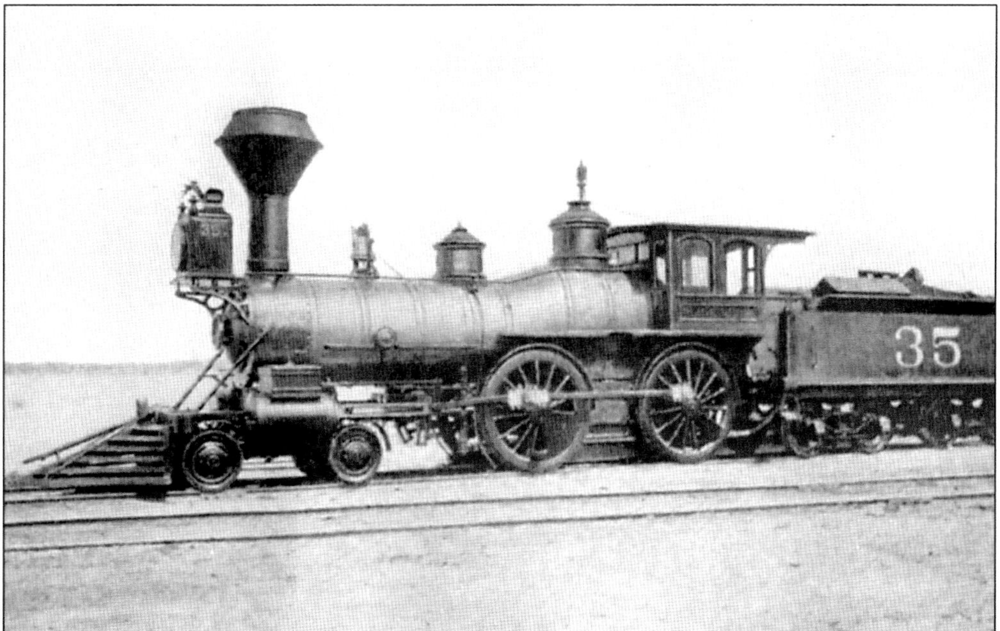

A Burlington 4-4-0 19th-century locomotive is pictured here.

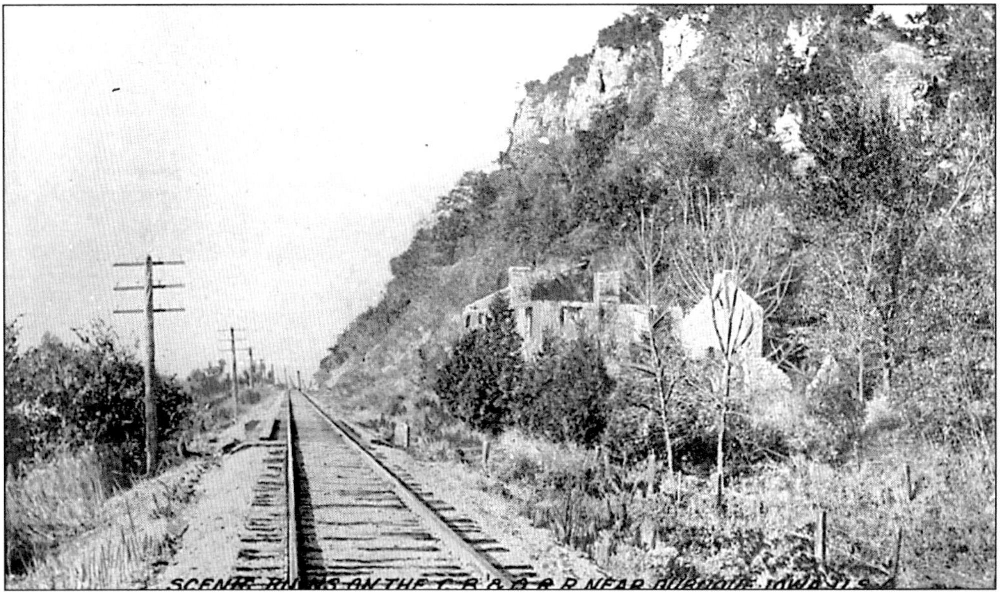

This image shows scenic ruins on the Chicago, Burlington and Quincy Railroad near East Dubuque, Illinois.

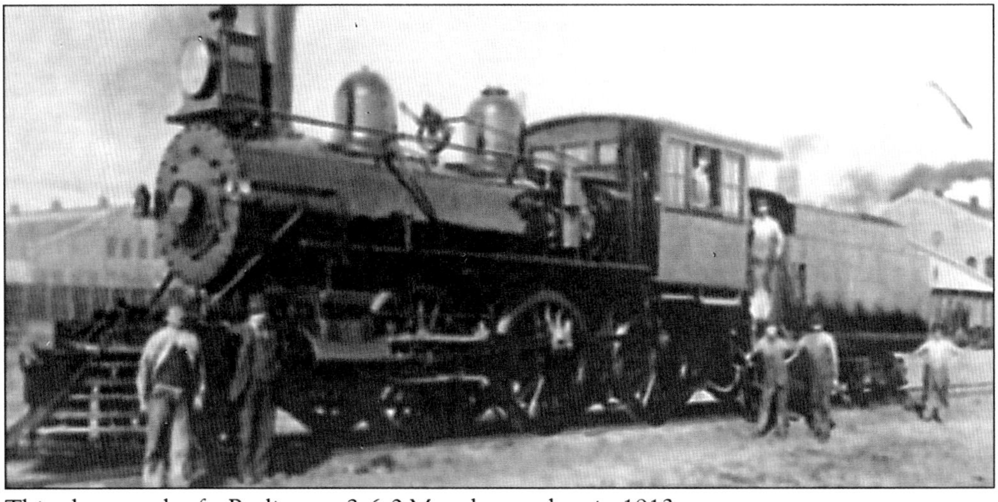

This photograph of a Burlington 2-6-0 Mogul was taken in 1913.

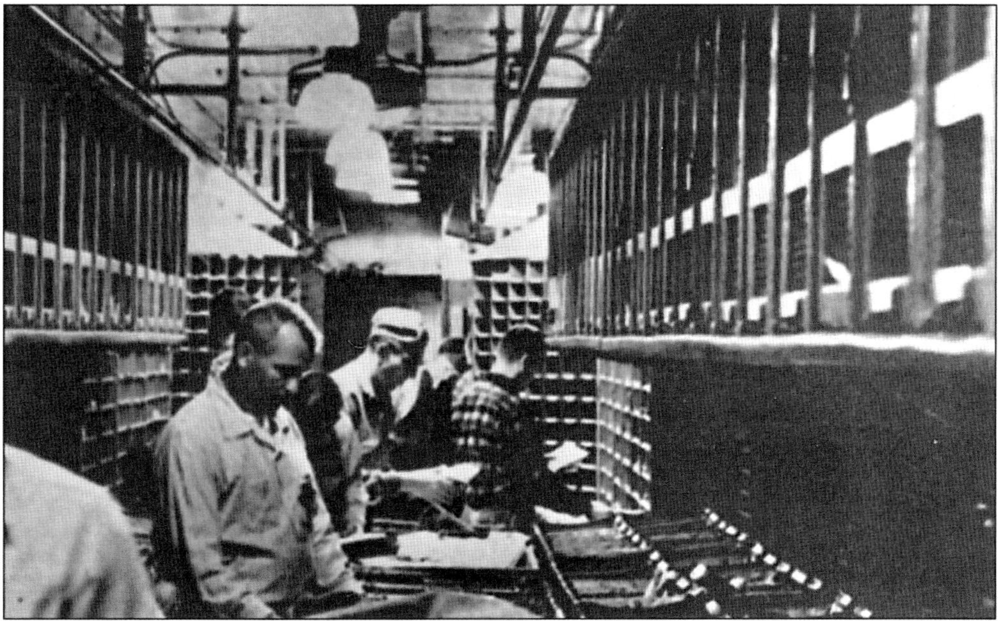
Postal clerks work in a Burlington Rail Post Office car.

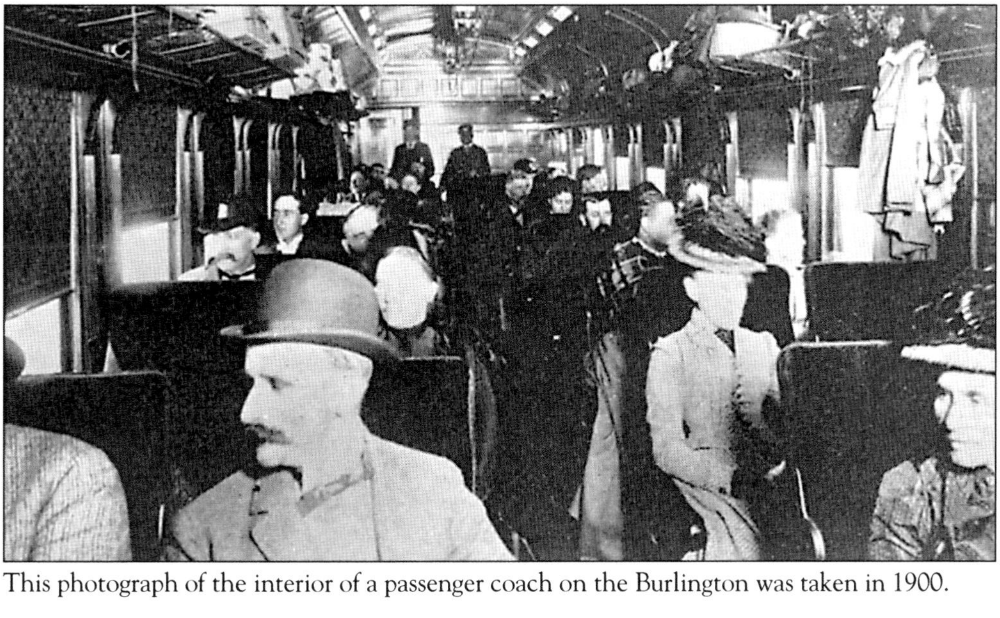
This photograph of the interior of a passenger coach on the Burlington was taken in 1900.

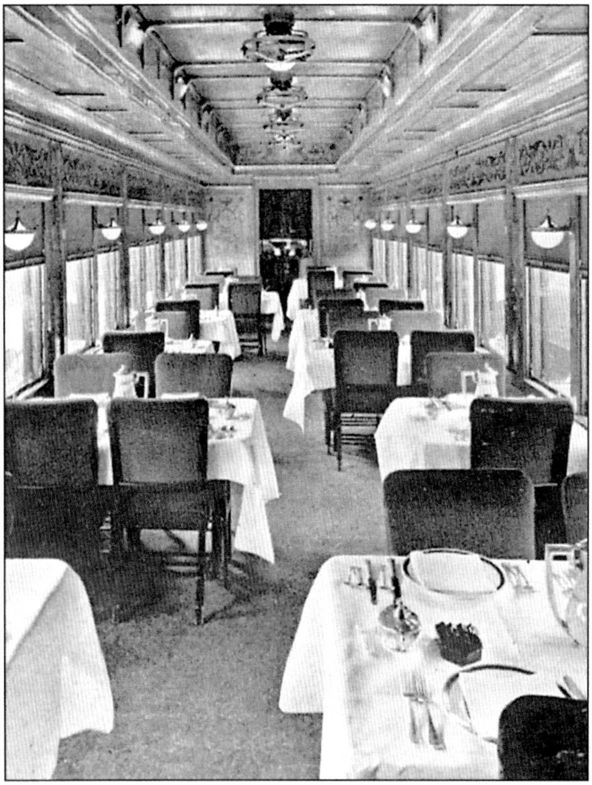

The Burlington's "Black Hawk" diner is shown here.

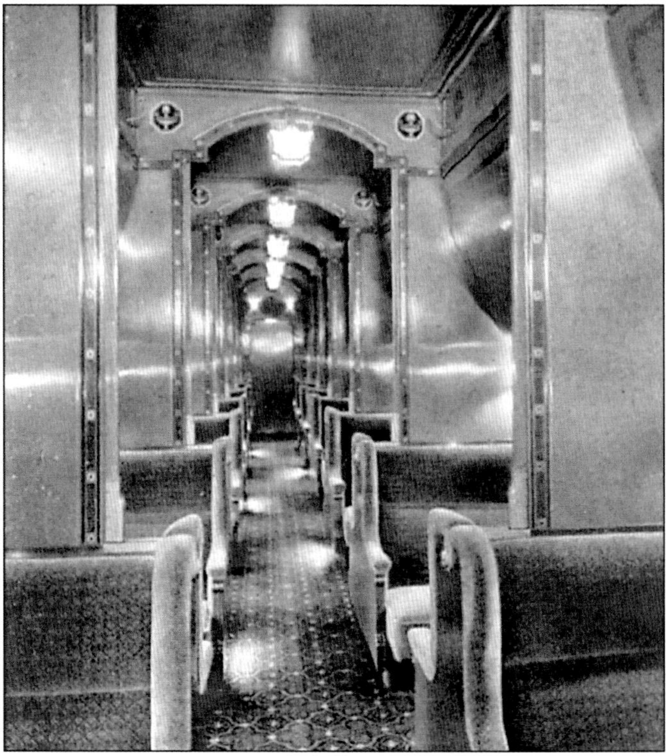

This is the interior of a Pullman sleeper.

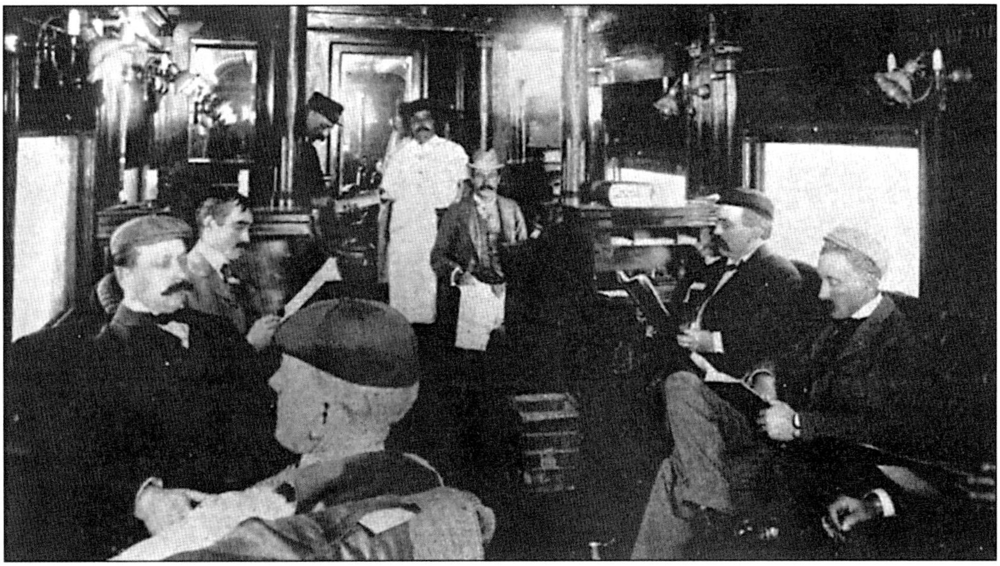

A parlor car on the Burlington is shown in this image from the early 1900s.

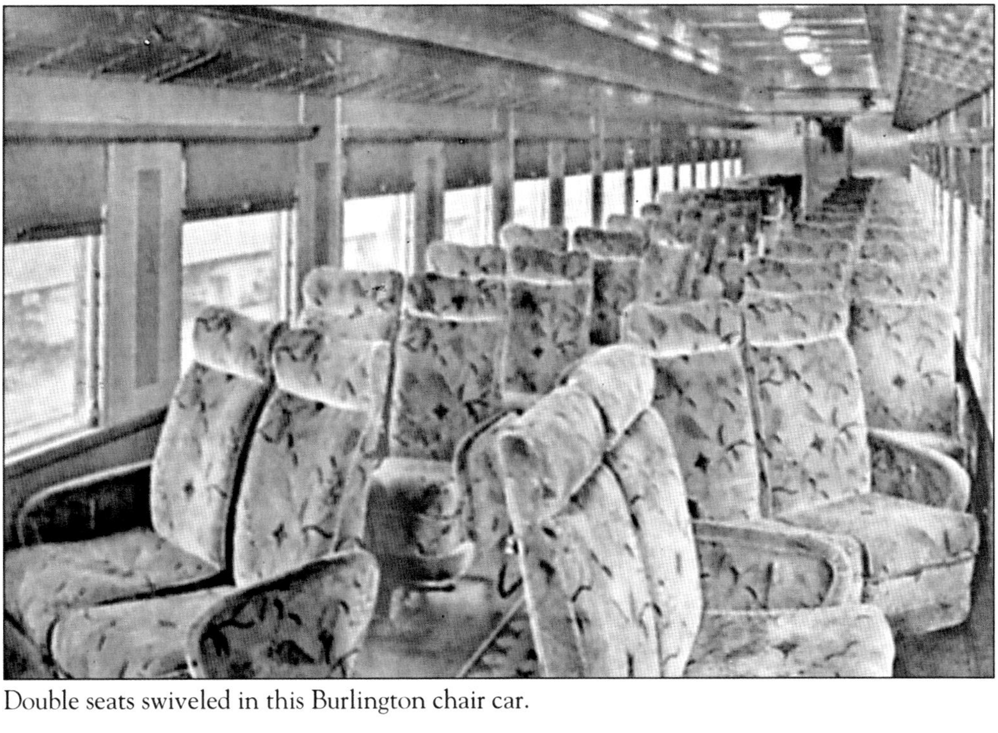

Double seats swiveled in this Burlington chair car.

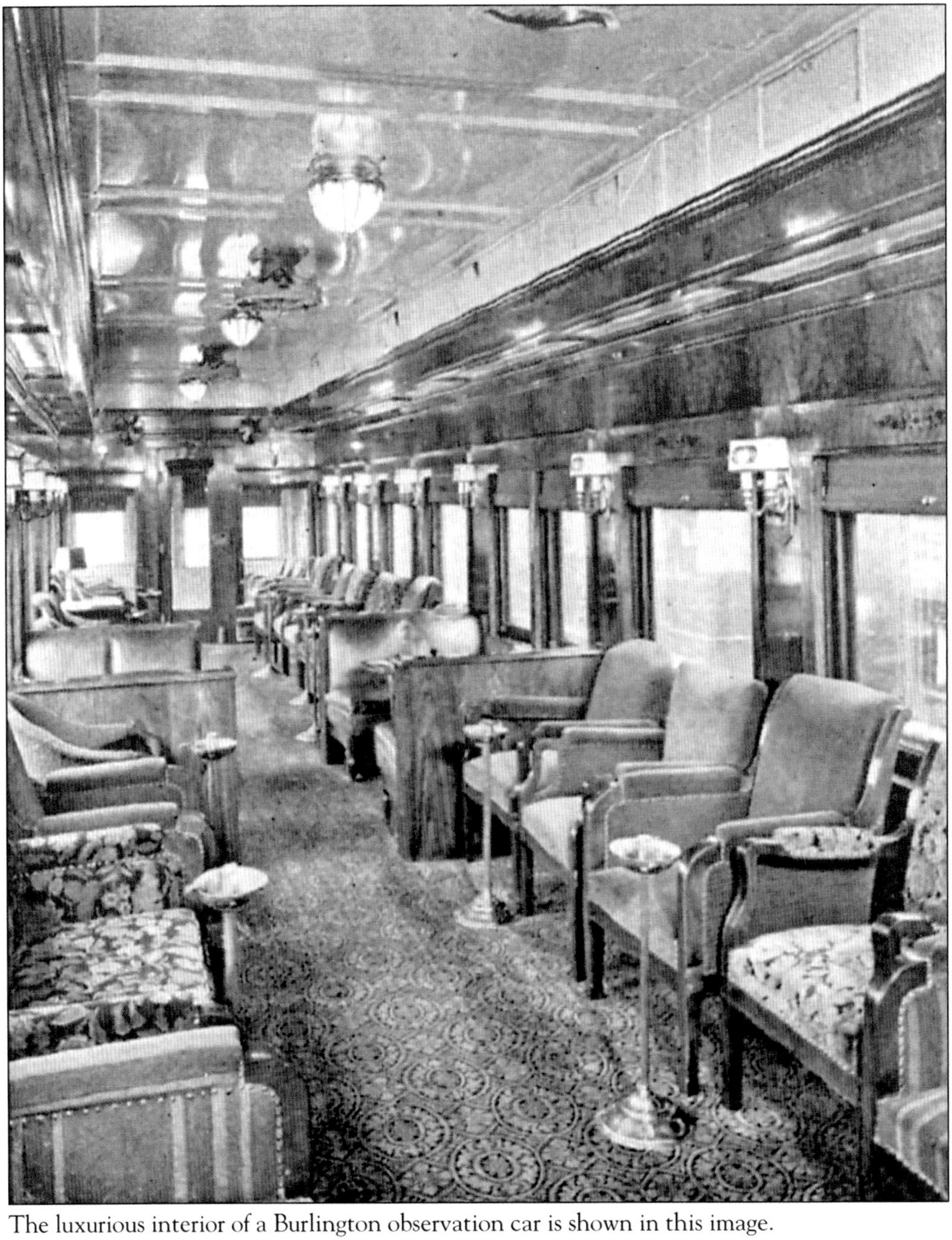

The luxurious interior of a Burlington observation car is shown in this image.

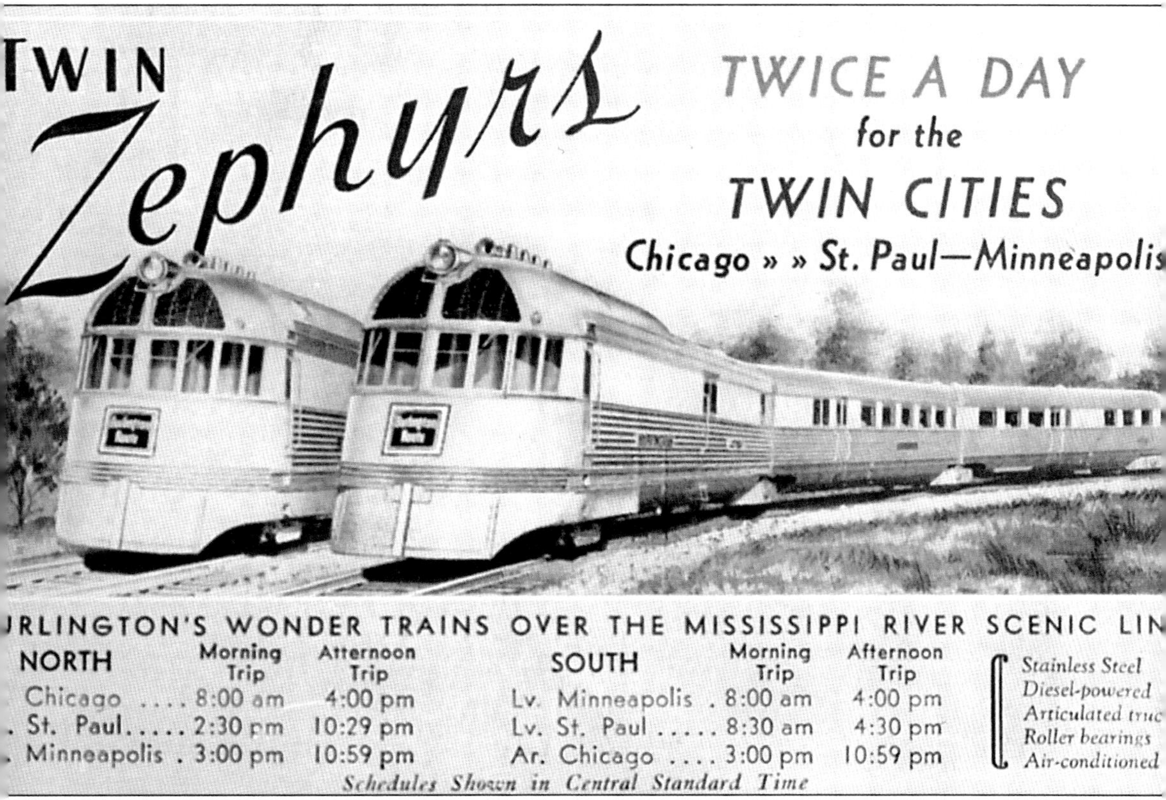

The Burlington used advertising to capitalize on its Twin Cities Zephyrs.

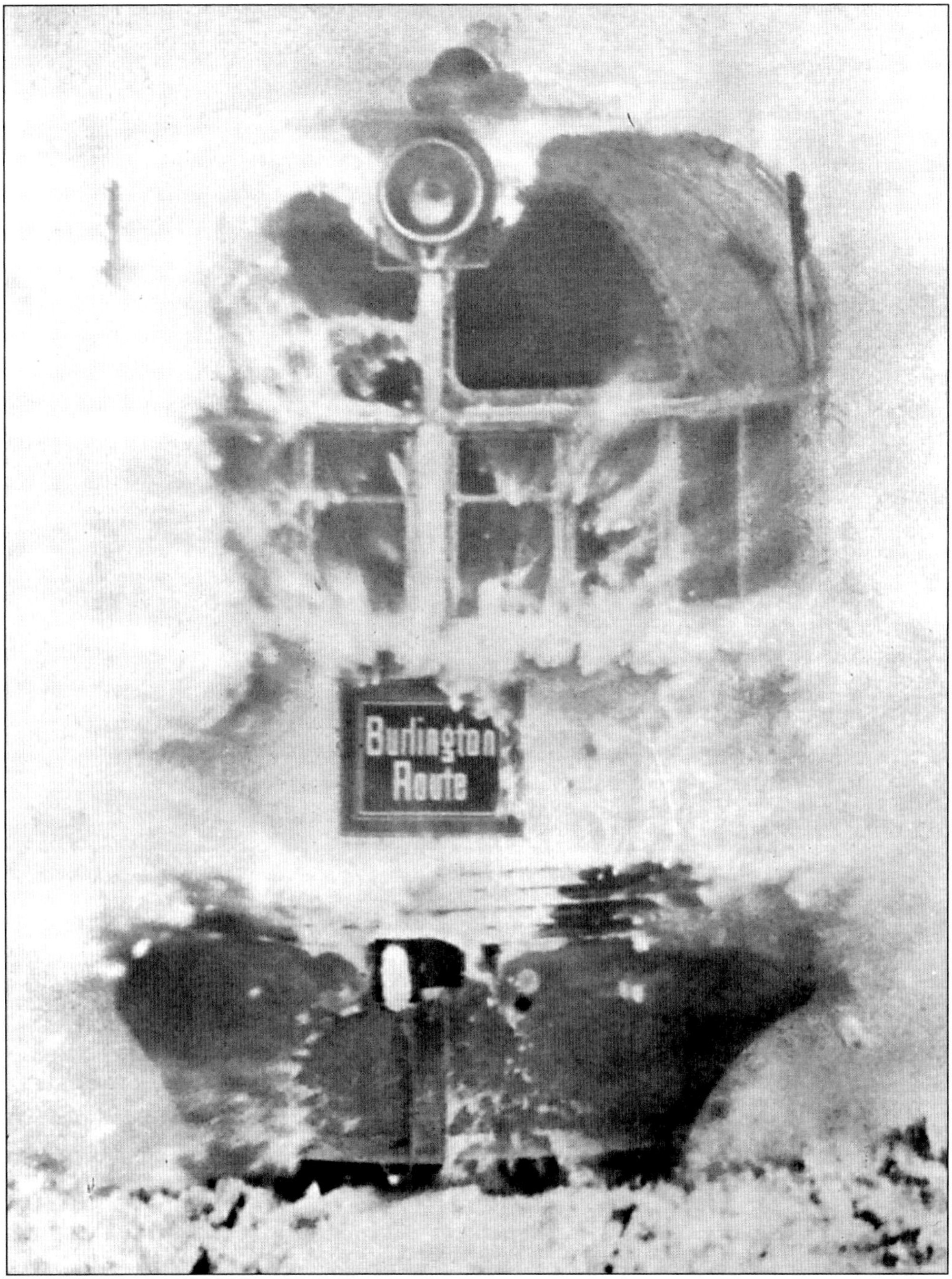

A Twin Cities Zephyr blasts through a snow drift.

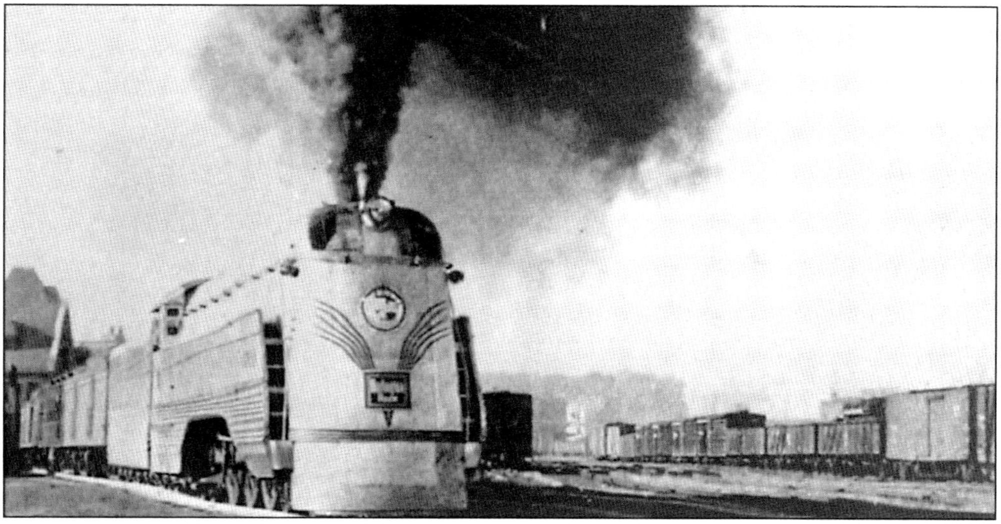

Aeolus, the name for the guardian of the wind god Zephyrus, was used as the name for the stand-by streamlined Zephyrs.

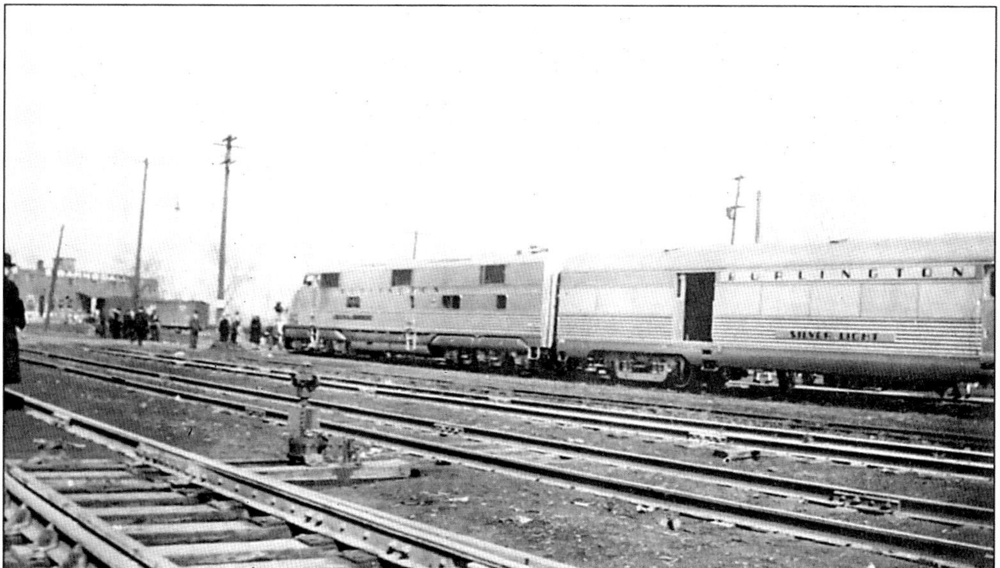

On March 17, 1940, a new E5 diesel and new passenger cars were on display at the Dubuque depot.

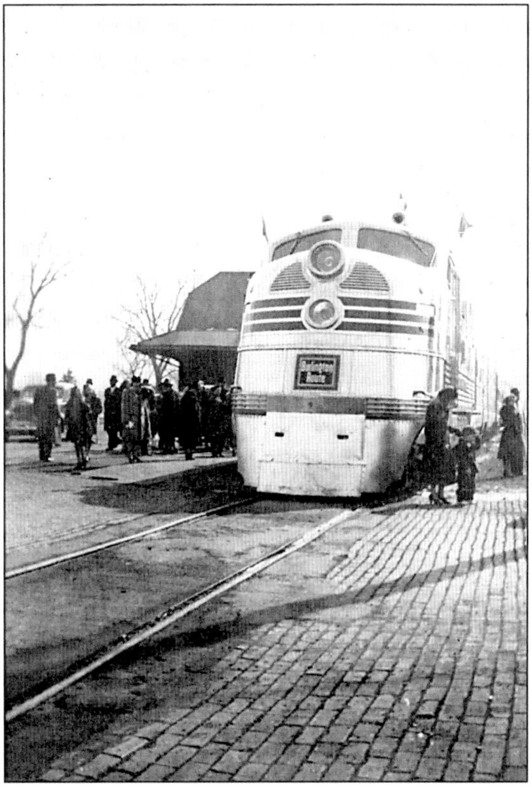

The front of the stylized E5 diesel locomotive from Electro Motive was used by the Burlington.

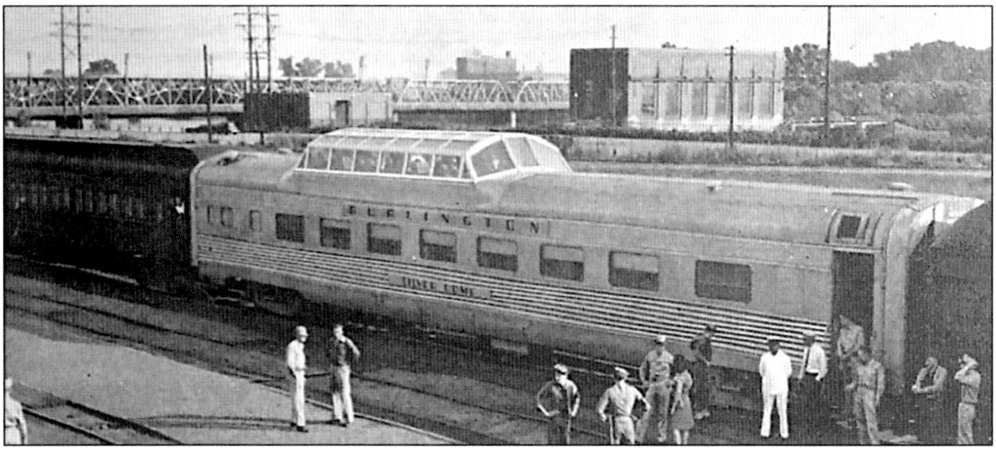

In 1945, the Burlington built the first vista dome passenger car in the nation.

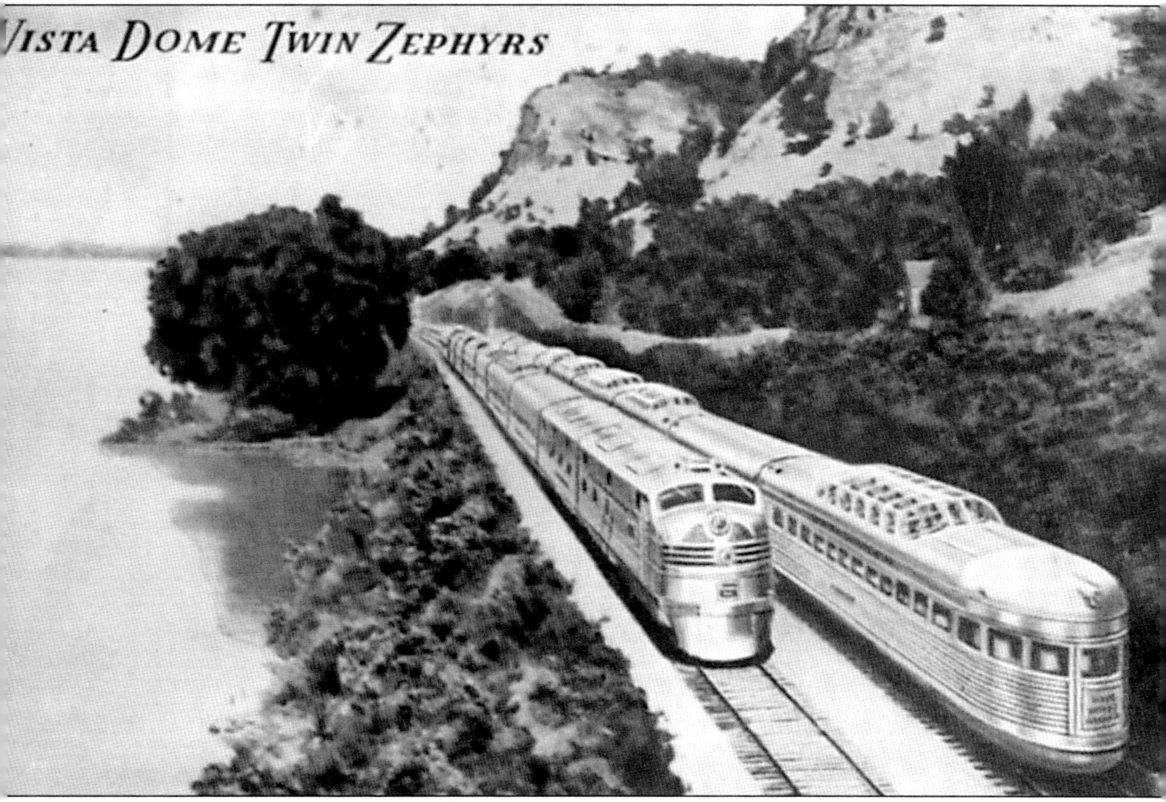

In this image, taken just after the end of World War II, Twin Cities Zephyrs pass north of East Dubuque, Illinois.

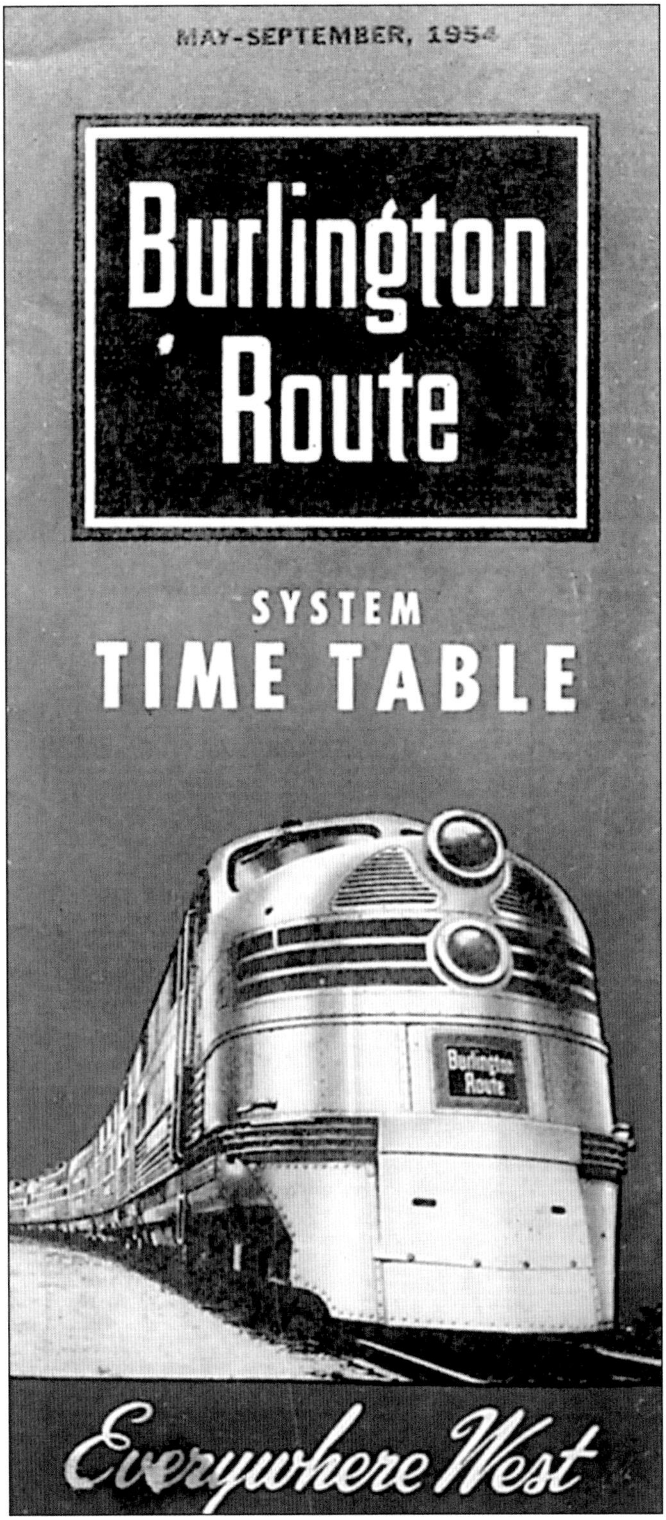

A 1954 Burlington timetable is shown here.

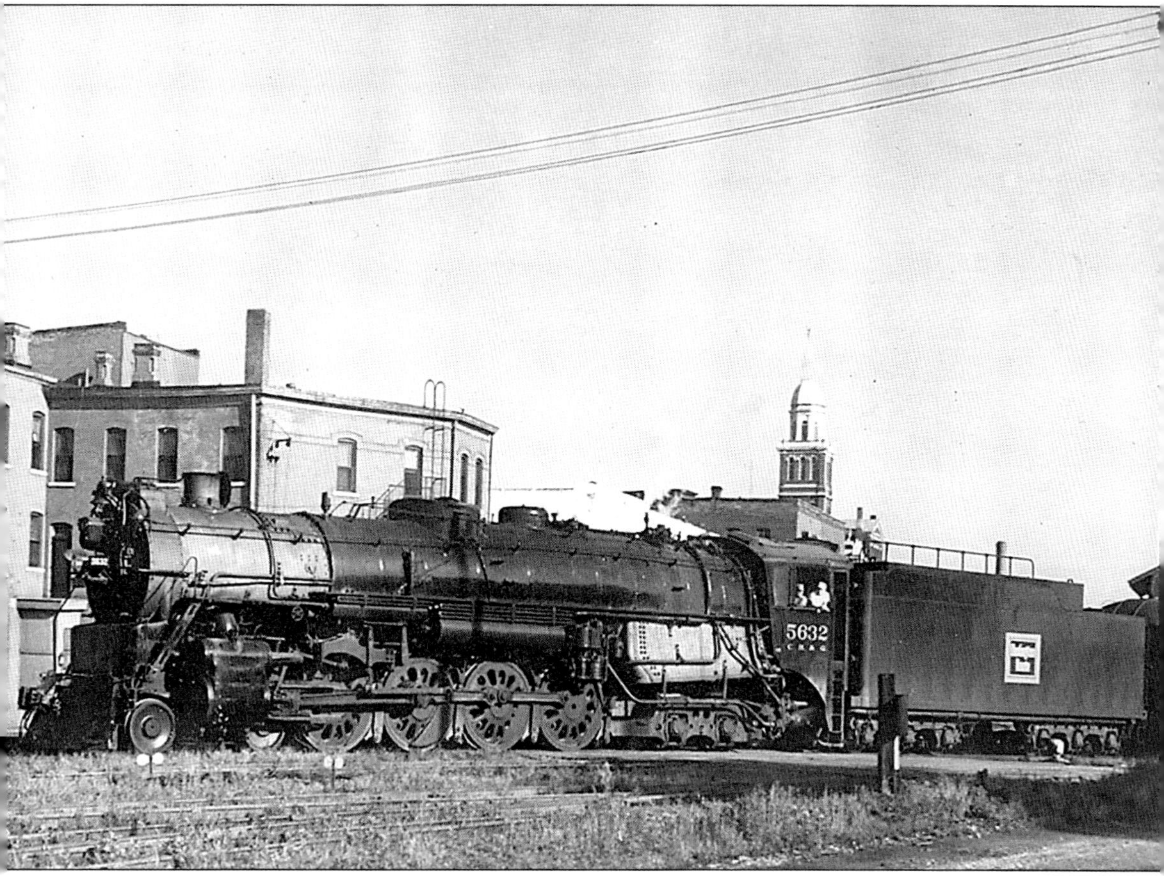

Chicago, Burlington and Quincy number 5632, a class 05 Northern 4-8-4, is pictured entering Dubuque with an excursion train in the late 1950s.

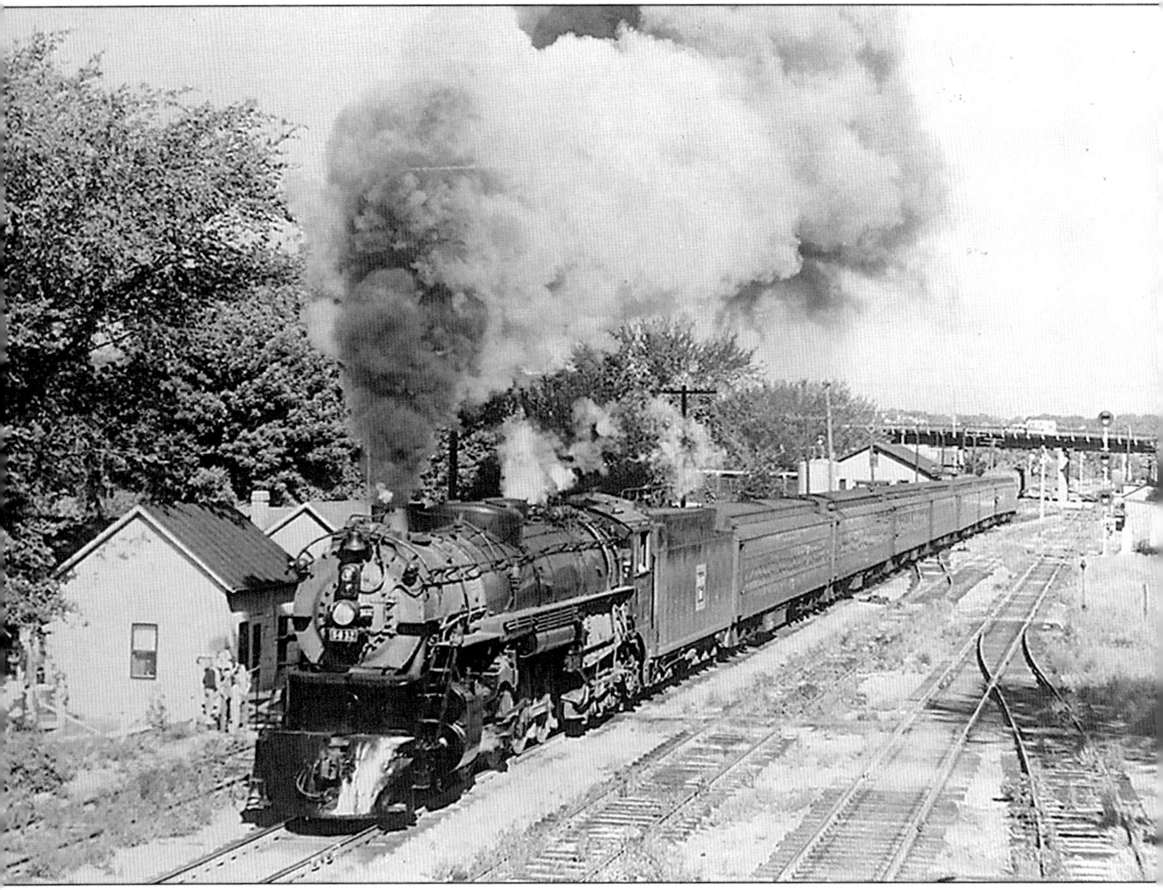

In this image, number 5632 leaves East Dubuque for Savanna, Illinois, with seven clerestory passenger coaches.

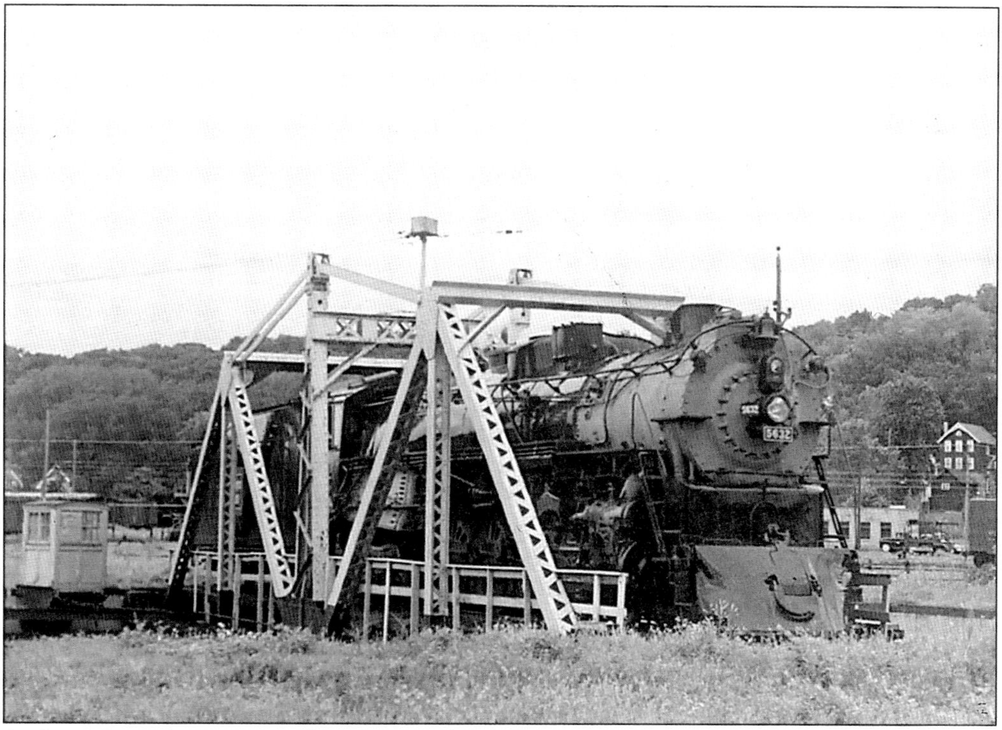

A class 05 Northern is turned at Savanna for the return trip to Dubuque.

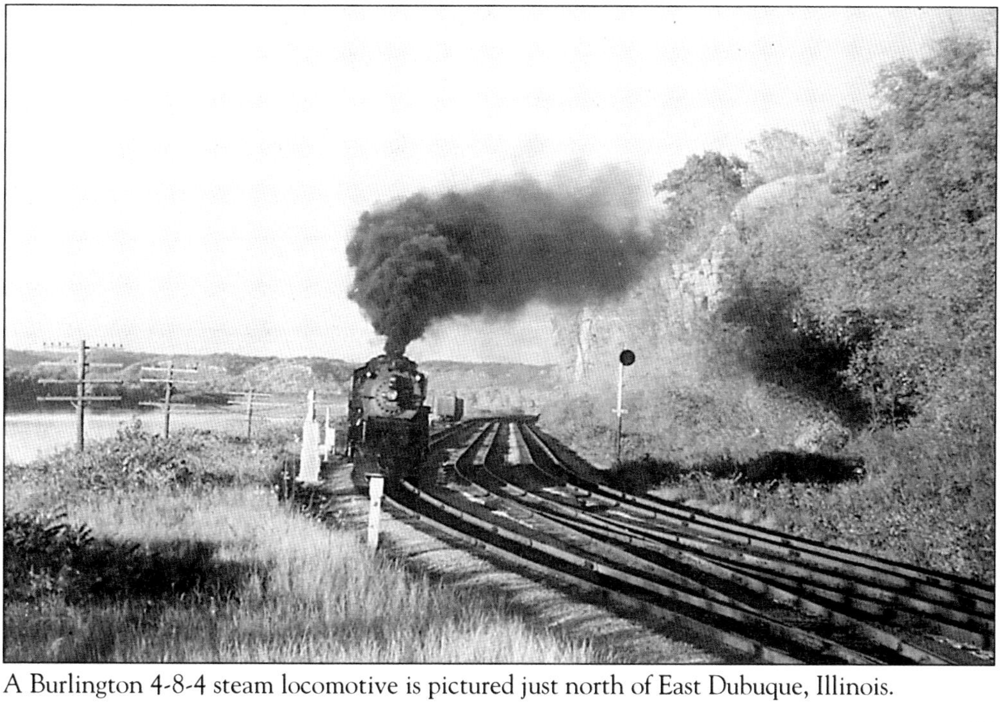

A Burlington 4-8-4 steam locomotive is pictured just north of East Dubuque, Illinois.

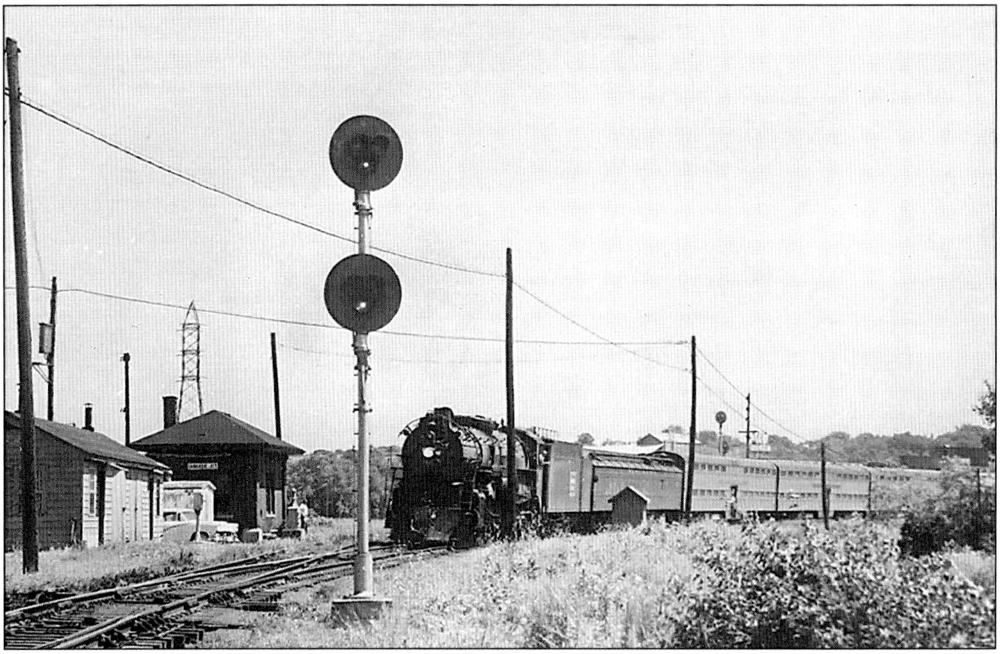

Number 5632 is pictured returning with another excursion train of commuter coaches in 1960s.

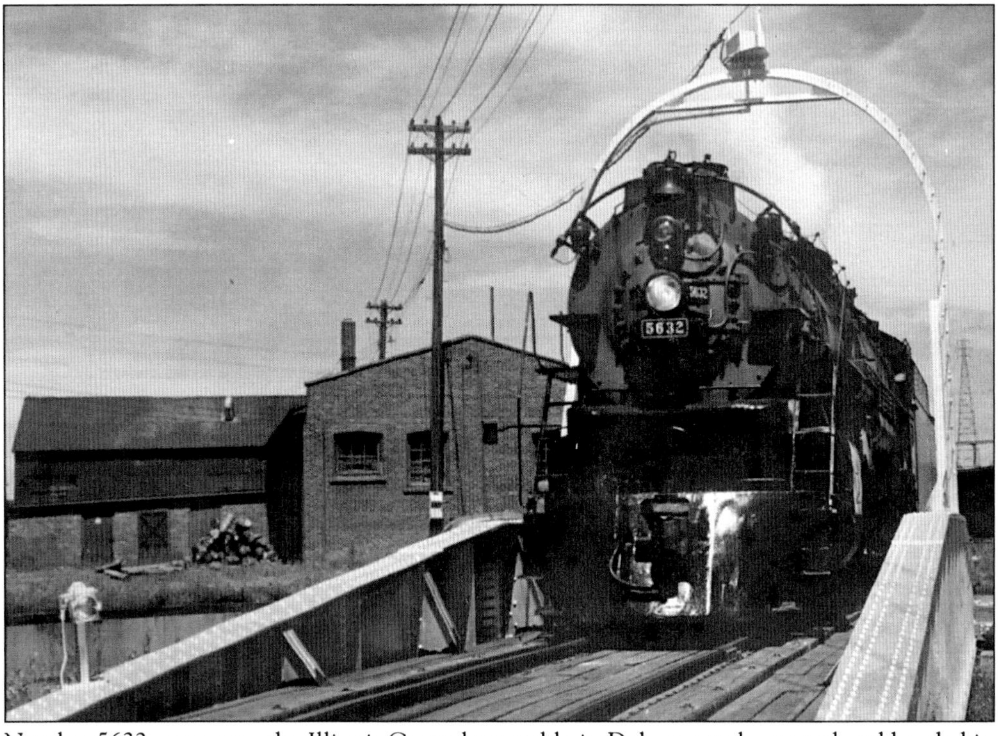

Number 5632 eases onto the Illinois Central turntable in Dubuque to be turned and headed in the opposite direction in 1960.

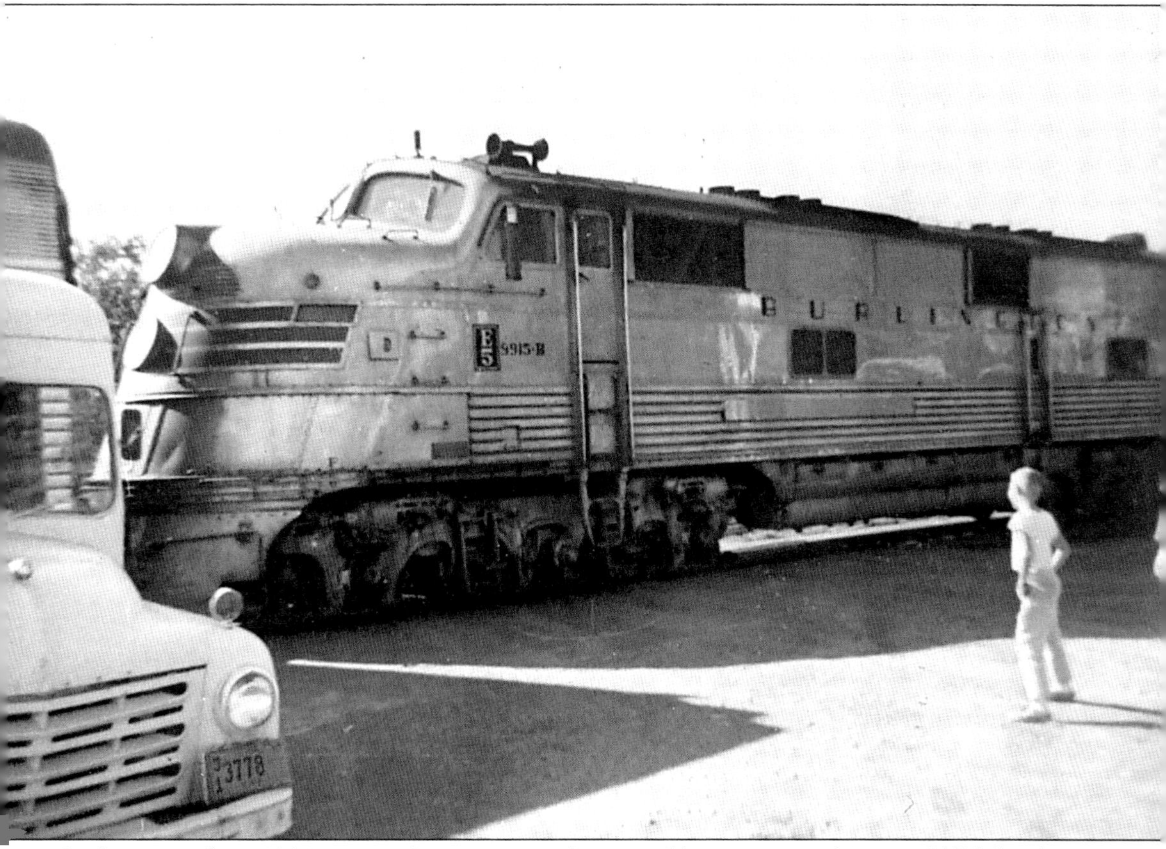

In this image from 1964, a young boy examines the second locomotive, a 24-year-old E5 diesel, which is on the point of the Twin Cities Zephyr at East Dubuque, Illinois.

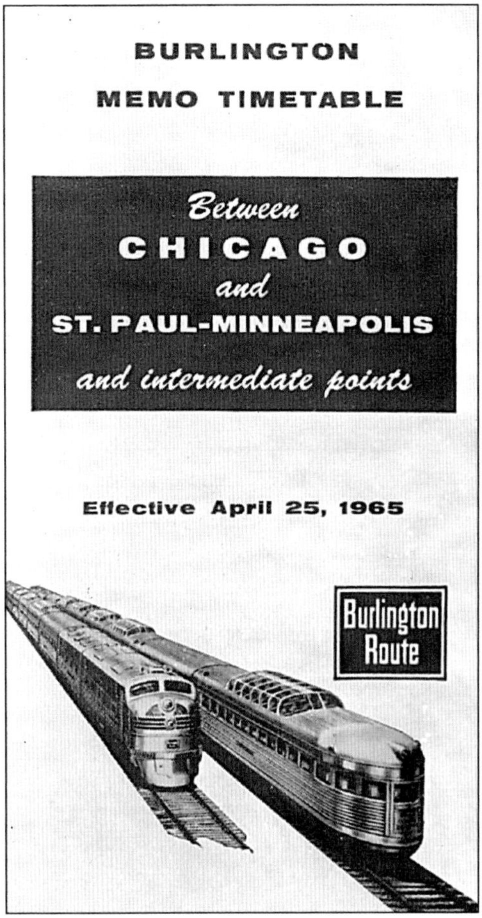

This Burlington Memo timetable is dated April 25, 1965.

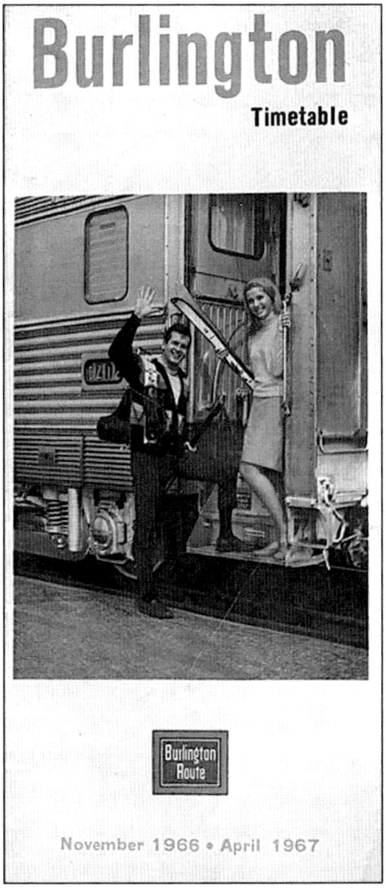

This Burlington timetable is from 1966 and 1967.

South of East Dubuque, Illinois, new ribbon rail is installed on the northbound (west) rails. These 1,428-foot-long rails helped cars' wheels cause a hissing noise, rather than the usual "clickity-clack" at the joints.

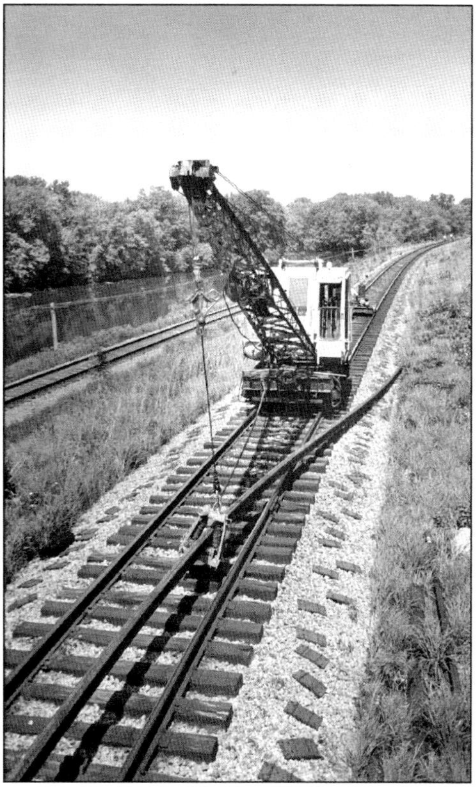

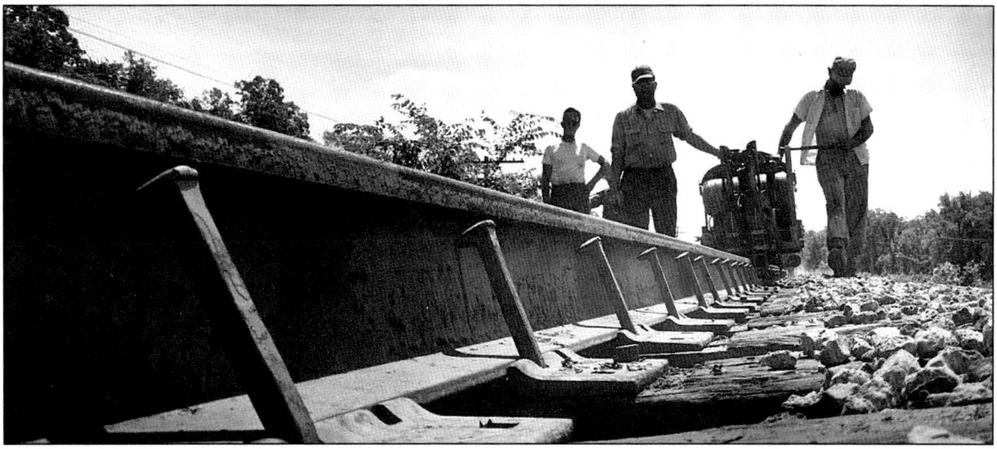

The spike setter positions the spikes to be set. The rail weighs 132 pounds per yard.

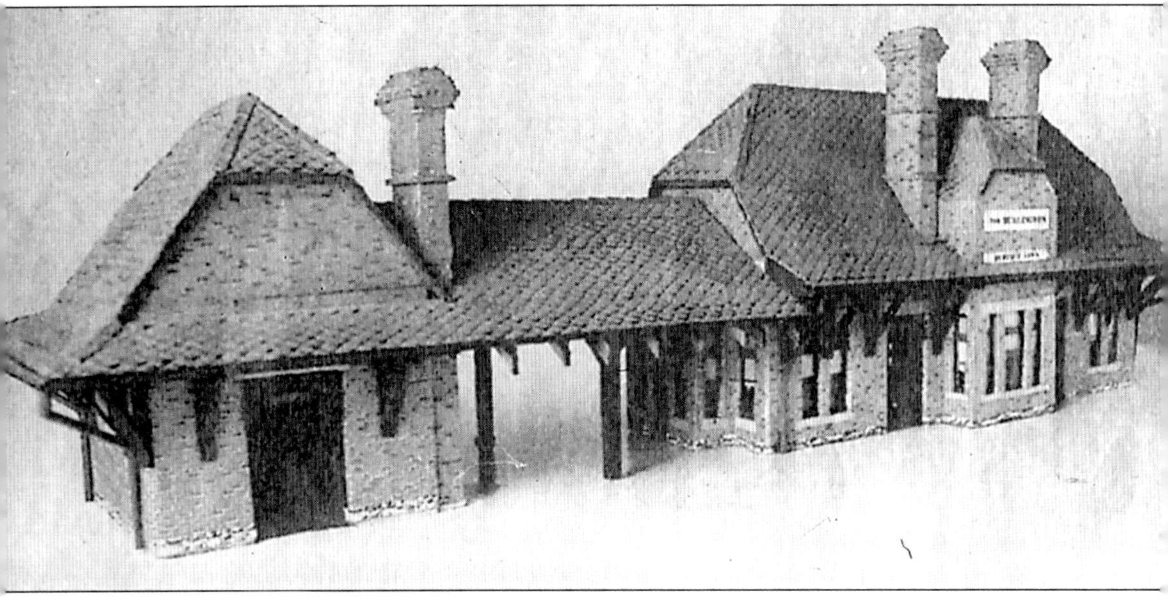

This is an image of a model of the Burlington depot in Dubuque, Iowa, as it appeared when built by the Chicago, Burlington and Northern Rail Road in 1881. In the 1940s, the cottage-style roof was removed and a modern exterior applied. In the 1990s, the building housed a boat museum, and was restored to its original appearance when the National River Aquarium and Museum was created. It currently houses a restaurant.

Four

The Chicago Great Western

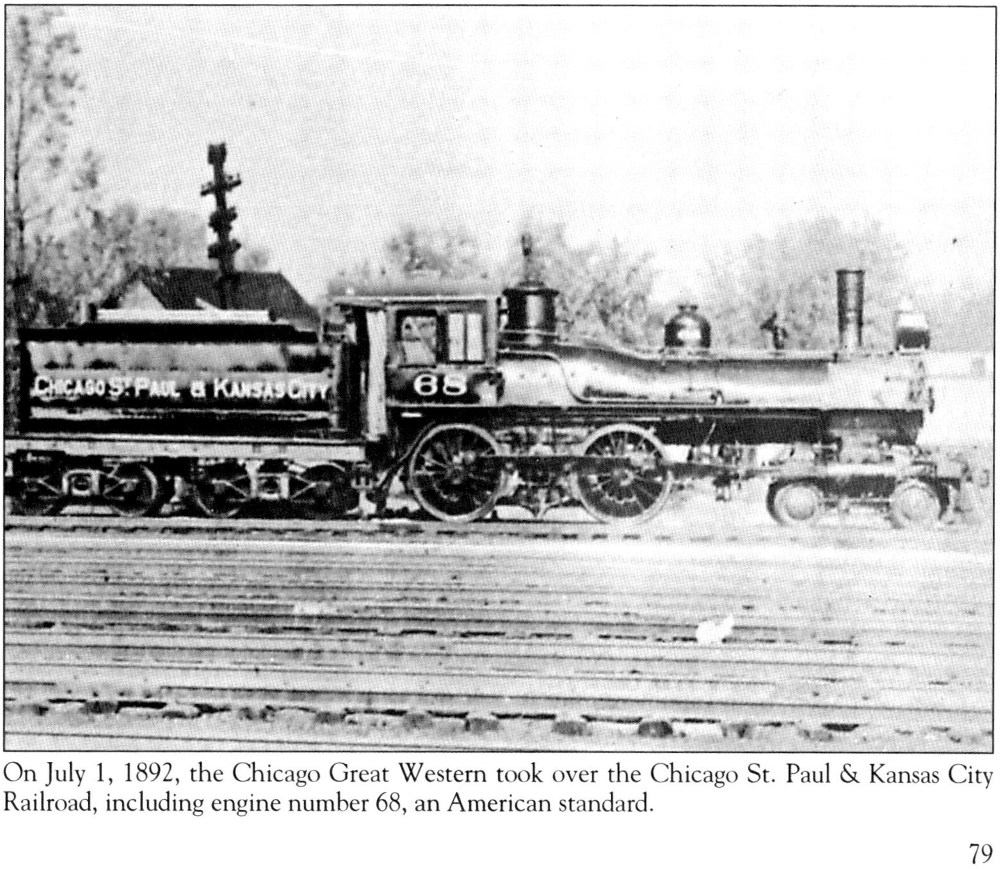

On July 1, 1892, the Chicago Great Western took over the Chicago St. Paul & Kansas City Railroad, including engine number 68, an American standard.

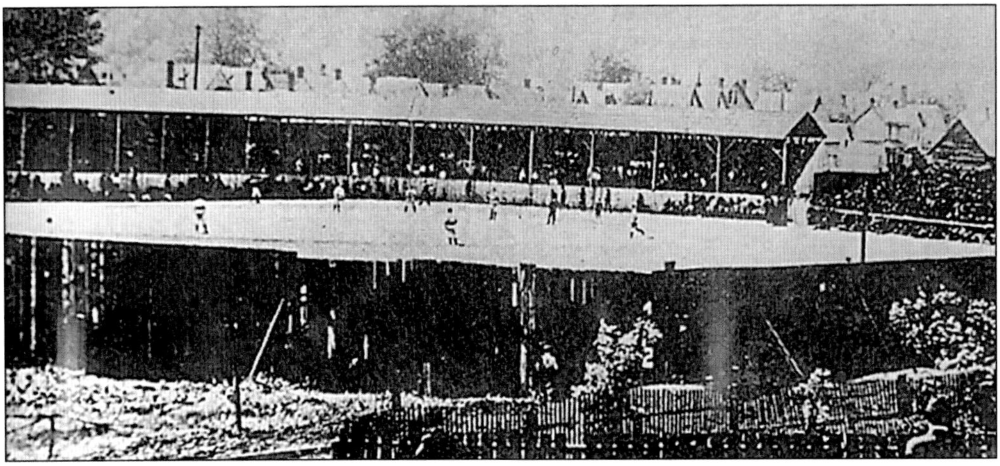

The Chicago Great Western tracks passed within a few feet of the outfield wall of the park on Jackson Street, as seen in this 1895 image.

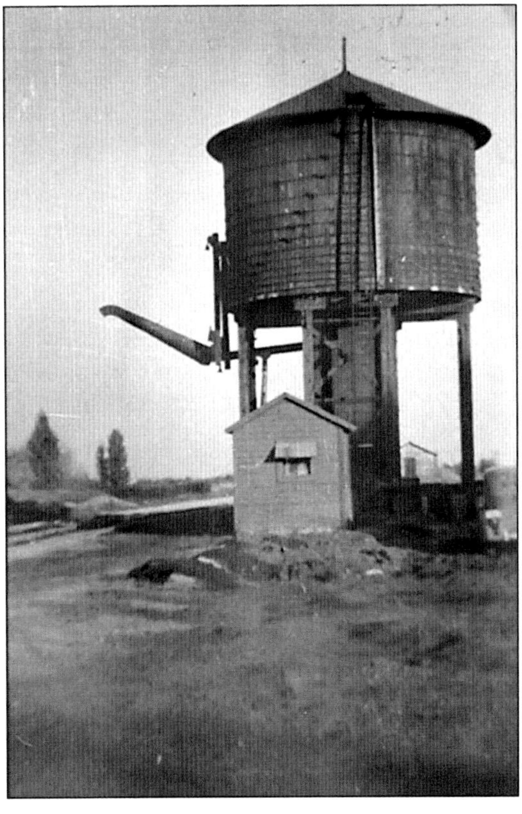

This is an image of a water tank where a locomotive could quench its thirst.

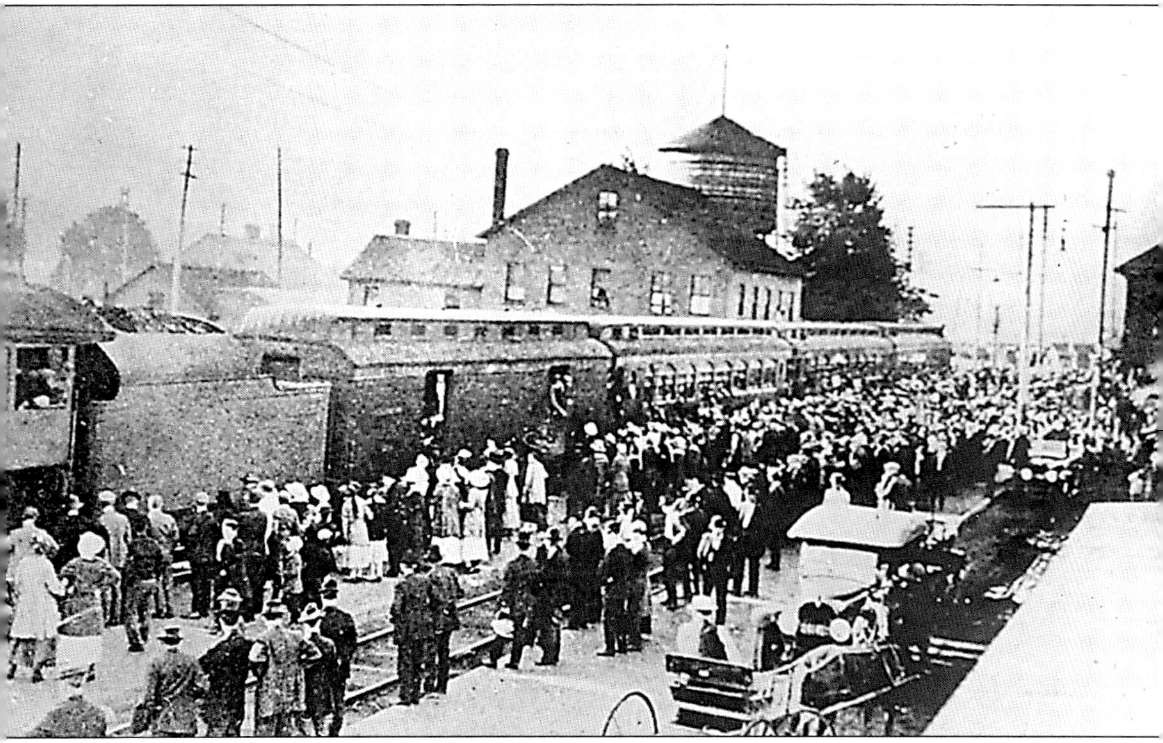

A four-car passenger train carries soldiers returning from World War I, stoppping in Dubuque to let some "dough boys" off.

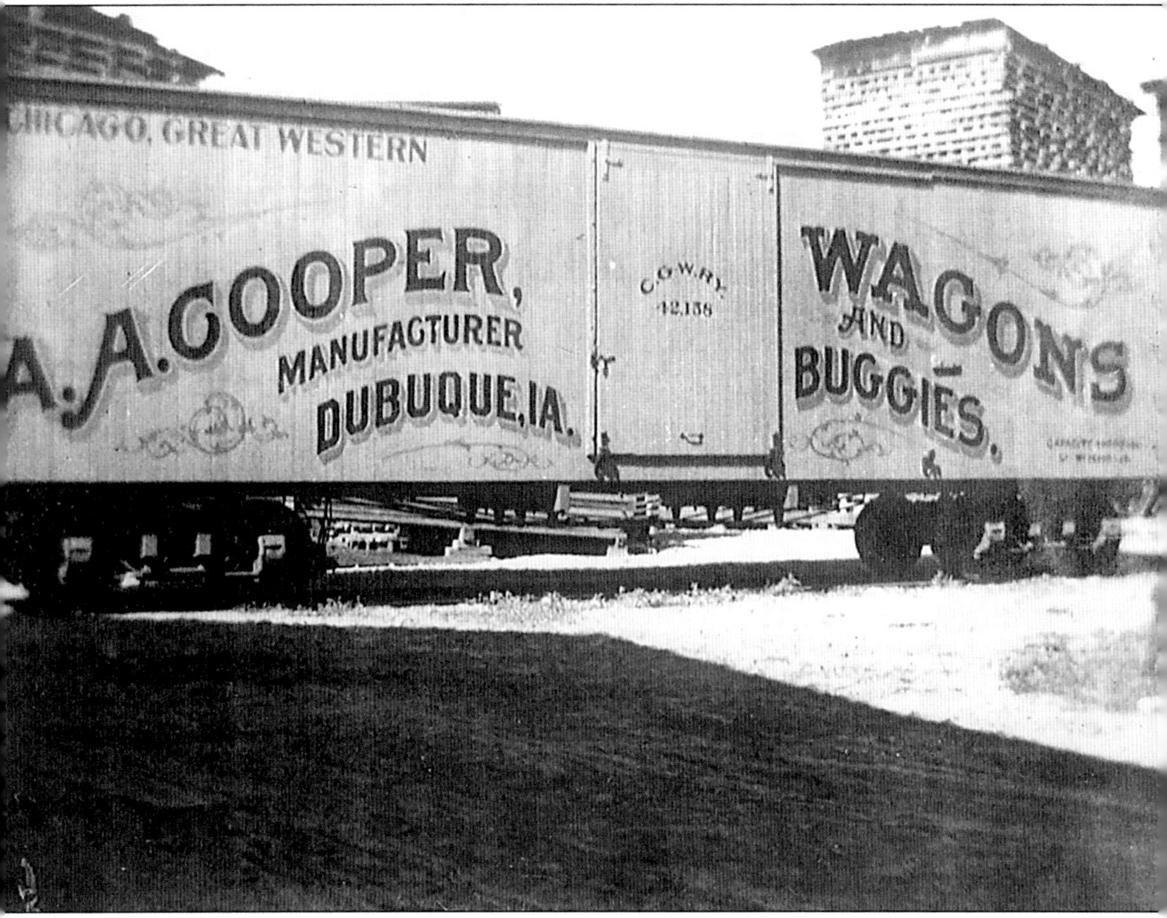

A. A. Cooper competed with the Studebaker Wagon manufacturer for many years. Cooper was approached by representatives of auto manufacturers and asked to convert his huge complex to accommodate the production of horseless carriages. He fervently believed that the automobile would not succeed, and refused.

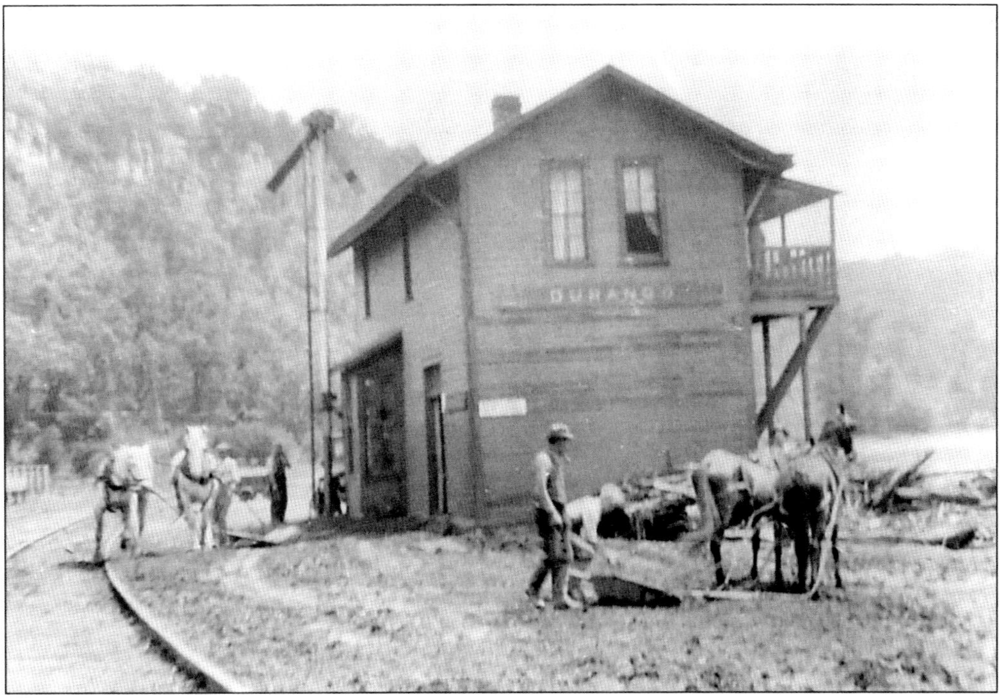

A team of horses pulls a scoop, helping to level the platform at Durango, Iowa. The white team is the power to level the ground in front of the station.

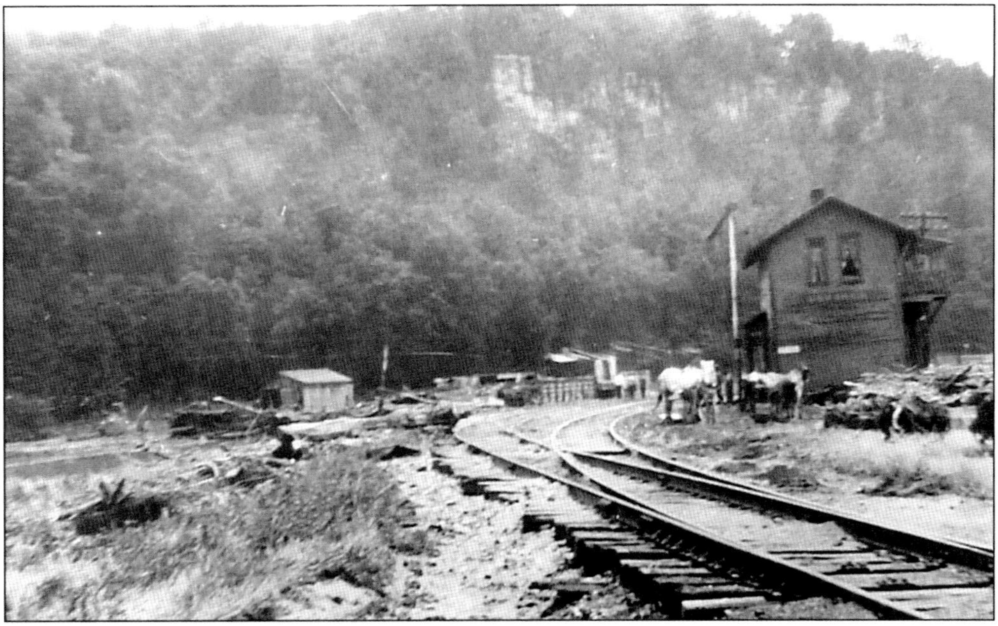

The work was slow but steady when men and horses worked together at any job in the 19th and early 20th century.

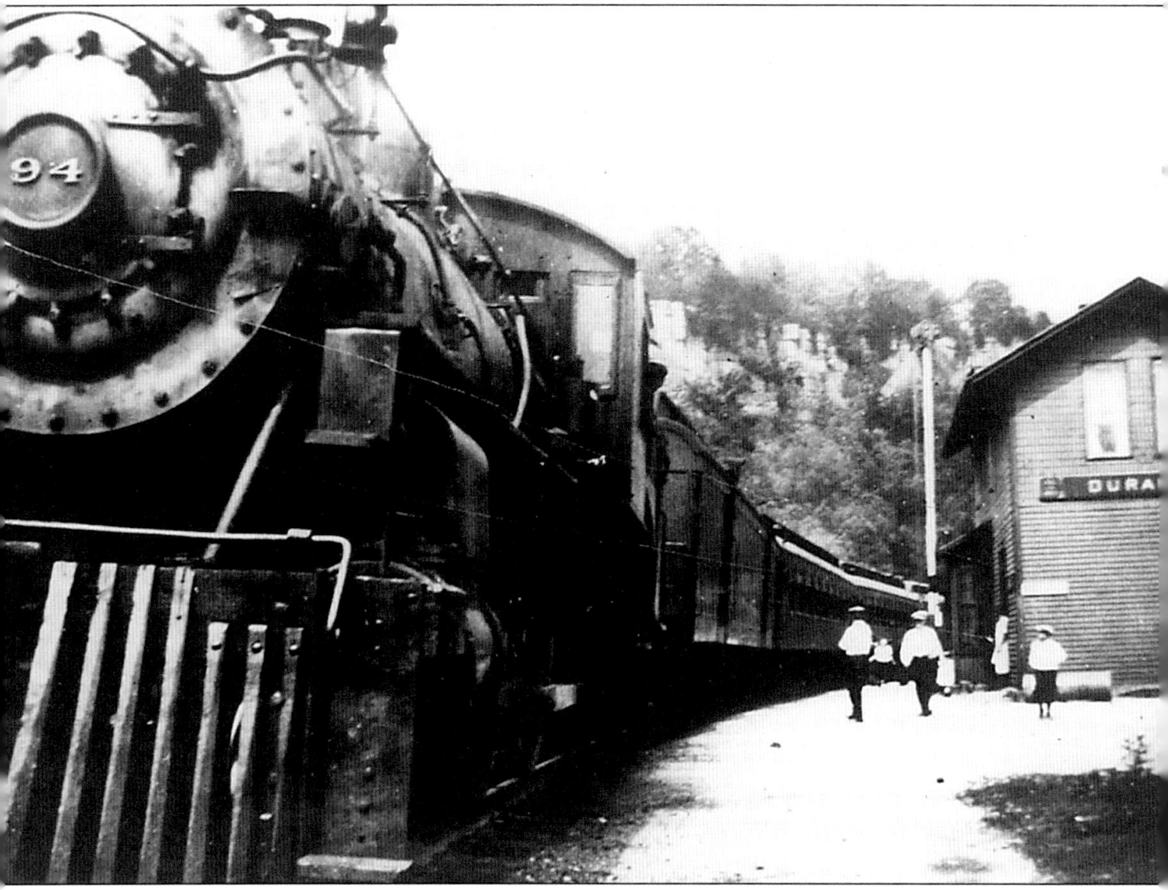

Engine number 94 and its passenger train stops at the completed platform at Durango, eight miles northwest of Dubuque.

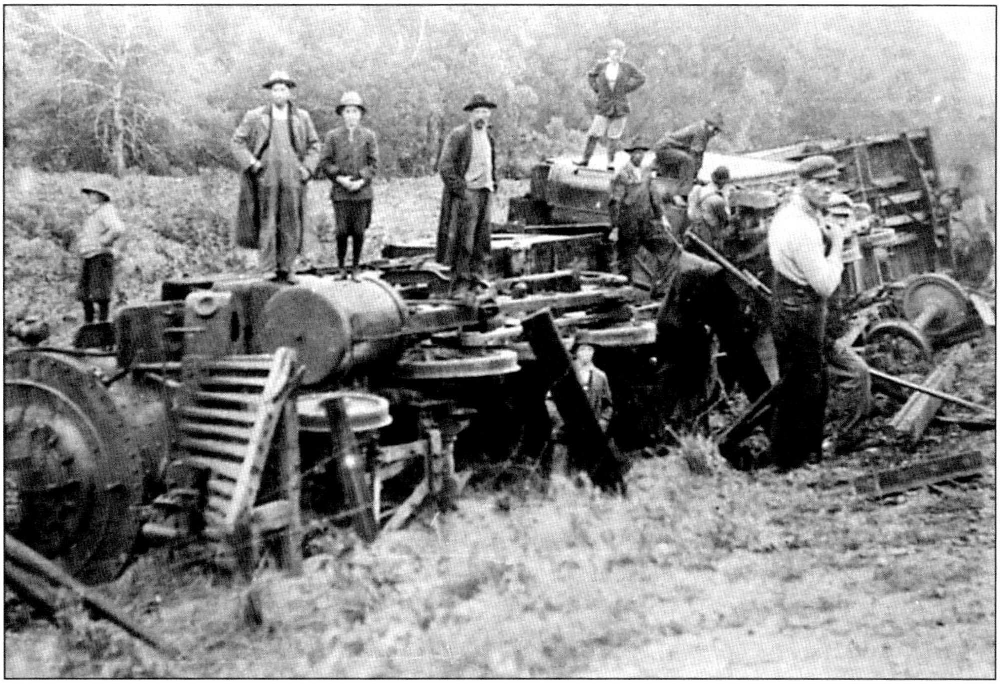

Engine number 327 lies on its side after a wreck at Graf, Iowa, in 1911.

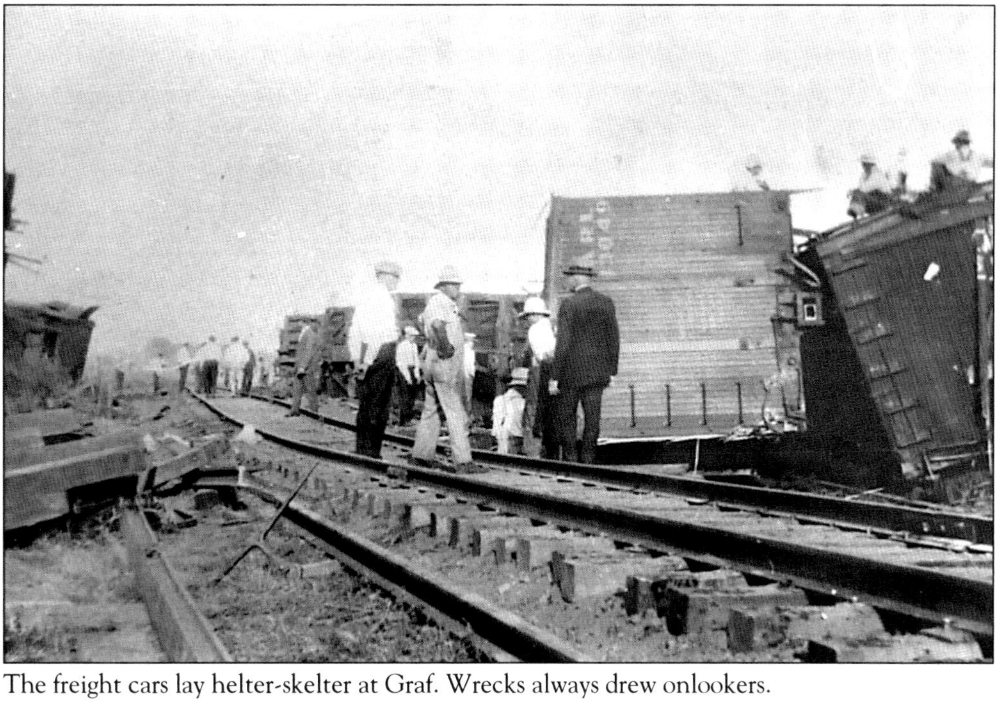

The freight cars lay helter-skelter at Graf. Wrecks always drew onlookers.

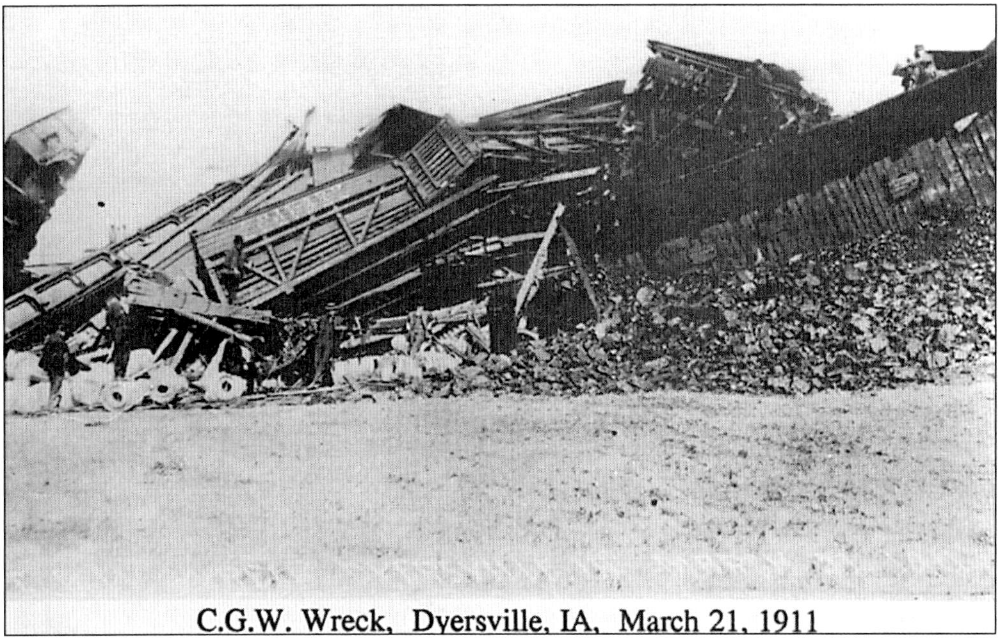

On March 21, 1911, another wreck on the Chicago Great Western occurred at Dyersville, Iowa. In this view the turmoil is evident.

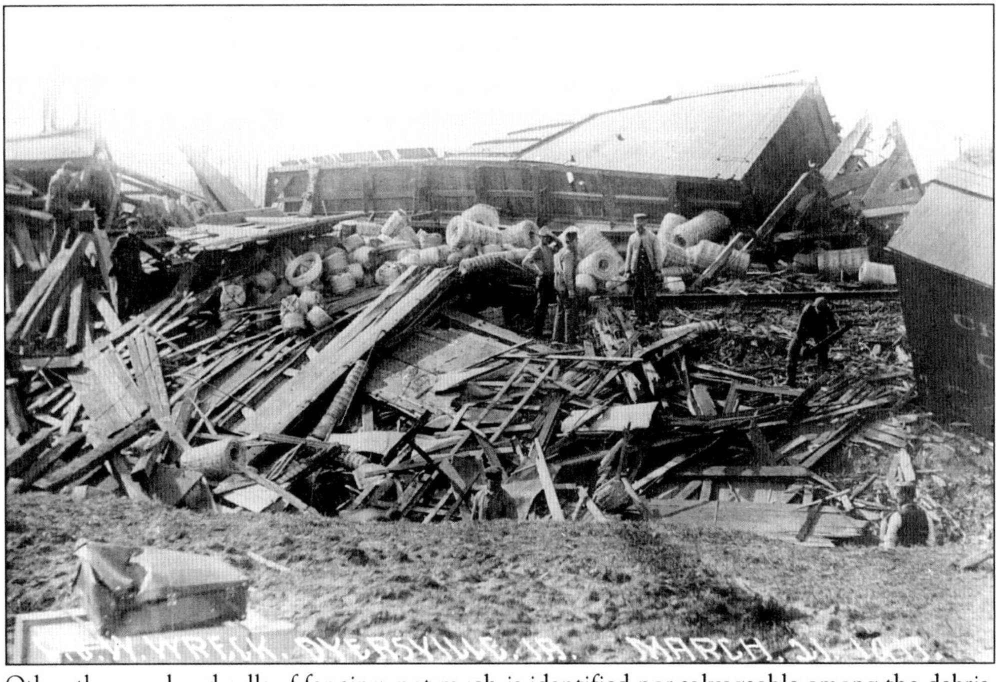

Other than coal and rolls of fencing, not much is identified nor salvageable among the debris. Wrecks were extremely costly to railroads.

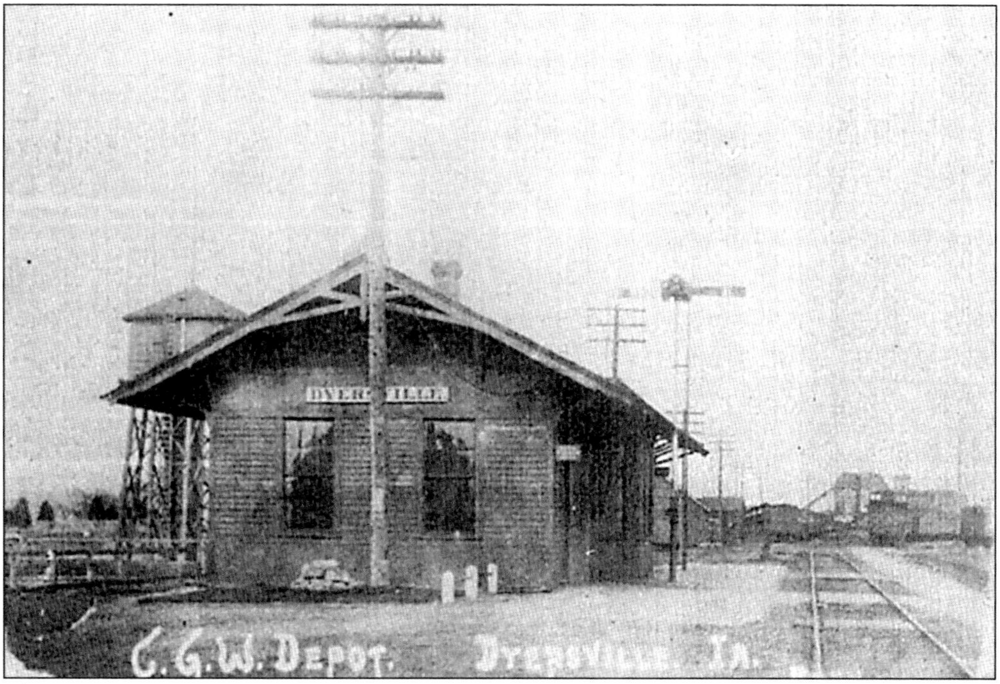

This photograph, taken at the Dyersville Chicago Great Western depot, provides a more peaceful scene.

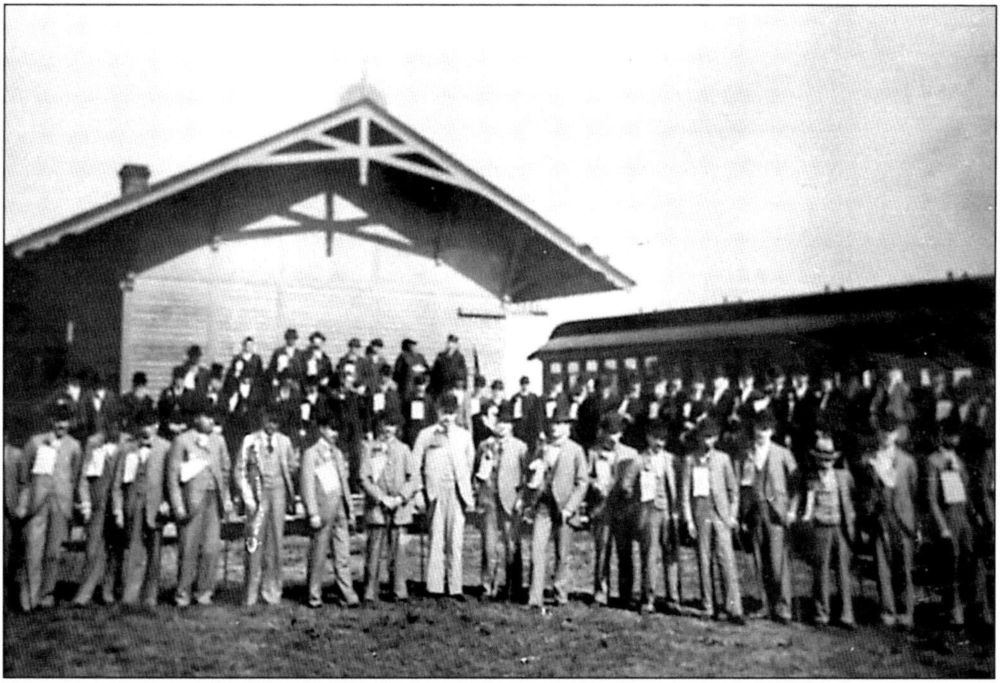

Also pictured at the Dyersville station, a group of men wearing similar tags pose for a photograph.

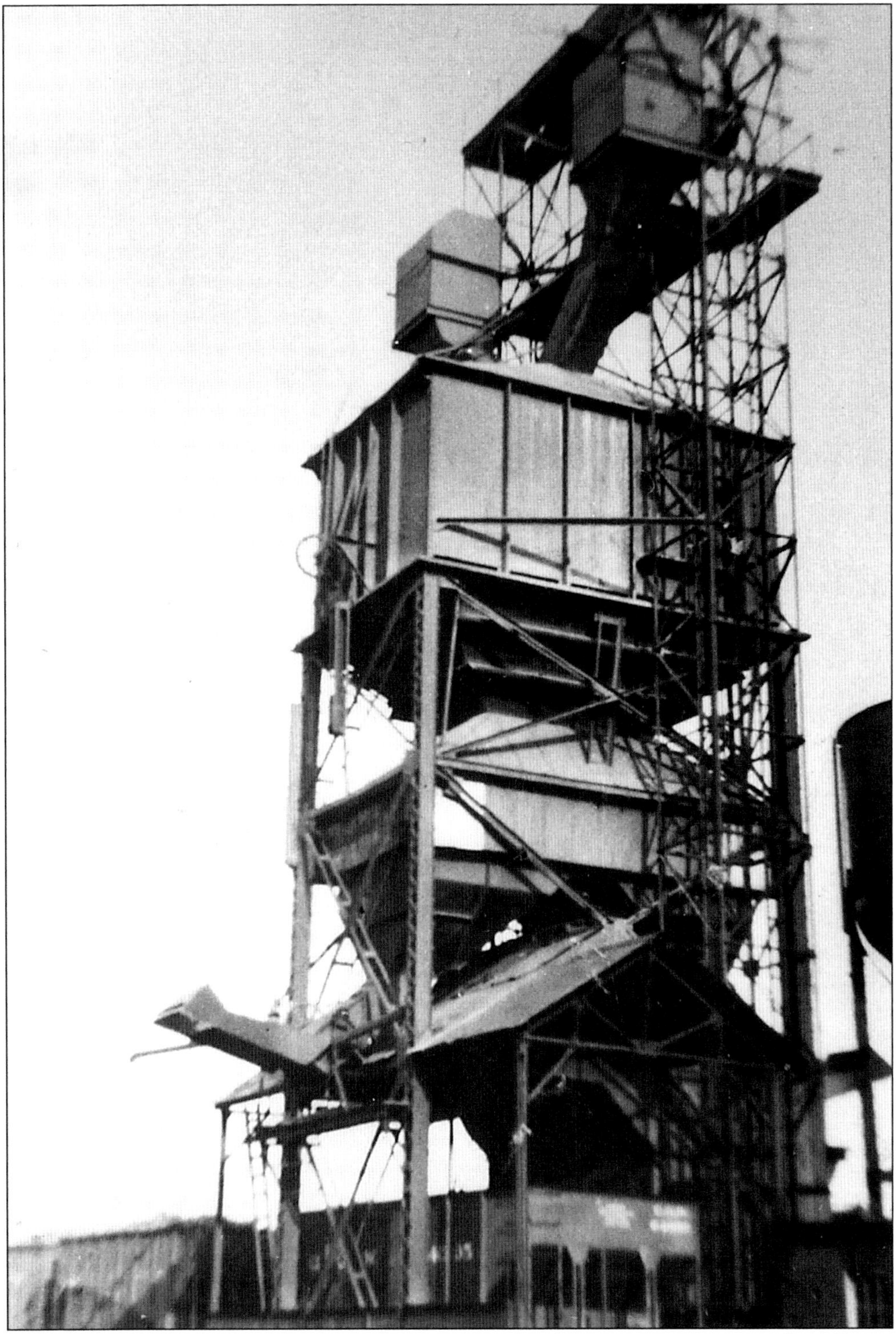

This image shows the coal tower at Graf, Iowa, west of Dubuque, in 1919. It gave the village a sense of importance whenever a train stopped for fuel or water.

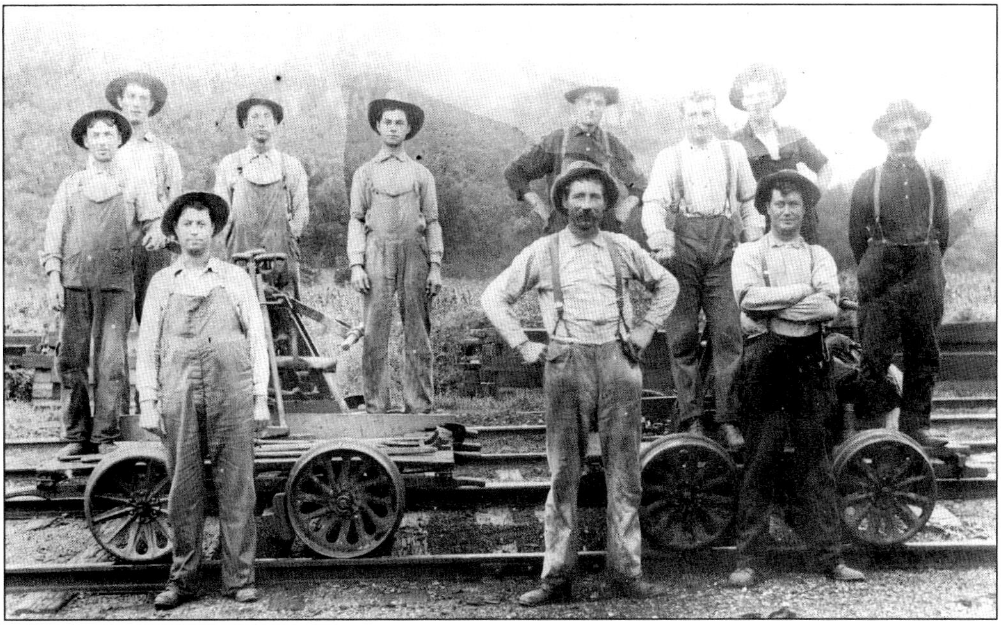

Members of an 11-man work gang pose on their hand cars at Durango, Iowa, before heading out to work.

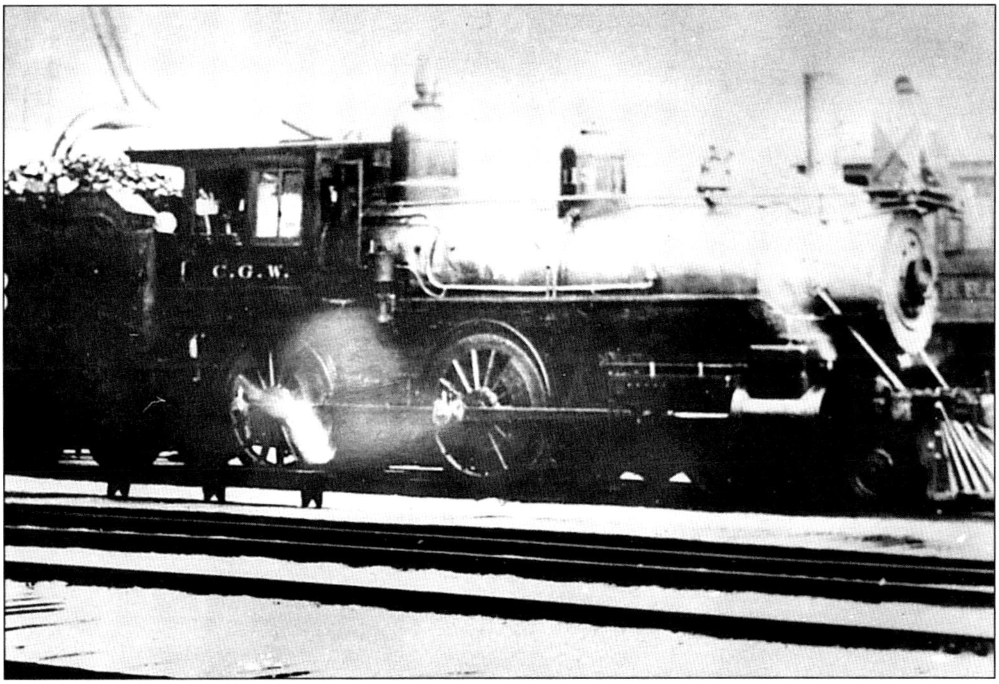

This is a photograph of engine number 113, a 4-4-0, pausing at Fairground in Iowa.

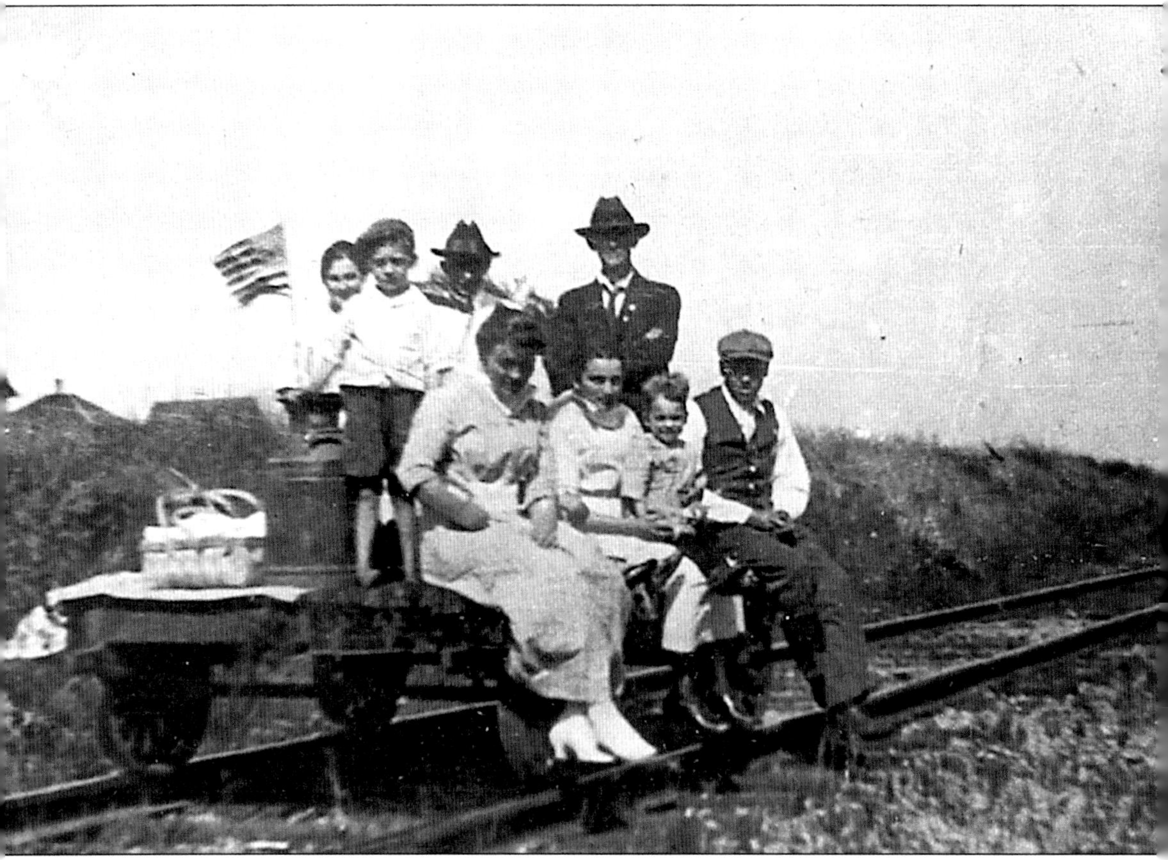

In the early 20th century, a quieter time, it was common for employees to have permission to use a hand car (like the one pictured above) to take their families on Sunday picnics.

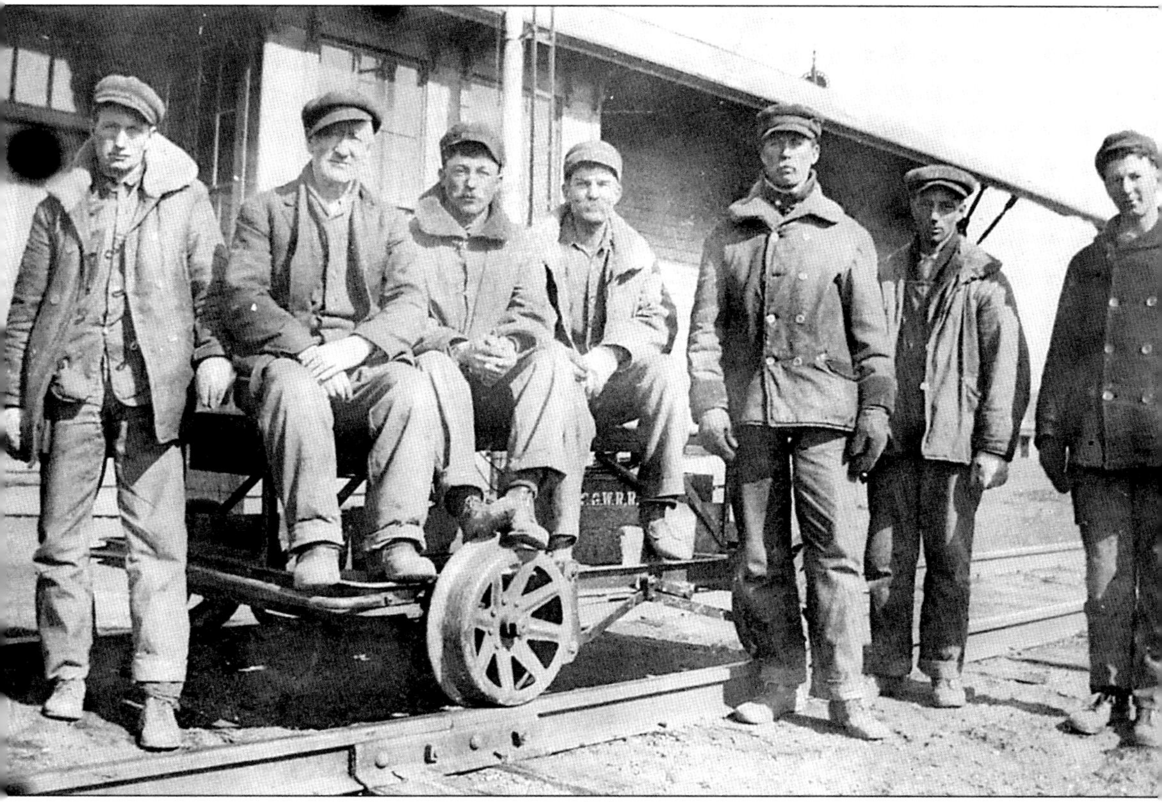

A section gang poses with their transportation before going to work. From left to right are Delmar Gunter, section boss Mr. Scott, Floyd Fertig, Bonder Auserkirk, Will Hutchinson, Earl Grones, and Willie Golliday.

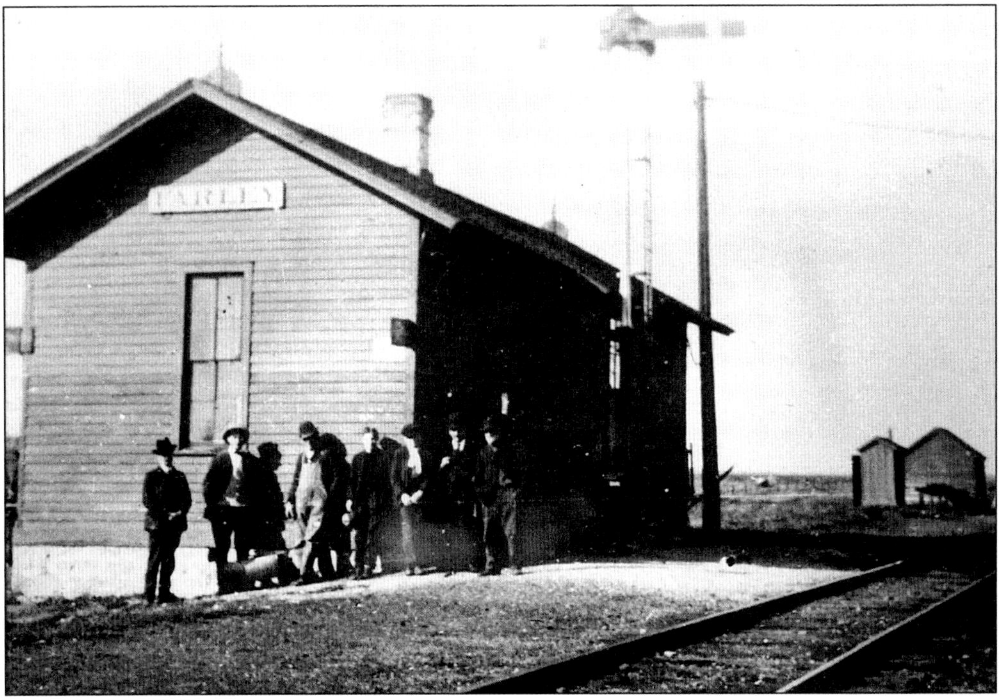

In this image, seven unidentified men pose next to the station in Farley, Iowa. The semaphore is signaling the next train to stop.

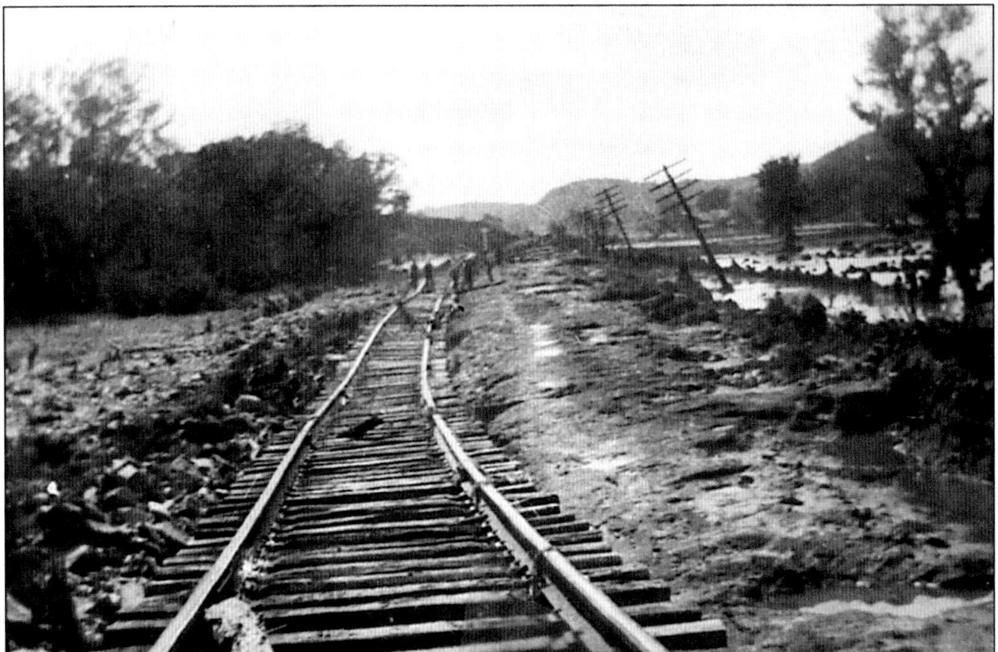

This 1925 photograph taken in Graf, Iowa, shows that water is one of the most powerful elements on earth, and that even a small river like the Little Maquoketa River can rip up and bend railroad tracks during a flood.

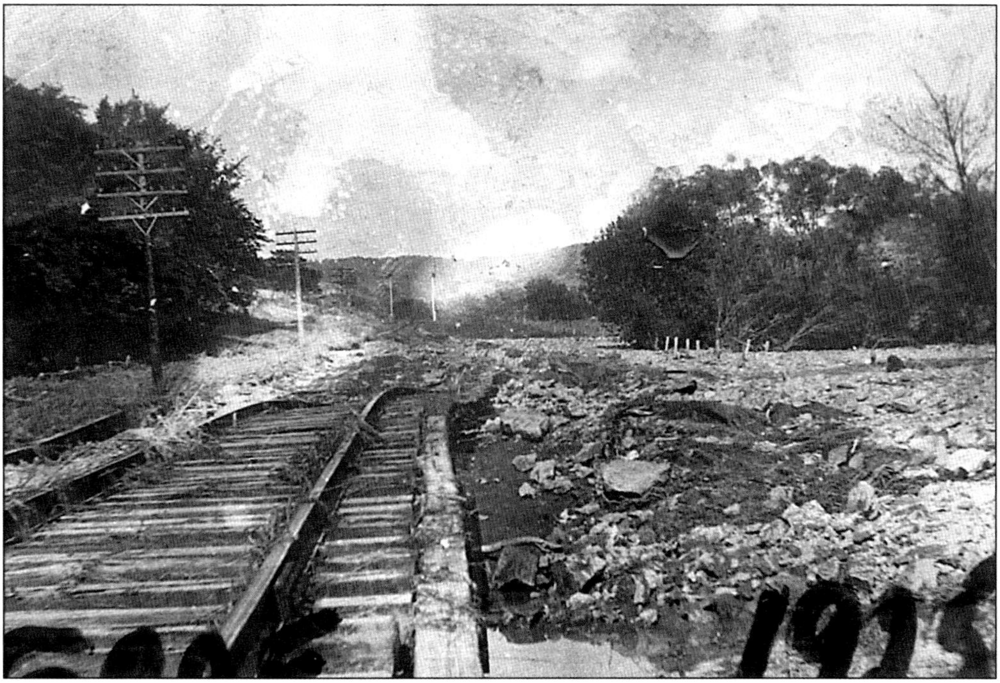

The 1925 flood caused extensive damage on the other end of the small town of Graf.

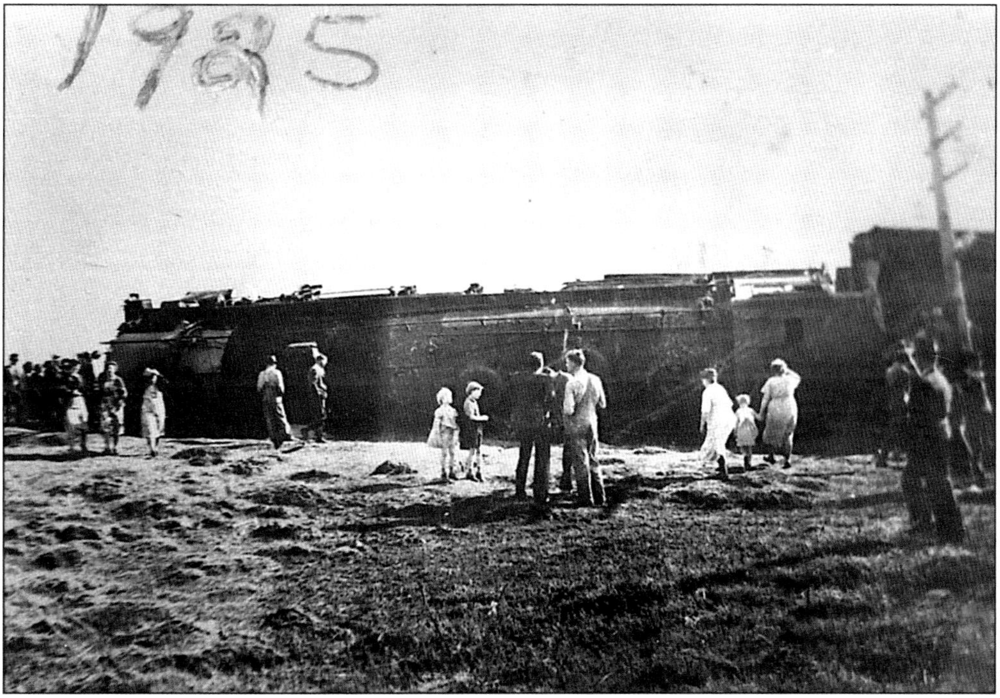

A huge locomotive tried to get through the water and rolled off the track.

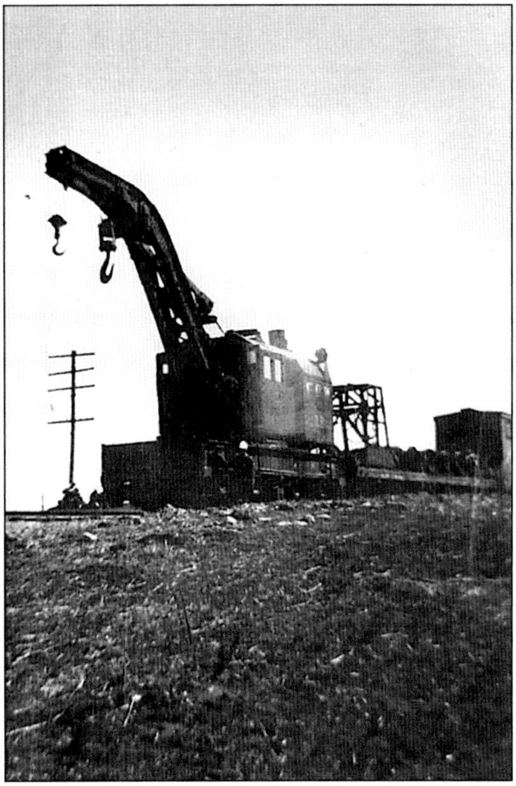

In the mess that resulted from the flood at Graf in 1925, the Chicago Great Western deployed its crane from Oelwein to help "right things."

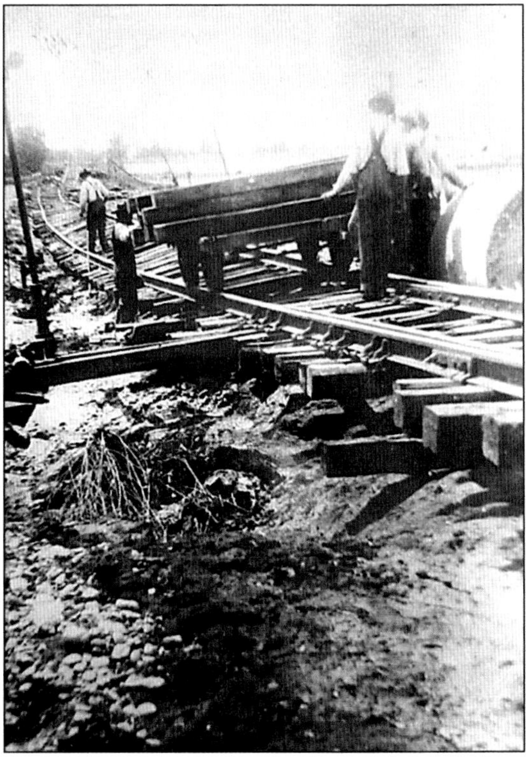

This work crew has a lot of grading and track-laying ahead; they will work long hours.

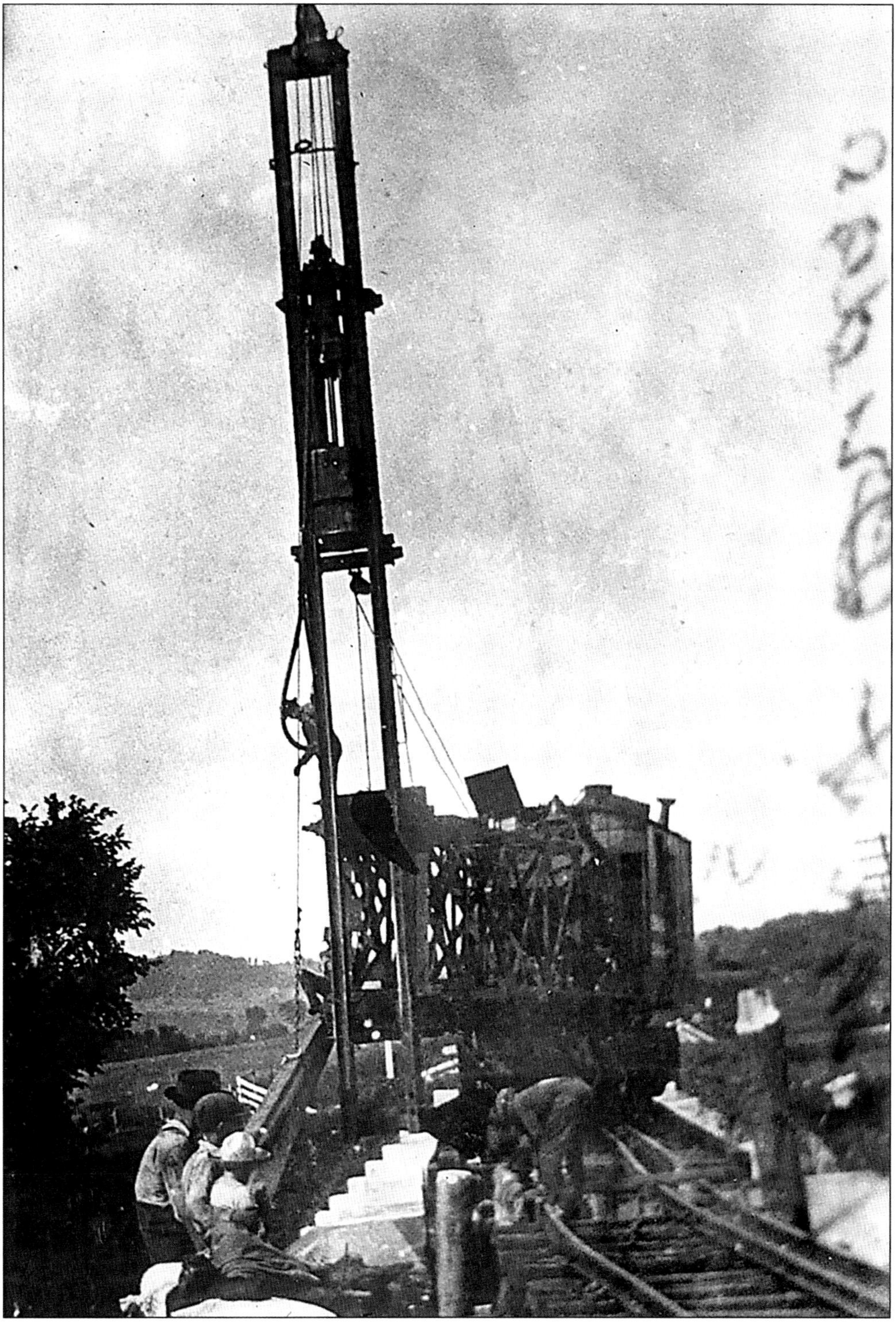

A piledriver works at securing a solid roadbed at a bridge near Graf.

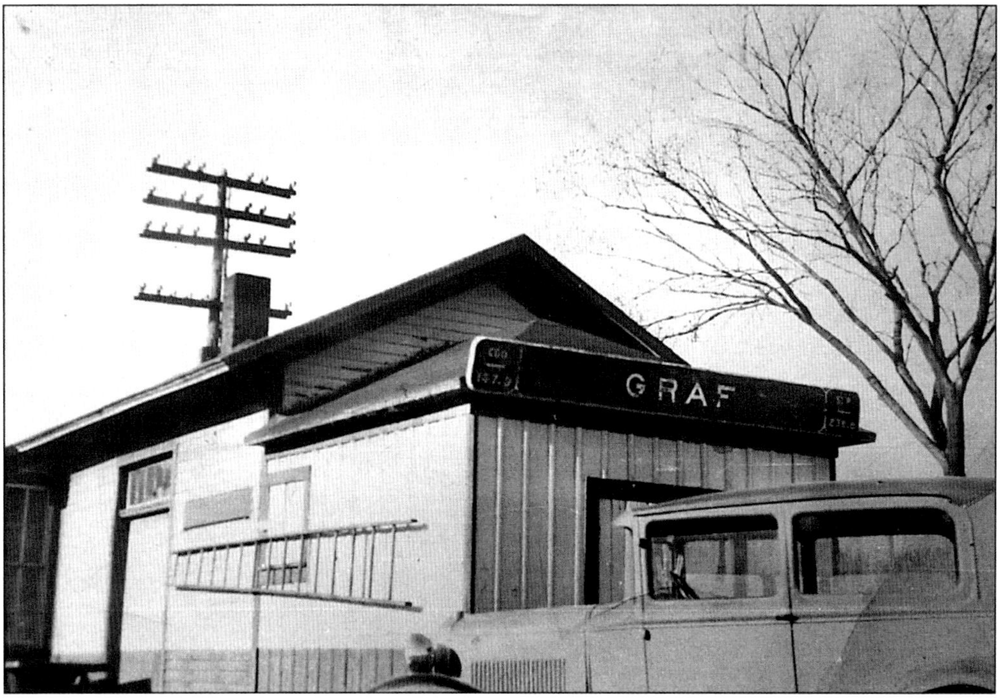

This is an image of the Chicago Great Western Rail Road station at Graf. The town was a great place to watch trains. Today, there are still homes in Graf, but no railroad.

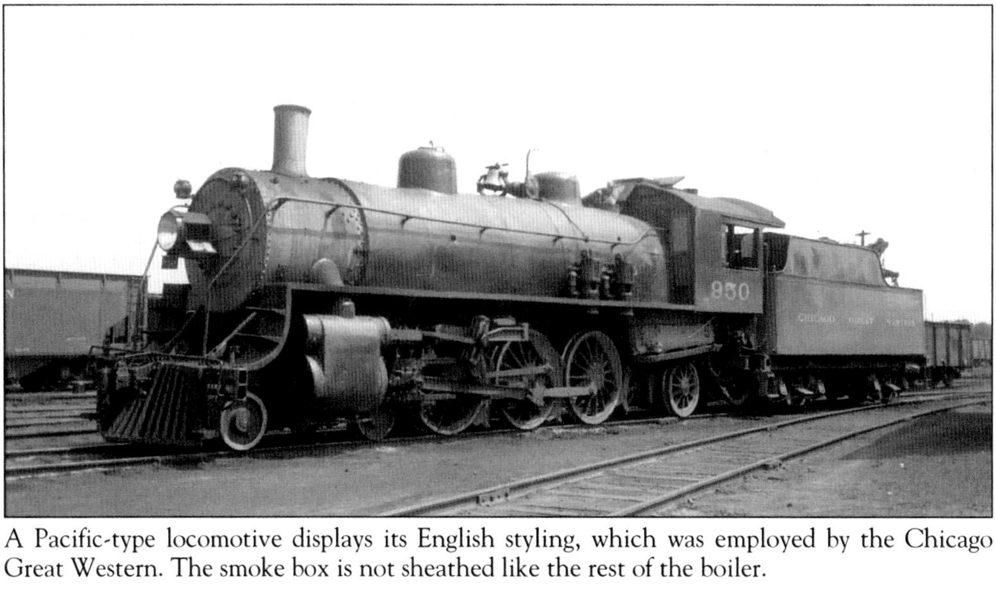

A Pacific-type locomotive displays its English styling, which was employed by the Chicago Great Western. The smoke box is not sheathed like the rest of the boiler.

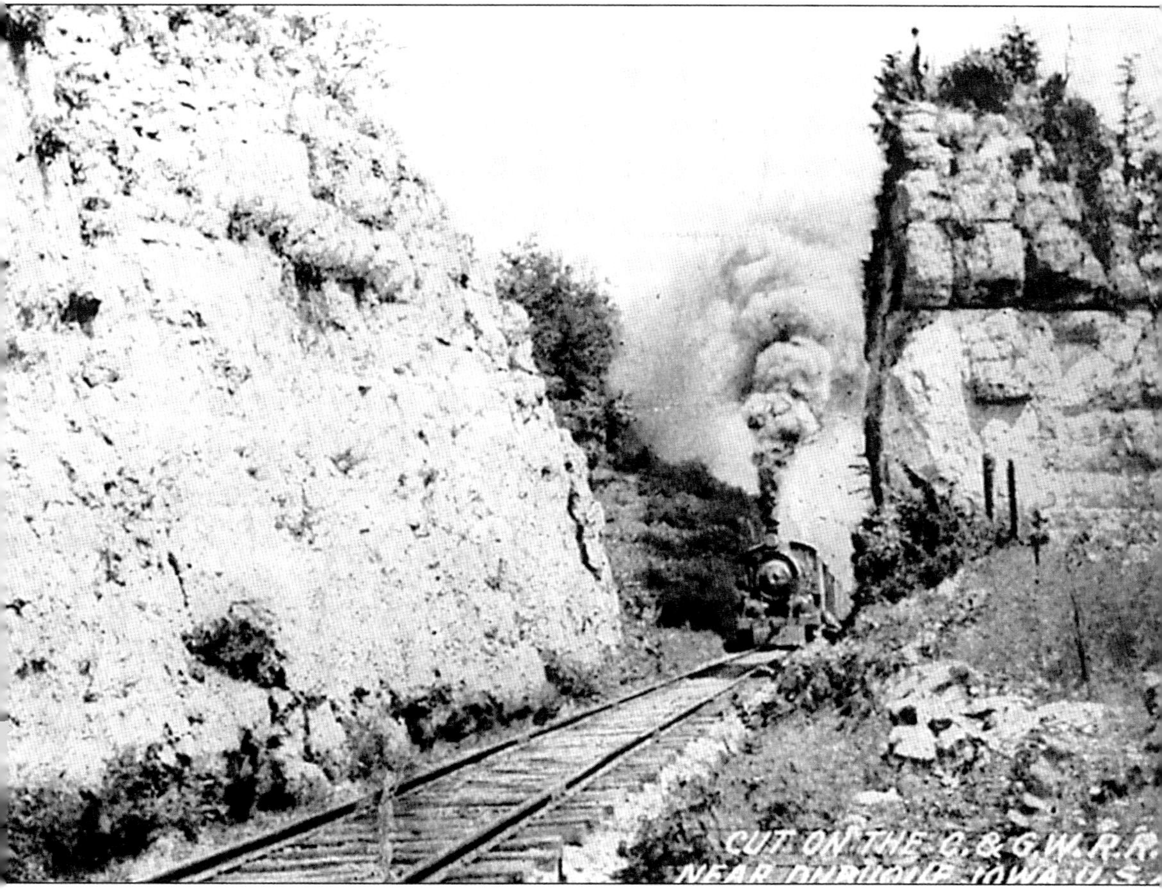

A Chicago Great Western locomotive charges triumphantly through a rock cut near Dubuque.

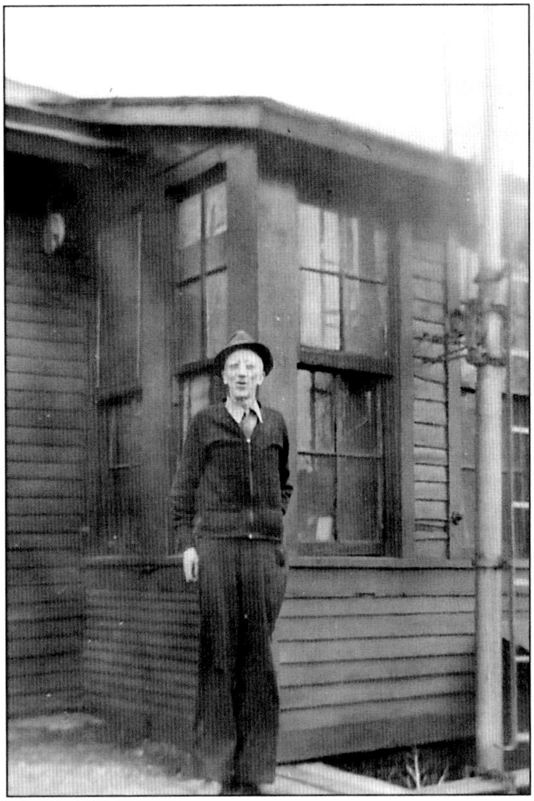

An operator who worked frequently at the fairground north of Dubuque is only remembered by his nickname, "Snapper."

Thru Train Schedules

Read Down — **Read Up**

Rochester Express Daily Ex. Sat.	*The Legionnaire* Daily	Between Chicago Rochester and Twin Cities	*The Legionnaire* Daily	
11.30 pm	6.30 pm	Lv.......Chicago.......Ar	8.15 am	....
4.26 am	11.30 pm	Lv......Dubuque......Ar	3.23 am	....
10.45 am	7.00 am	Ar......Rochester Lv	9.30 pm	....
....	7.10 am	Ar...... St. Paul Lv	8.20 pm	....
....	7.50 am	Ar.... Minneapolis Lv	7.45 pm	....

THE LEGIONNAIRE.....De luxe, all-steel train, consisting of luxurious Pullman Observation-Lounge Car, with library and writing facilities; inviting Club Buffet; roomy, immaculate Diner; latest improved Pullmans and comfortable Chair Cars.

Valet service—reasonable charges for pressing both ladies' and men's apparel.

Pullmans may be occupied until 8.00 a.m. at Rochester.

ROCHESTER EXPRESS...Pullmans; Coaches, and Cafe Car serving breakfast.

A 1929 timetable shows that "the Legionaire," a night train, stopped in Dubuque at 11:30 p.m. westbound, and 3:23 a.m. eastbound. The CGW had pride in its passenger trains.

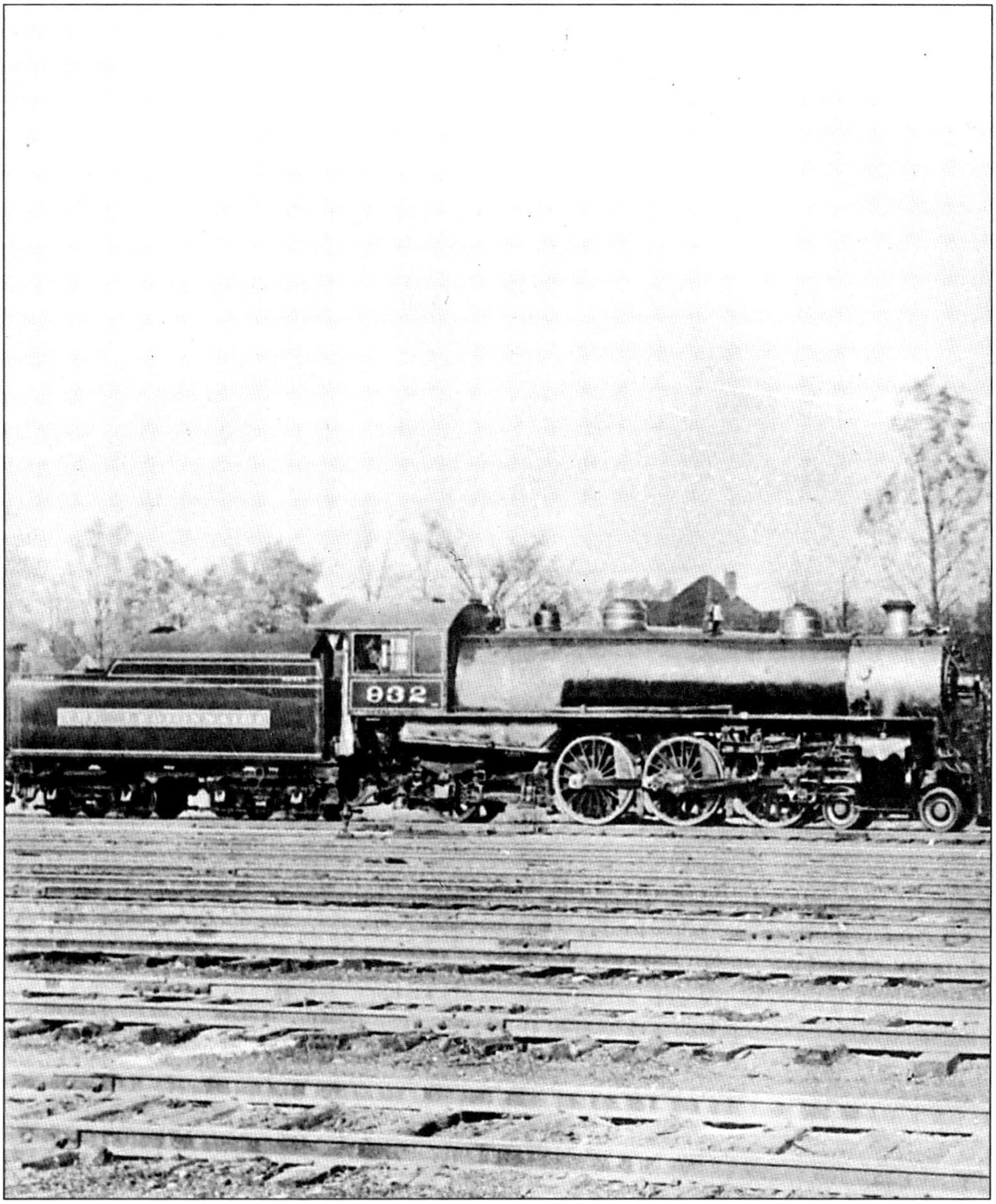

In this image, number 932, a spiffy English-styled Pacific with a capped stack, pulls "the Legionaire." The train's name was carried on the flanks of its tender.

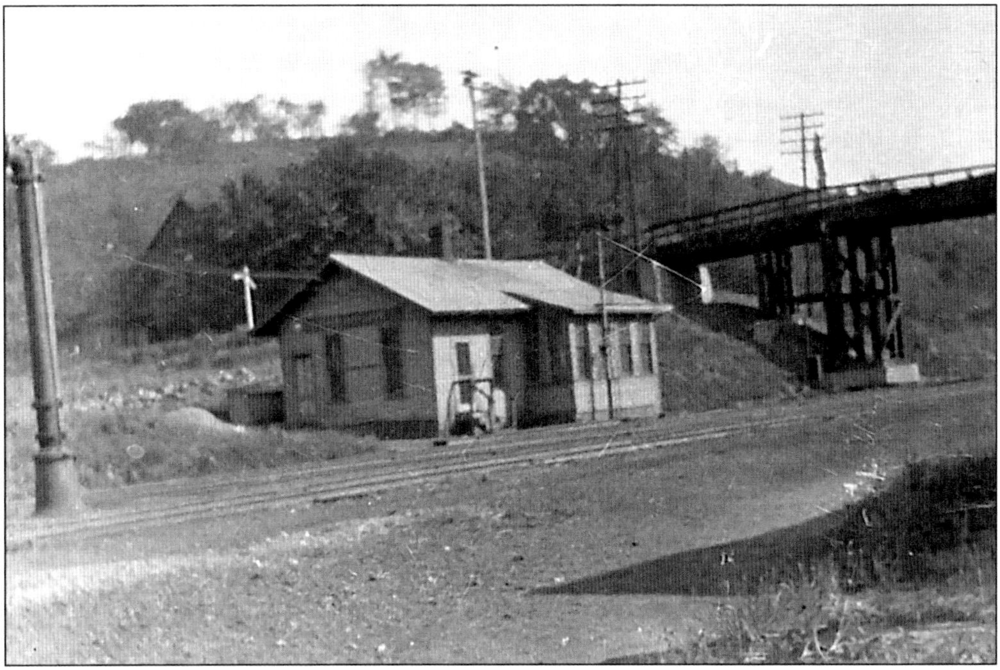

A view of Fairground shows the sunshine on the area immediately north of the wooden viaduct, and south of the water column where locomotives could get a drink.

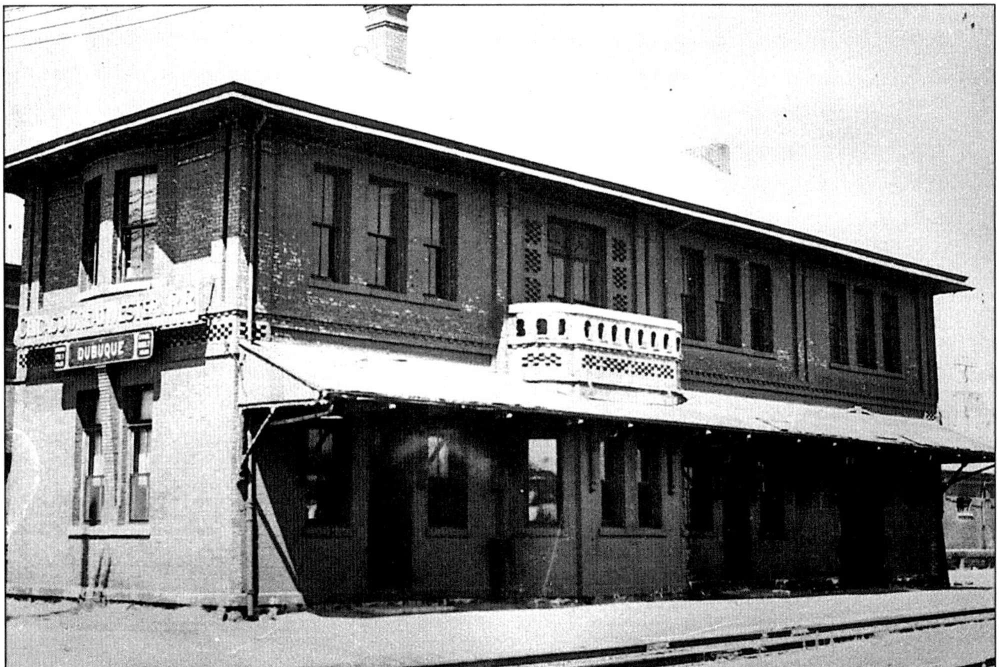

The Minnesota and Northwestern Railroad designed and built the Dubuque station, which went with Minnesota and Northwestern property when the Chicago Great Western took over.

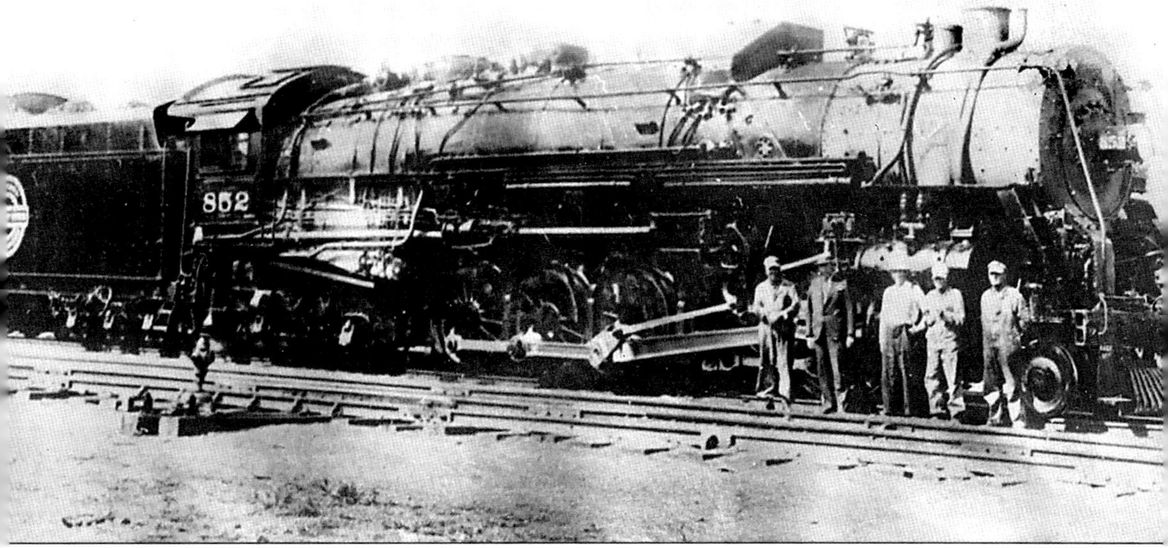

Ole Hartman, Ted Olson, Mike Rogge, John Trower, and Bill Bradfield stand next to a Texas-type engine number 852. The behemoth locomotives in the 800 series put a lot of other locomotives out of work.

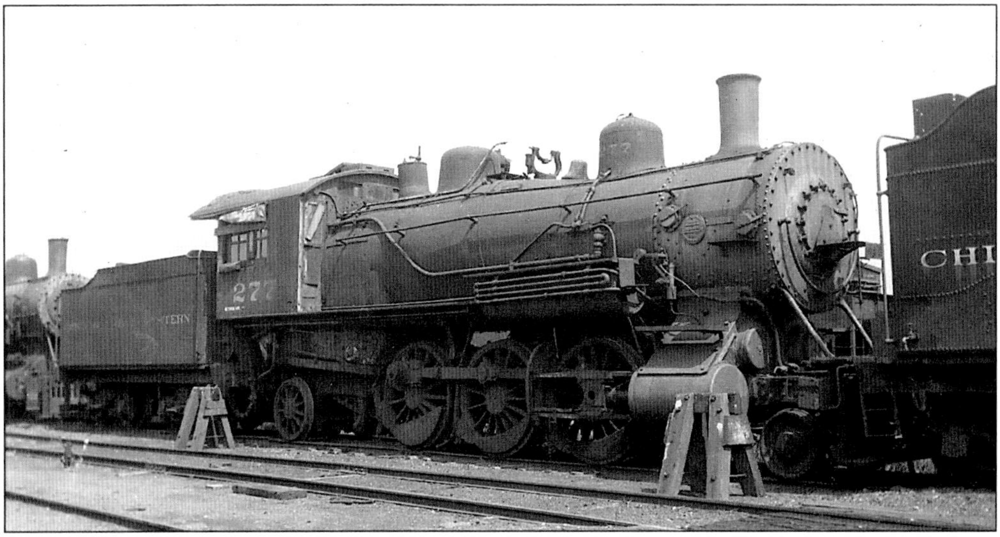

This is an image of locomotives on the rip track waiting for the torch.

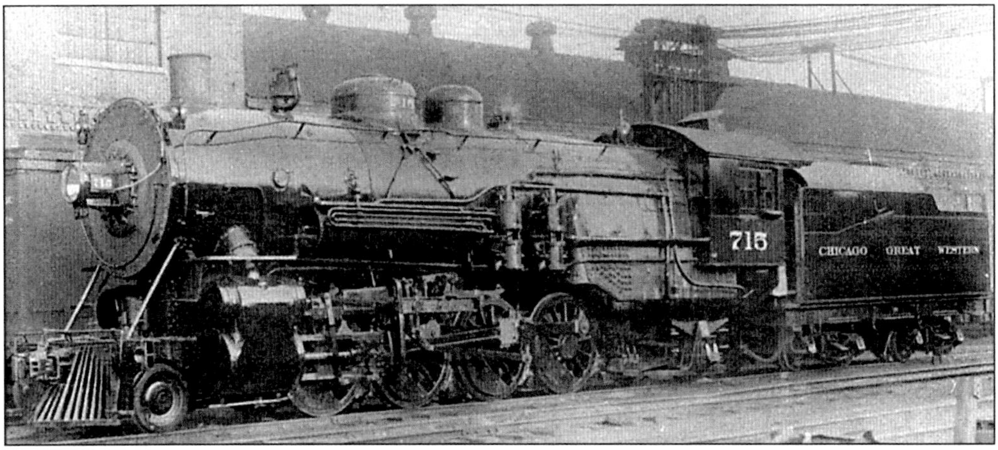

The Mikado 2-8-2 types, such as number 715, worked along with the 800s.

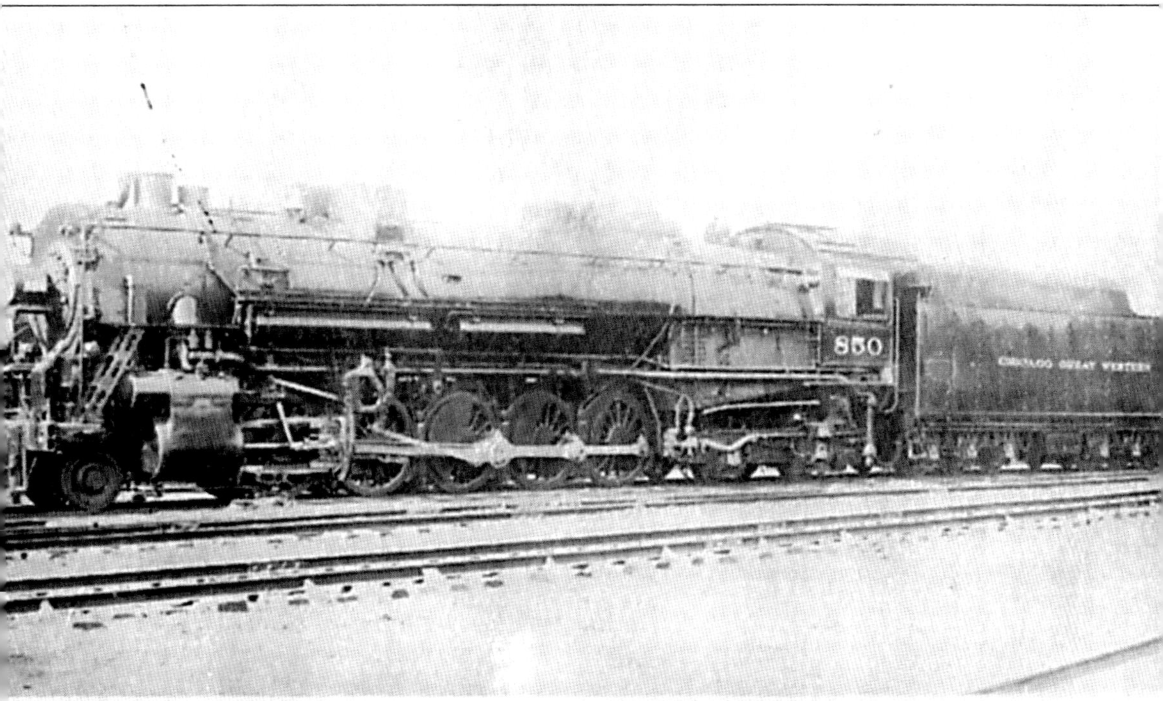

ONE OF 50 TEXAS TYPE FREIGHT ENGINES USED BY C.G.W.
— COURTESY OELWEIN MUSEUM

The appearance of the fireman's side of number 850 is considerably different than that of the engineer's side.

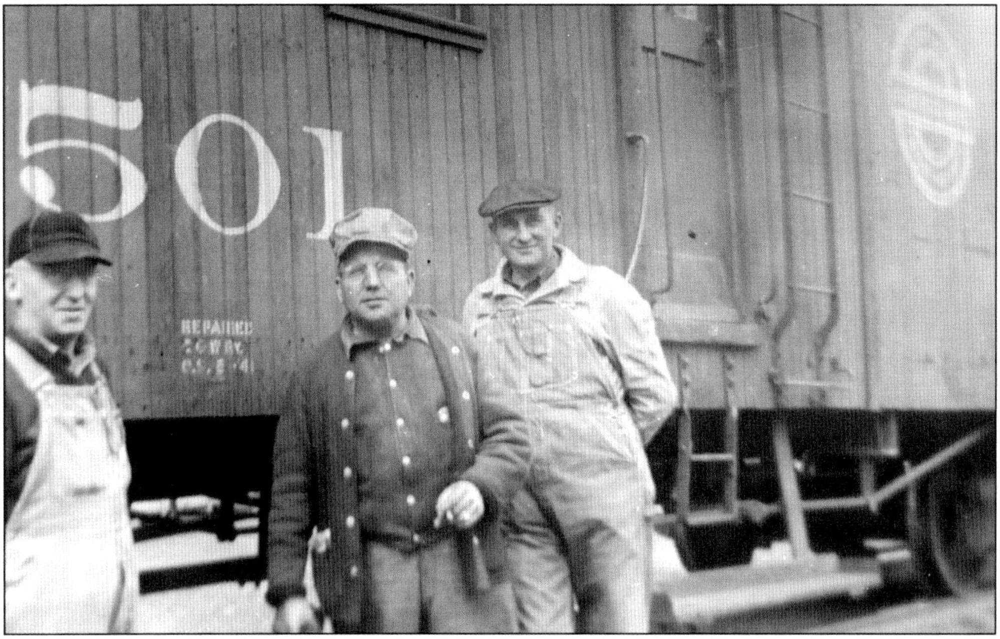

Three men pose next to work car number 501 in Dubuque. The man on the left is "Fuzzy" (last name unknown) and beside him is Jake Myers. The third man is unidentified.

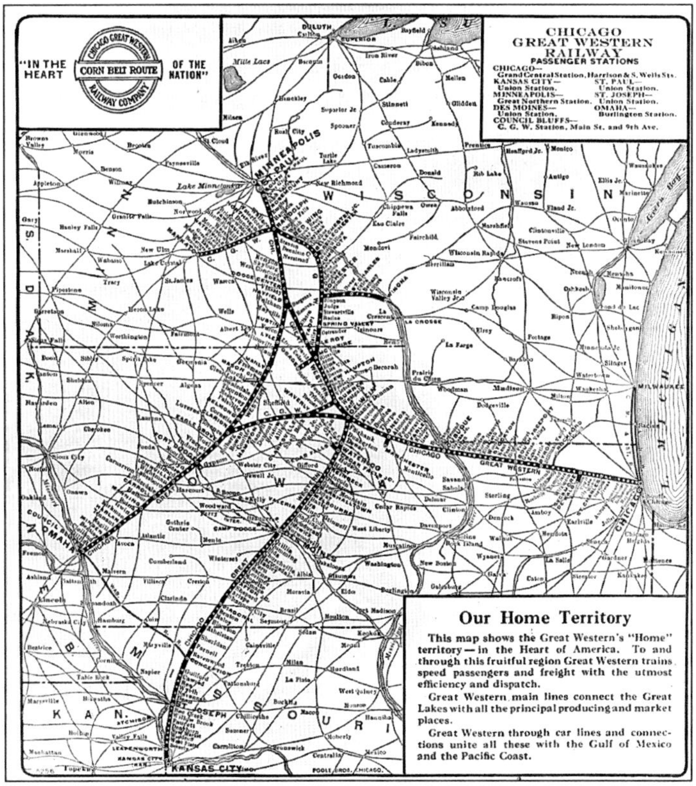

This is a map of the Chicago Great Western's territory from a 1944 timetable.

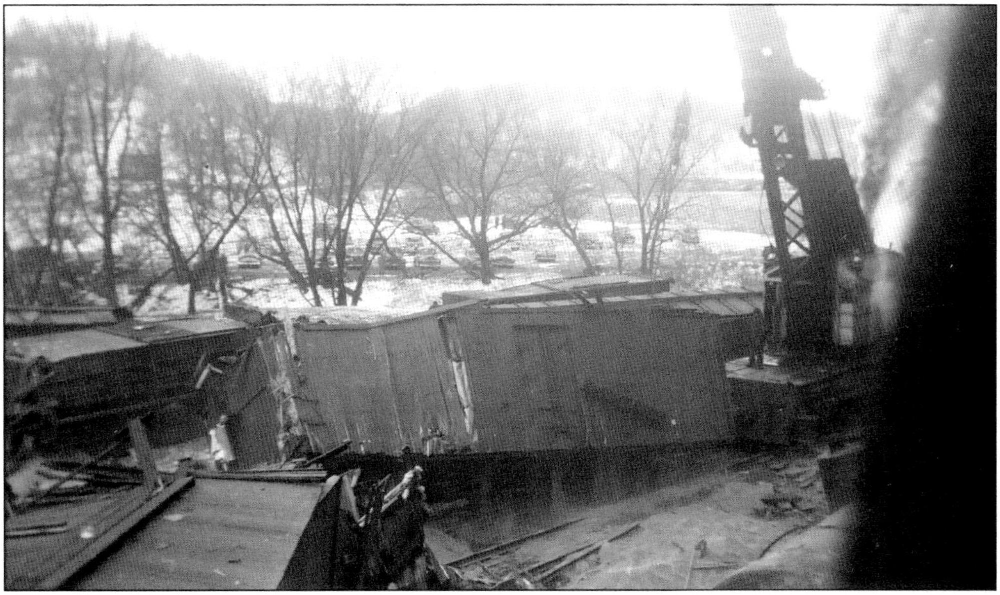

On a winter night in 1942, a Chicago Great Western freight train derailed southeast of Durango, Iowa. Several looters made off with sides of beef from a wooden refrigerator car that had split open.

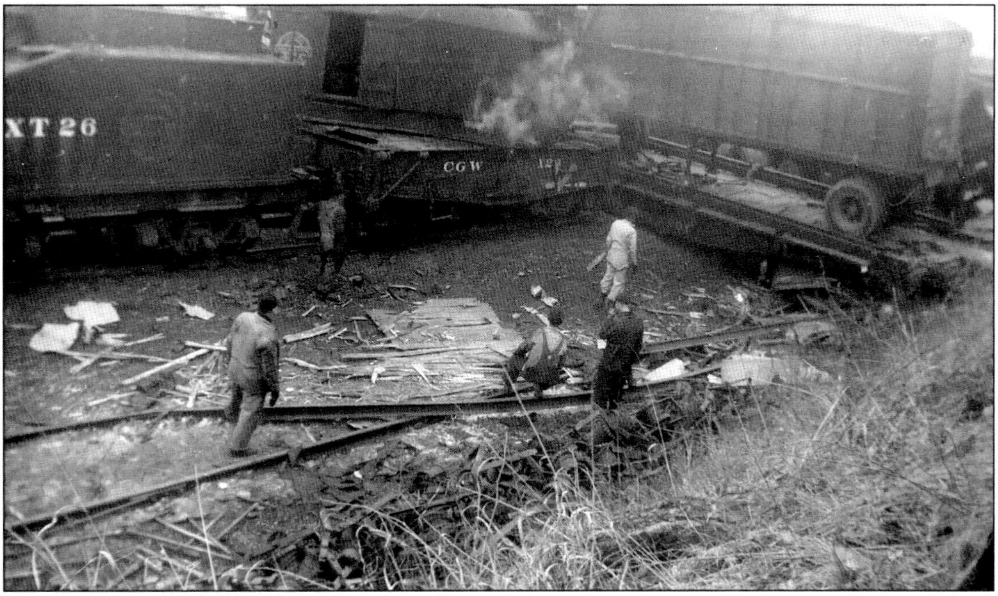

The Chicago Great Western crane and its tender work to remove the debris. Rails were twisted like soda straws when the cars left the track.

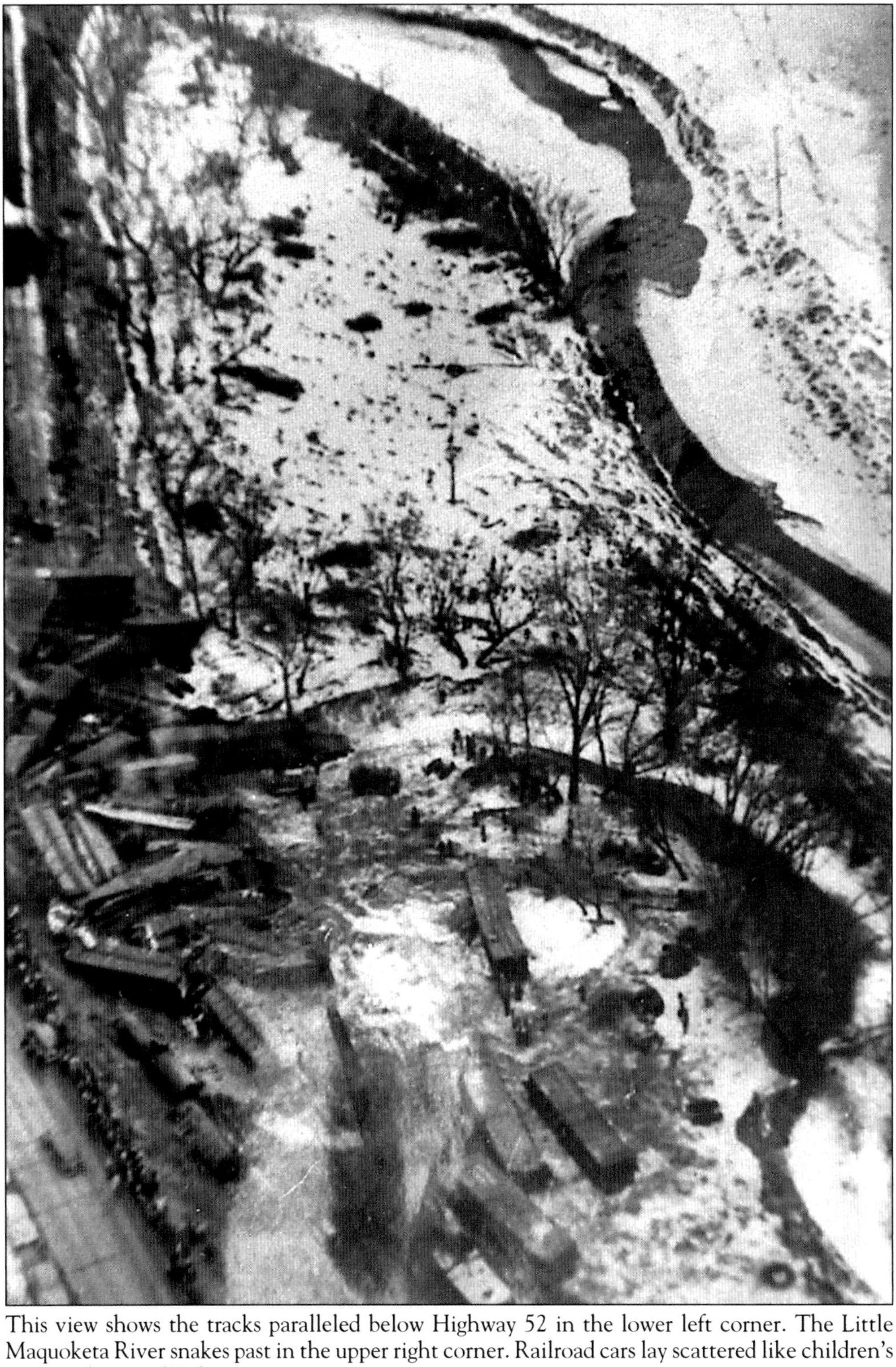

This view shows the tracks paralleled below Highway 52 in the lower left corner. The Little Maquoketa River snakes past in the upper right corner. Railroad cars lay scattered like children's toys northwest of Dubuque.

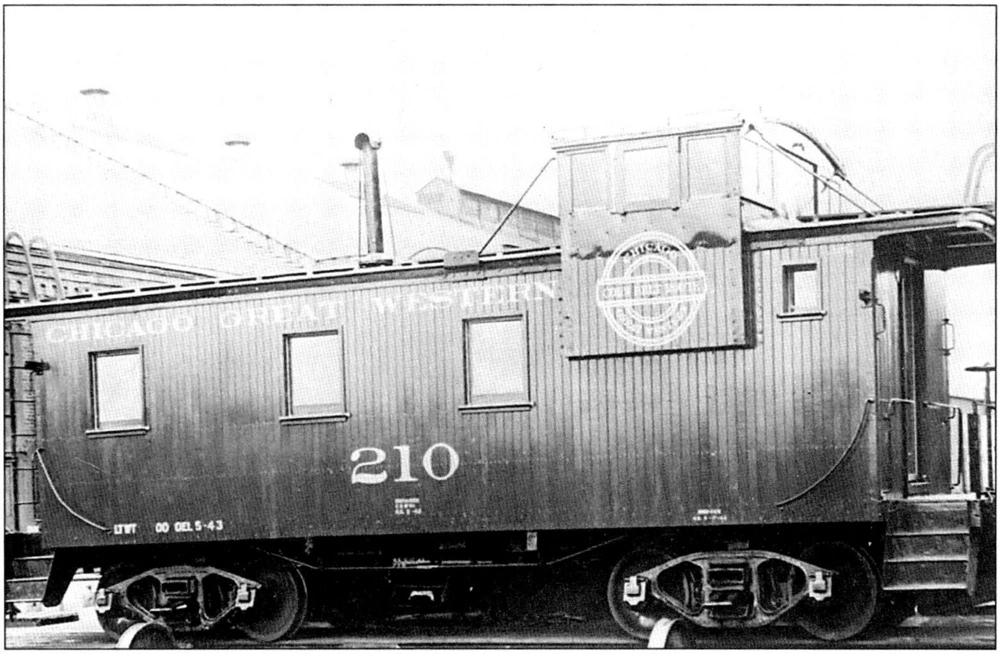

Caboose number 210 was backshopped at Oelwein, Iowa, in May, 1943. In this photograph, it sits on the transfer table ready to go back to work.

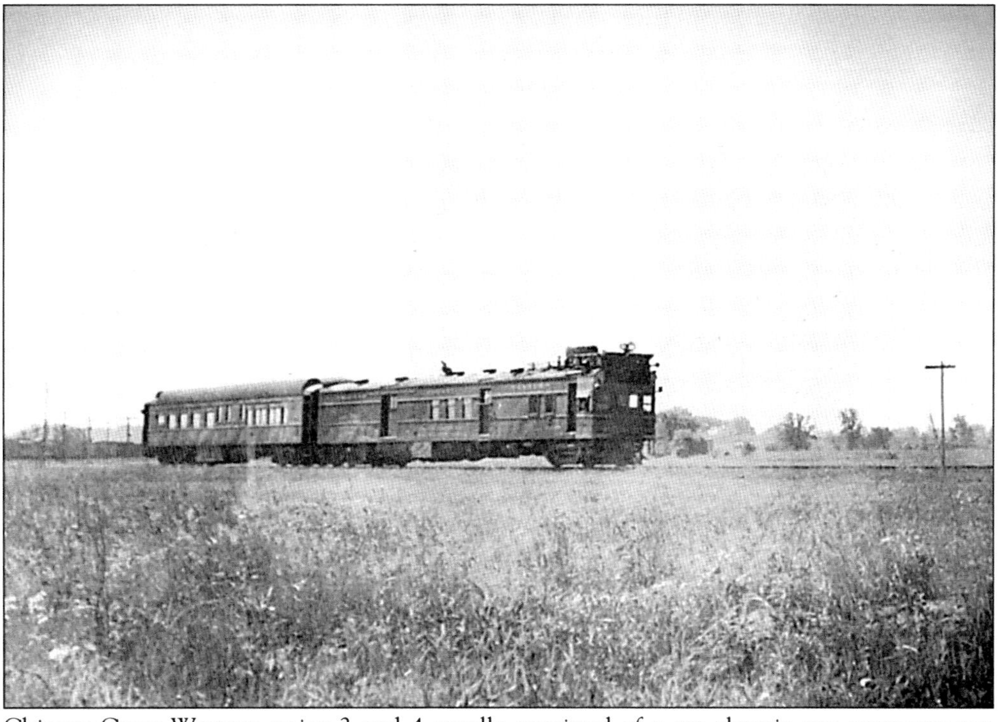

Chicago Great Western trains 3 and 4 usually consisted of a gas electric one-passenger car, going from Oelwein, Iowa, through Dubuque to Chicago, and back.

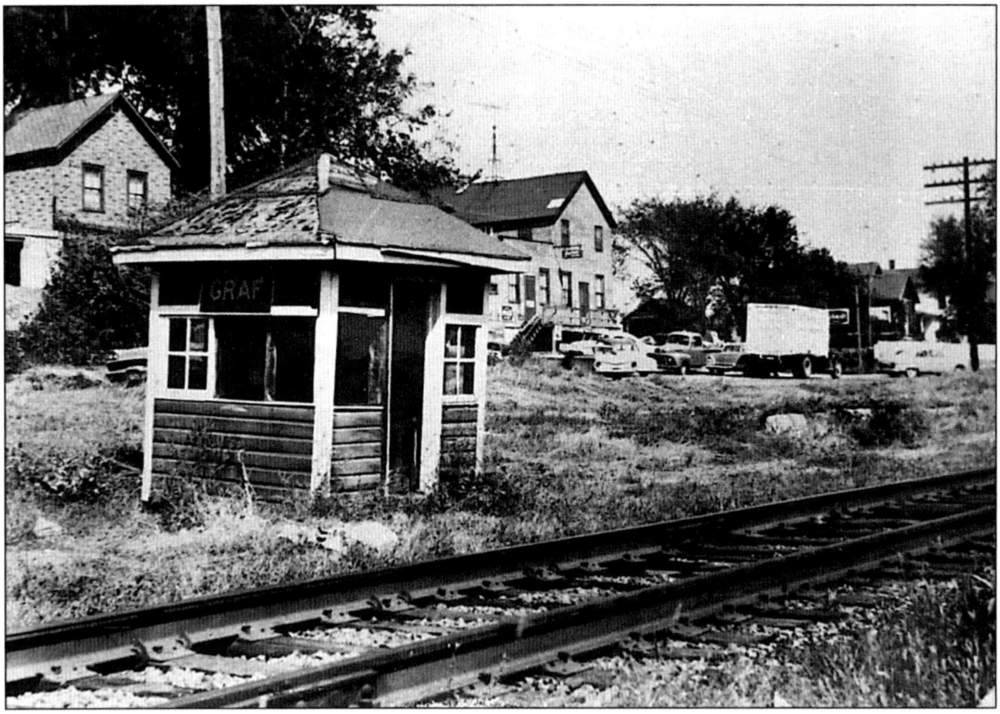

In the mid- to late 1950s, any stop in Graf, Iowa, became a slow-down for six- and seven-unit diesels.

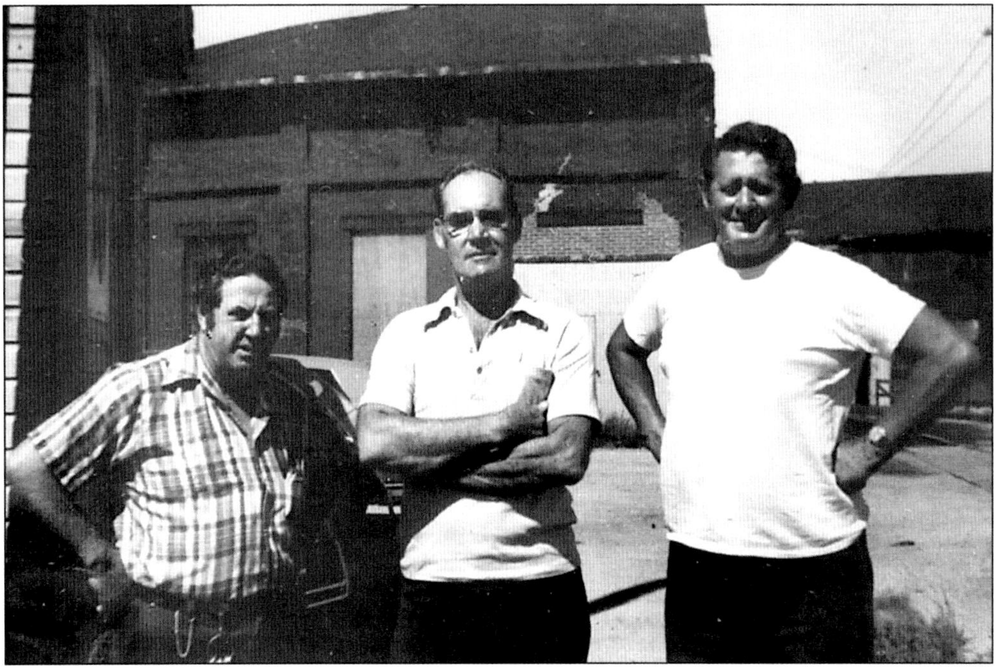

Three employees of the Chicago Great Western have their picture taken at the Chicago, Milwaukee, St. Paul & Pacific roundhouse and yards in Dubuque. From left, they are Tom Grace, Tom Goin, and Chuck Finch.

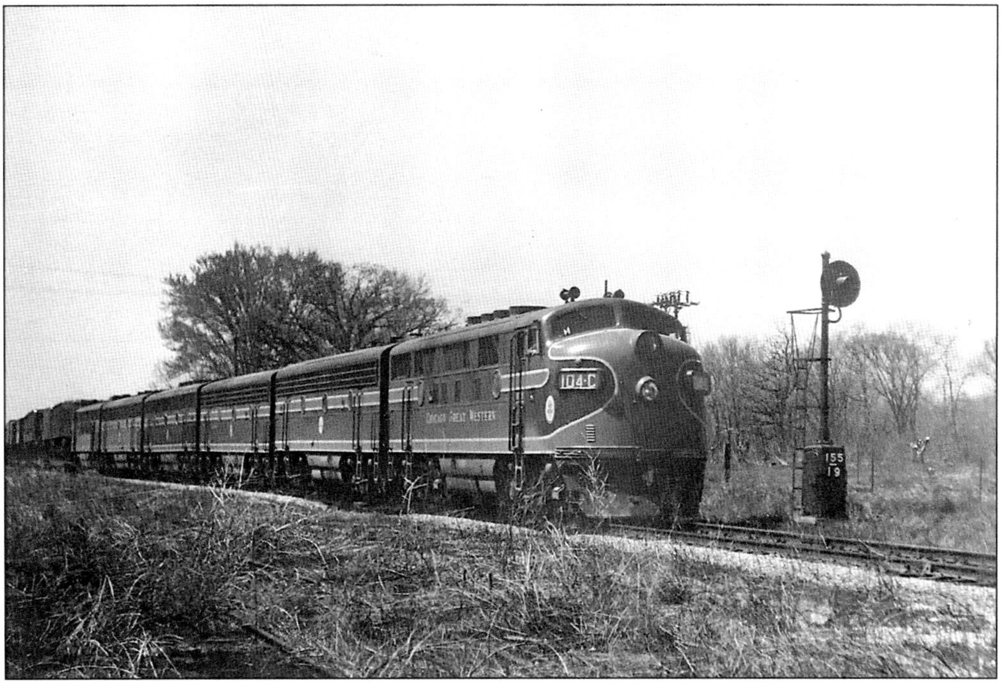

A six-unit F3 diesel pulls approximately 100 cars through the rolling Midwestern countryside. Nine- and ten-unit diesels became common on the Chicago Great Western.

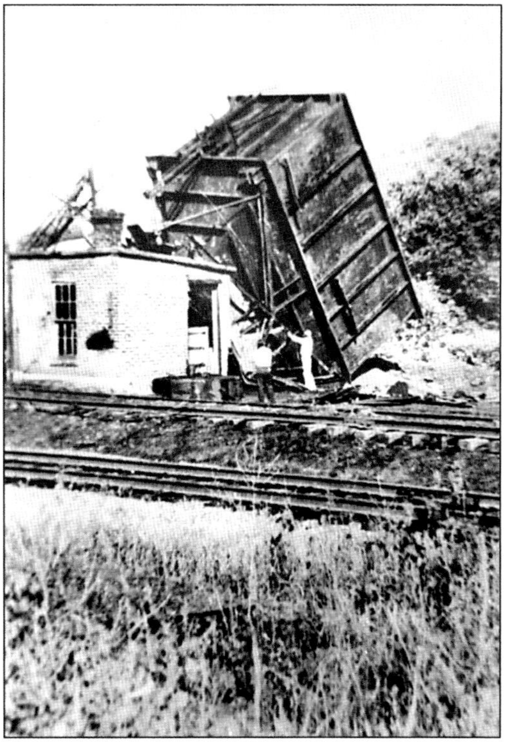

The coal tower at Graf, Iowa, was demolished on August 11, 1950.

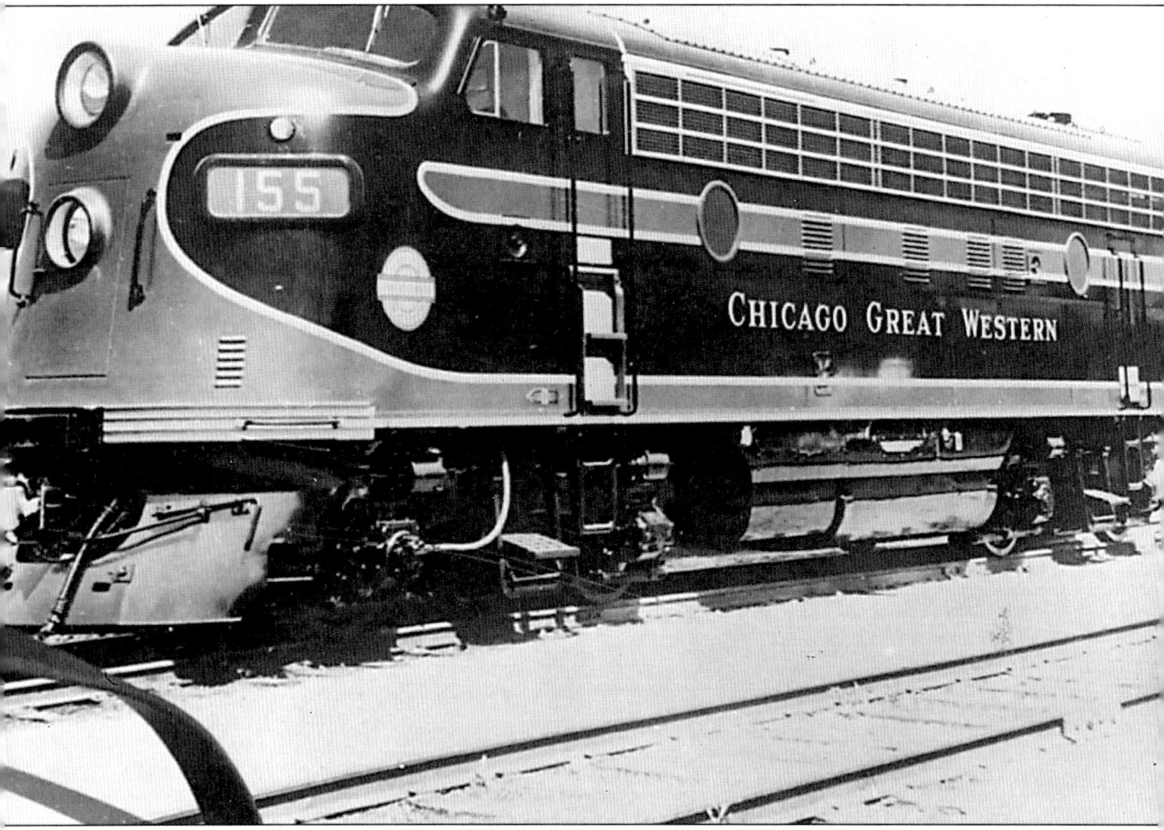

One hundred shares of five percent preferred stock in Chicago Great Western Railway Company shows that the railway still had value.

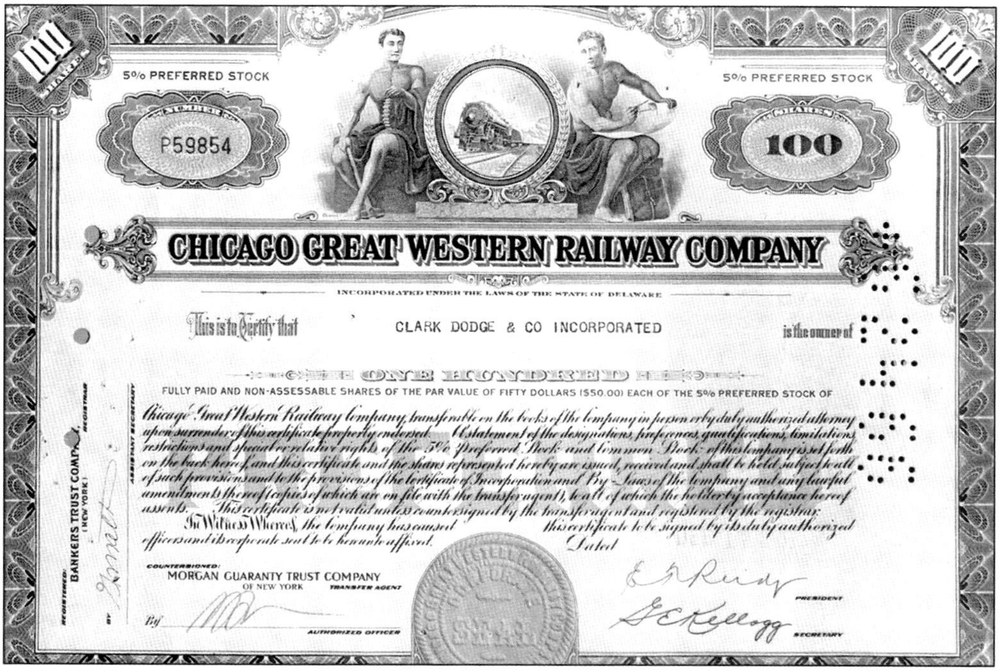

5% PREFERRED STOCK

5% PREFERRED STOCK

NUMBER P59854

SHARES 100

CHICAGO GREAT WESTERN RAILWAY COMPANY

INCORPORATED UNDER THE LAWS OF THE STATE OF DELAWARE

This is to Certify that CLARK DODGE & CO INCORPORATED is the owner of

ONE HUNDRED

FULLY PAID AND NON-ASSESSABLE SHARES OF THE PAR VALUE OF FIFTY DOLLARS ($50.00) EACH OF THE 5% PREFERRED STOCK OF

Chicago Great Western Railway Company, transferable on the books of the Company in person or by duly authorized attorney upon surrender of this certificate properly endorsed. A statement of the designations, preferences, qualifications, limitations, restrictions and special or relative rights of the 5% Preferred Stock and Common Stock of this Company is set forth on the back hereof, and this certificate and the shares represented hereby are issued, received and shall be held subject to all of such provisions and to the provisions of the Certificate of Incorporation and By-Laws of the Company and any lawful amendments thereof (copies of which are on file with the transfer agent), to all of which the holder by acceptance hereof assents. This certificate is not valid unless countersigned by the transfer agent and registered by the registrar.

In Witness Whereof, the Company has caused this certificate to be signed by its duly authorized officers and its corporate seal to be hereunto affixed.

Dated

COUNTERSIGNED: MORGAN GUARANTY TRUST COMPANY OF NEW YORK TRANSFER AGENT

By AUTHORIZED OFFICER

PRESIDENT

SECRETARY

REGISTERED: BANKERS TRUST COMPANY (NEW YORK) REGISTRAR

BY ASSISTANT SECRETARY

In the 1960s, three SD-40s could pull as much as six F3 units did in the 1950s.

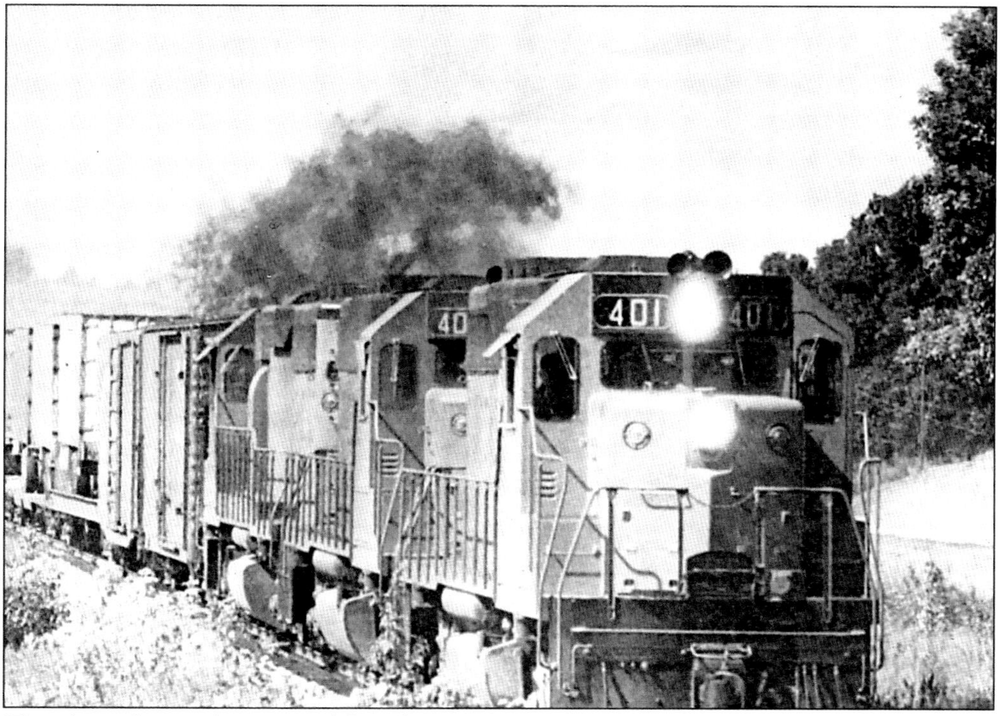

This photo shows a late view of the Chicago Great Western station at Dyersville, Iowa.

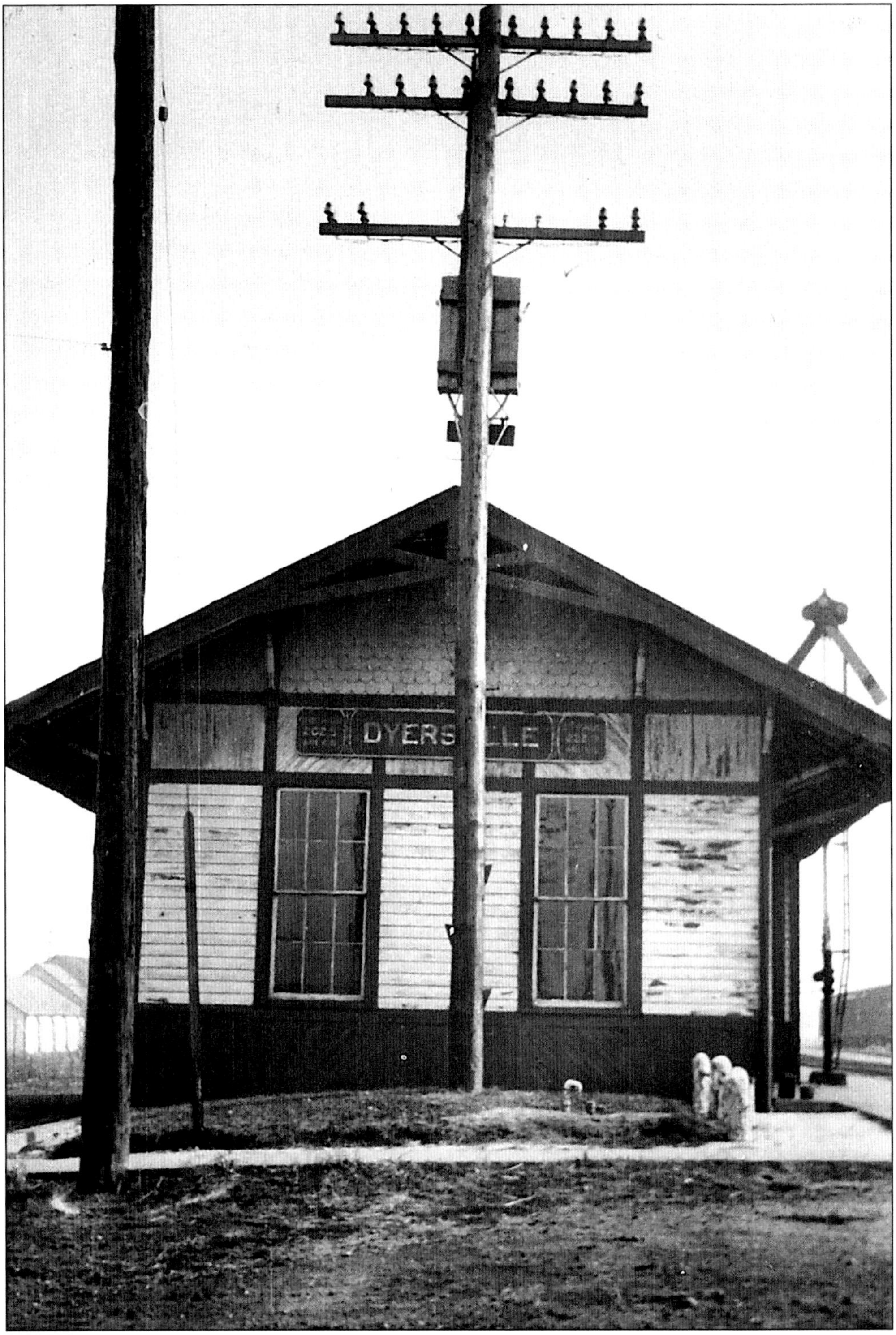

In this image, the Chicago Great Western Railway's Dubuque station shows its age. The upper floor's windows have been boarded over, and its operations moved to Oelwein.

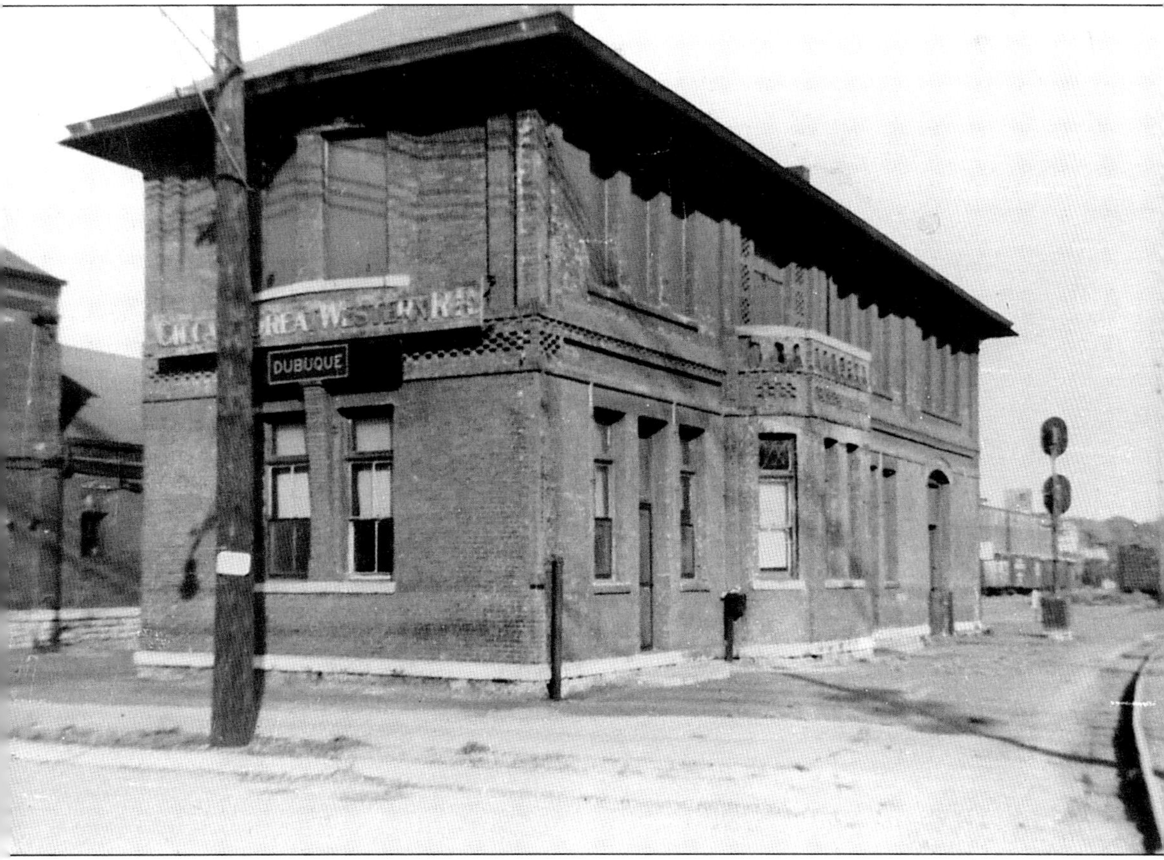

Train number 91 passes Fairground. The Chicago Great Western will always be remembered for its multiple diesel units.

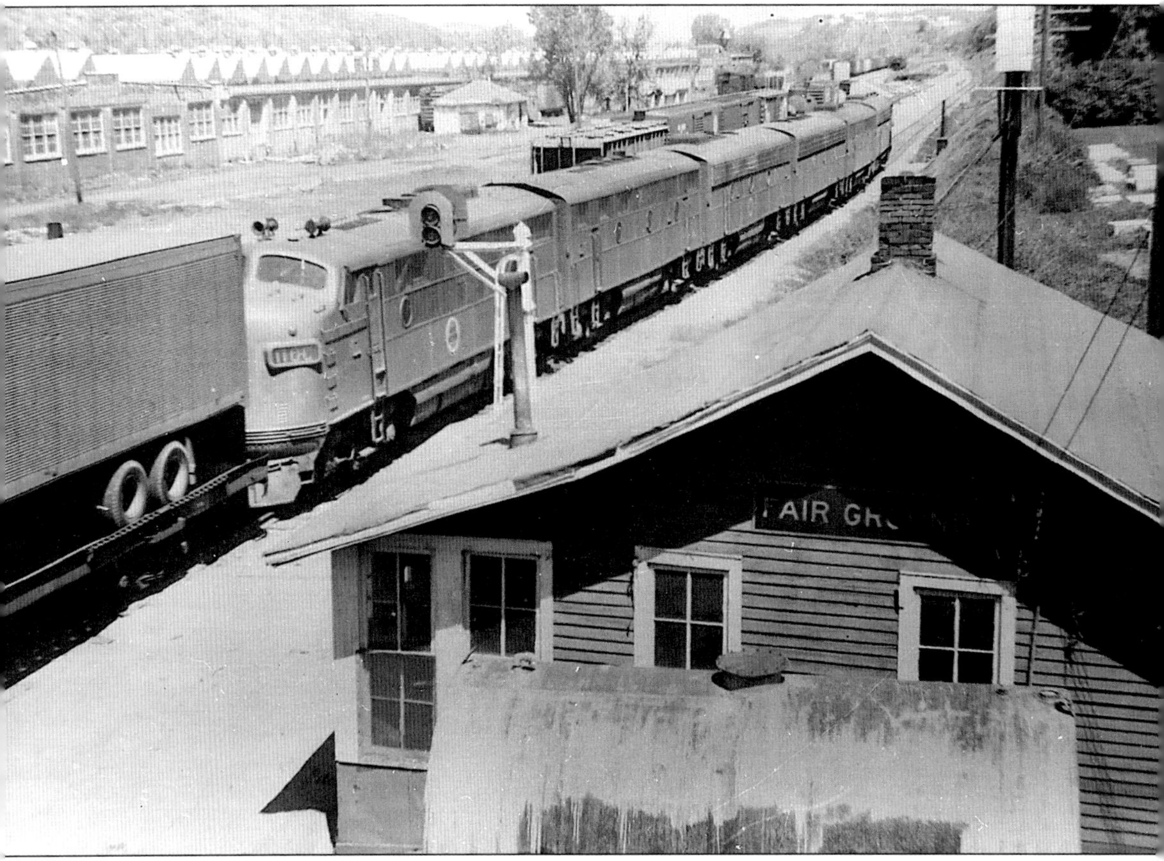

Dubuque's public transportation system began with horse-drawn cars in 1868. Although the flooding Mississippi couldn't stop the horses, Dubuque's hills eventually did.

Five

The Trolleys and Funiculars

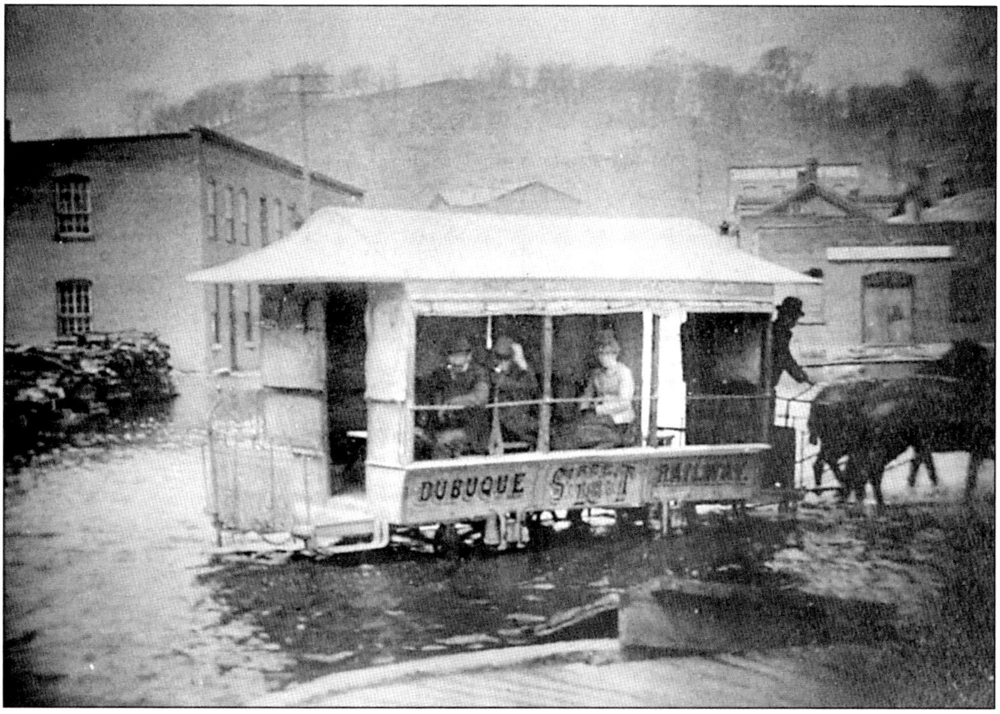

J. K. Graves began using a steam-powered car to pull a small passenger vehicle in 1883. It proved to be unreliable on some of Dubuque's hills, even once track was installed.

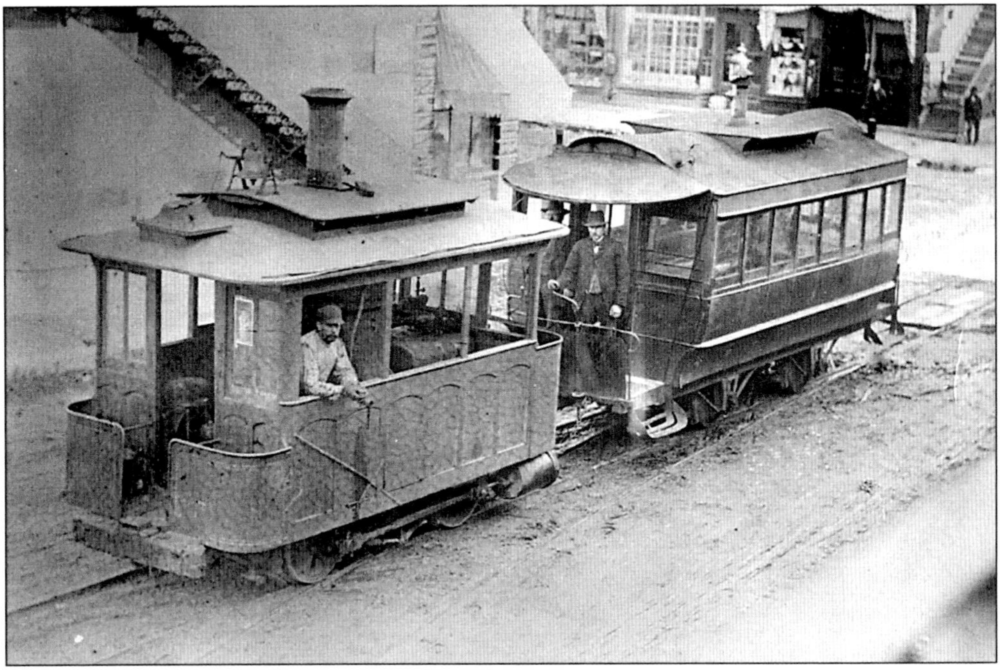

With an electric overhead catenary system to deliver power to the cars, Dubuque's first trolley cars, such as number 2, began serving the public on November 25, 1889.

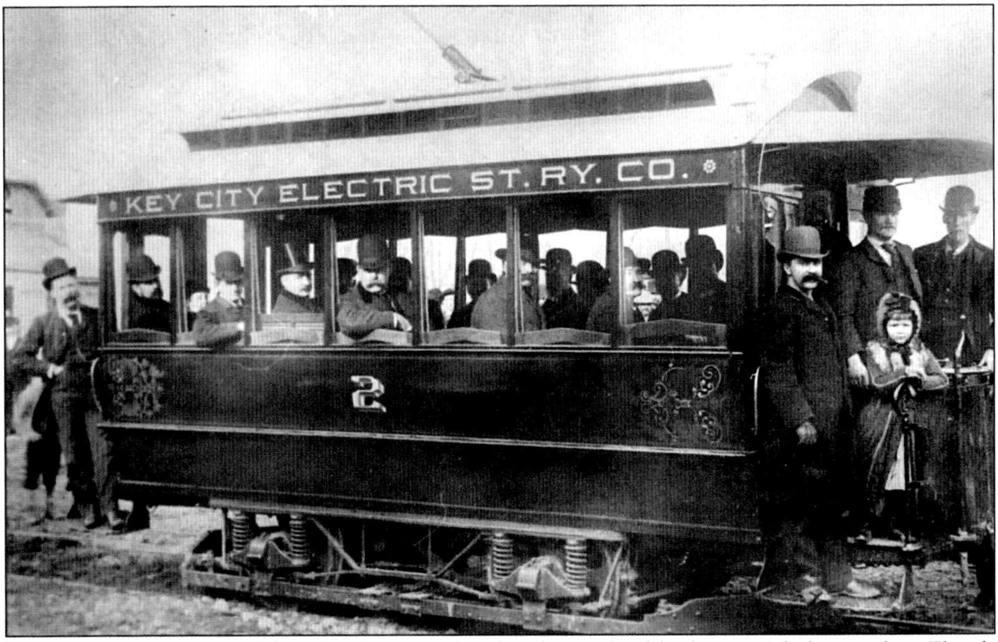

Dubuque's main thoroughfares had been surfaced with wooden blocks, set tightly together. Floods would float some of the blocks away, which were later replaced, but they proved unsuitable for trolley cars and were replaced with brick. Main Street was resurfaced in 1892.

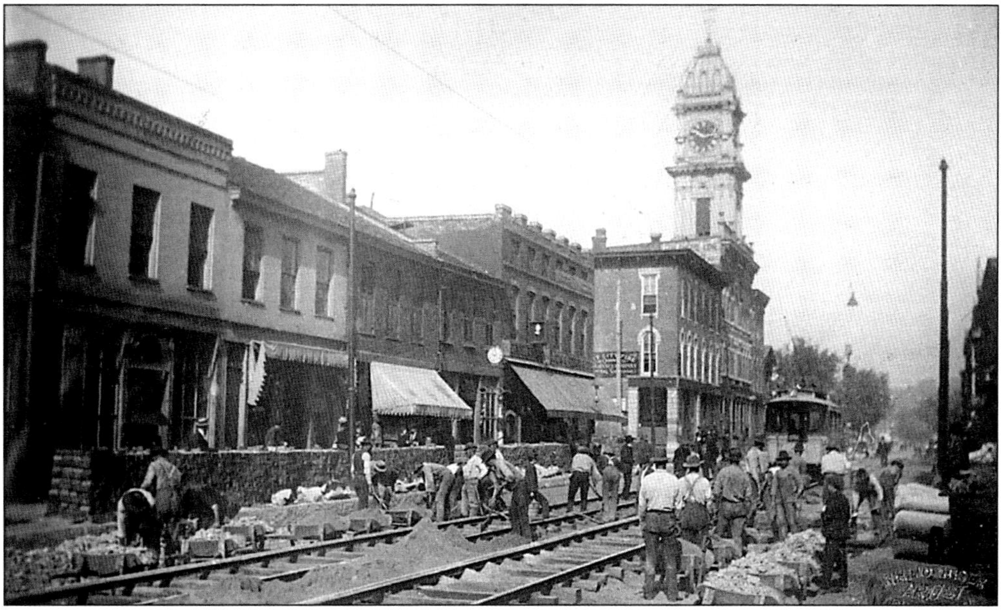

Once the street work was finished, the trolleys rolled down Main Street and along their appointed routes. Here, a southbound trolley heads for Fourth Street.

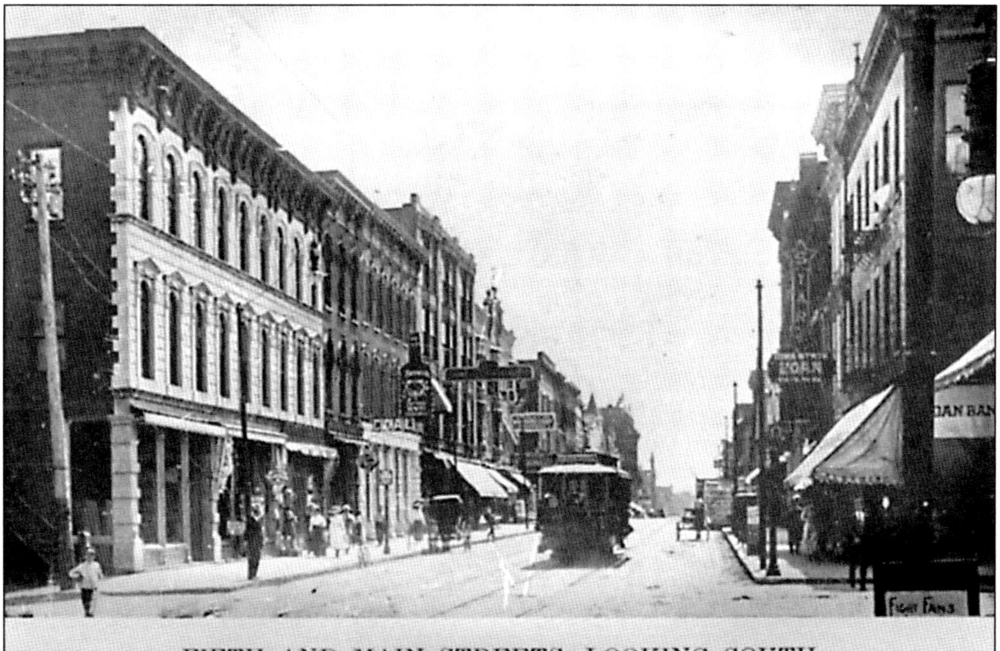

This is an image of Dubuque Light and Traction Company's trolley number 15 in a residential neighborhood in 1897. The company operated from 1894 to 1897.

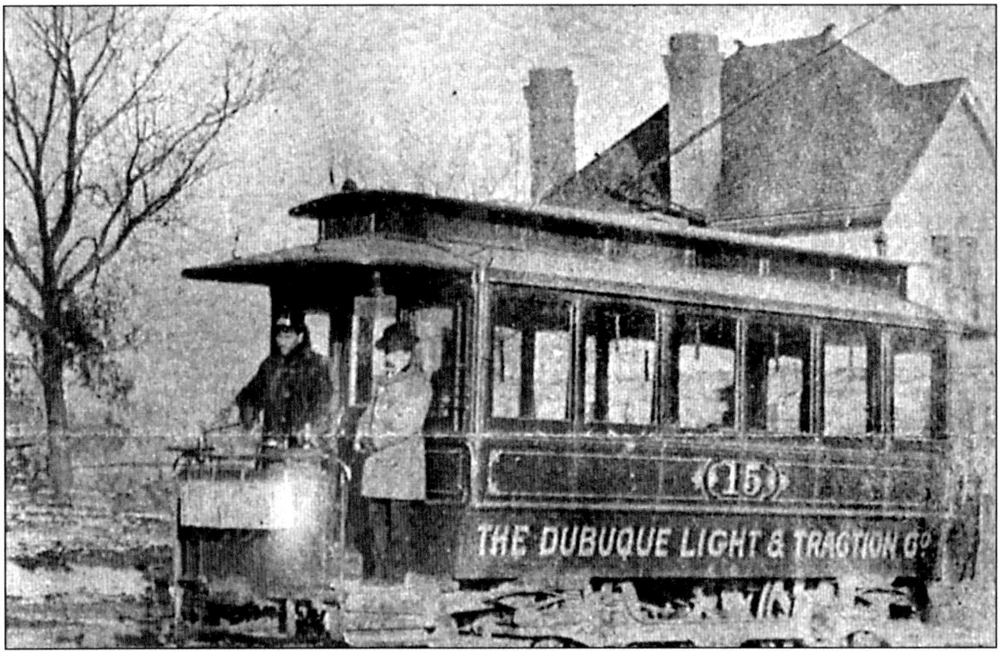

This photo shows a summer open-air car, number 81, which was built by the St. Louis Car Company for the Union Electric Company of Dubuque.

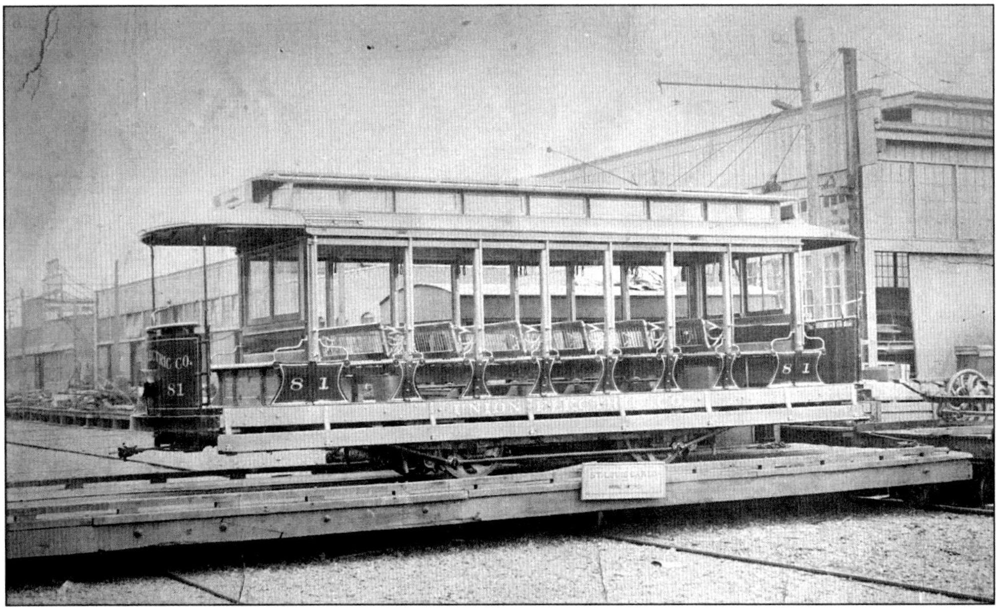

On Easter Sunday, April 23, 1905, the motorman on car 66 lost control. He and 16 passengers rode the trolley downhill until it jumped the tracks and struck a building. No one was injured.

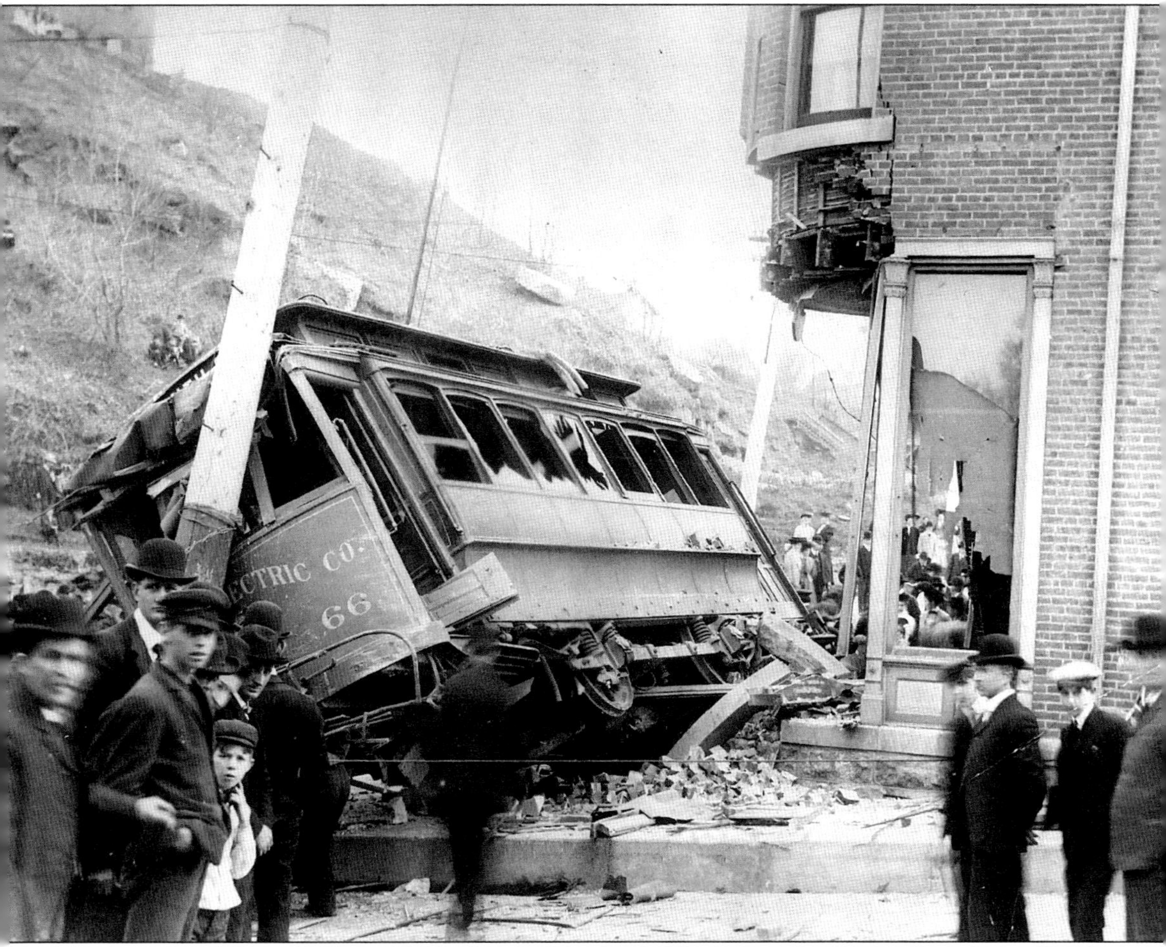

Photographer E. L. Egelhof captured this image of Union Park, which was north and west of Dubuque, in 1906. What a great way to spend a leisurely Sunday afternoon!

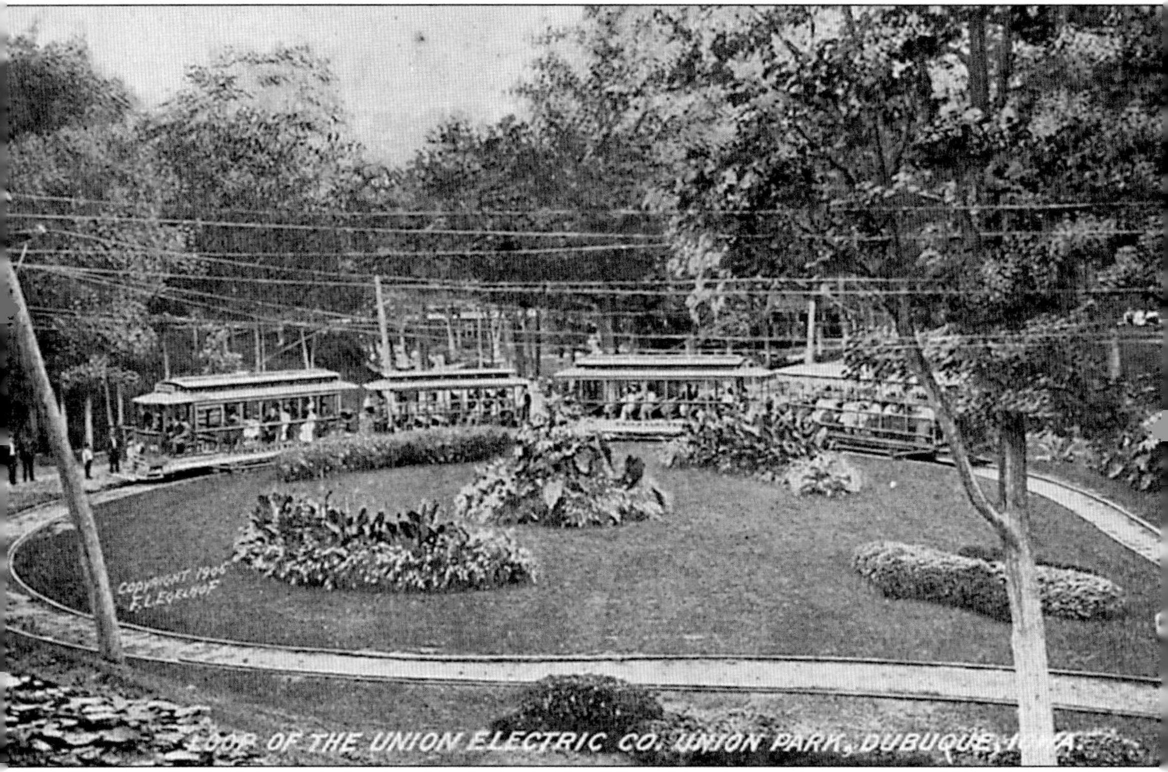

A few years later, a passenger platform and more buildings had been erected. There were daily shows at the theater, dances at the dance hall, rides, picnic areas, and a rustic outdoor bandstand.

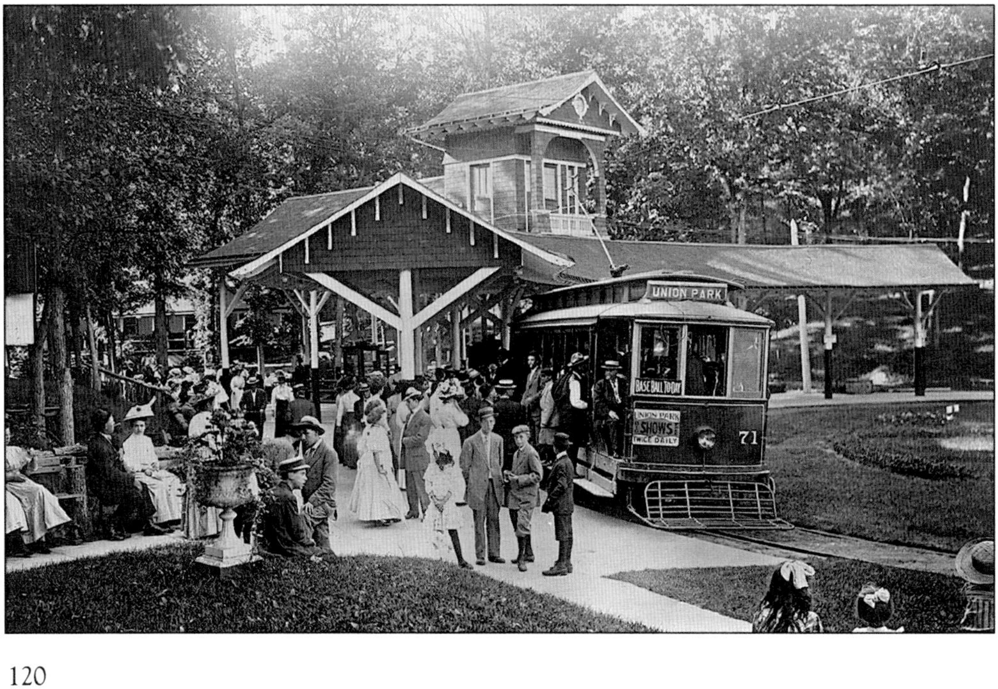

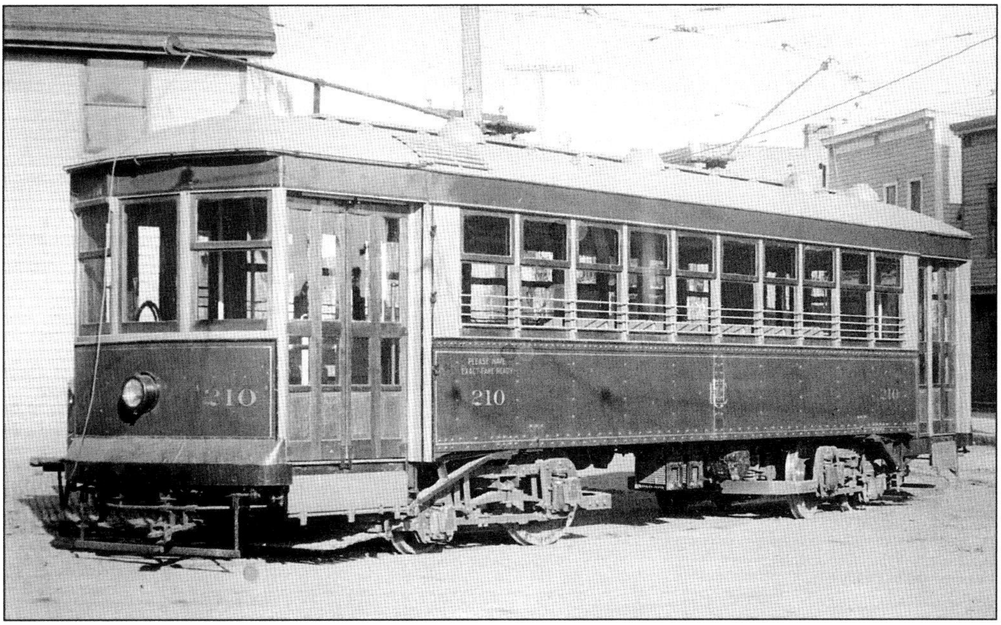

Number 210, a larger, more comfortable trolley, seated more passengers than other trolley cars. This photograph shows number 210 turning a corner.

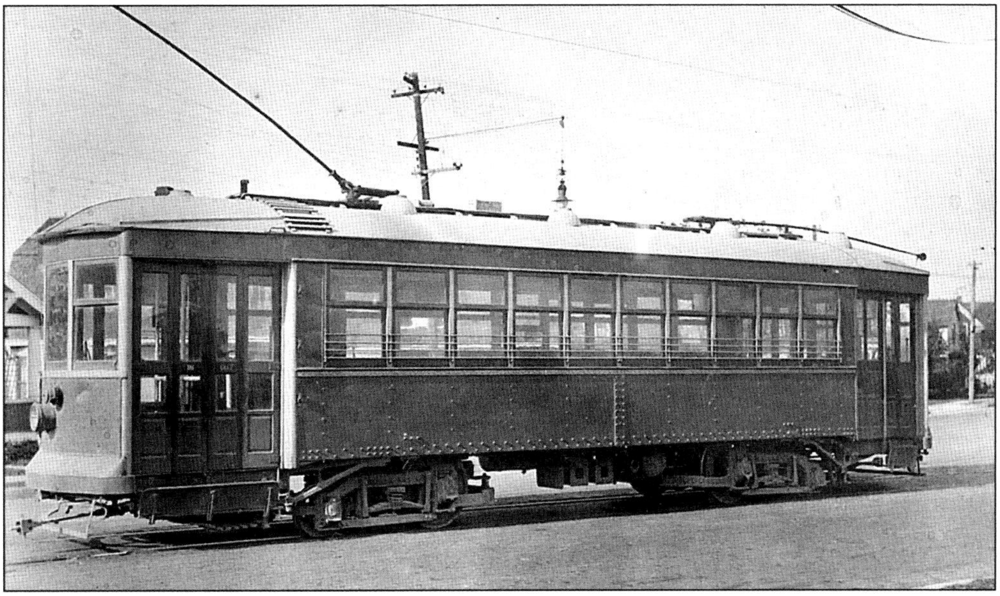

This image of trolley number 212 displays its wider doors than the four-wheeled trolleys and the steps that folded down to allow passengers to step aboard.

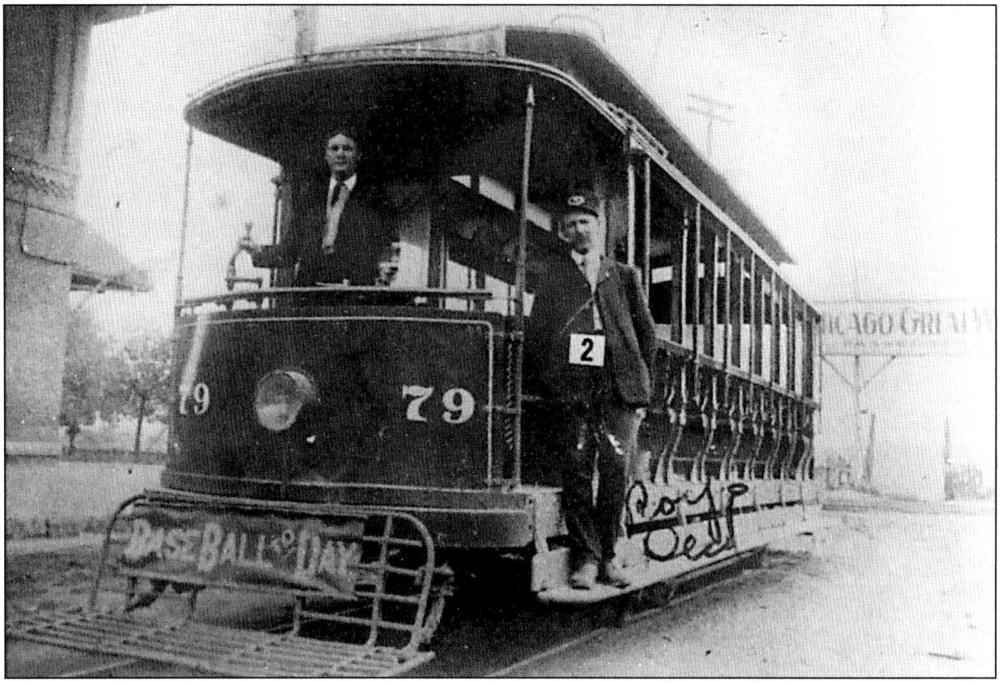

Open-air trolley number 79 poses with its two-man crew, a conductor and a motorman, at the Chicago Great Western depot in Dubuque in 1925.

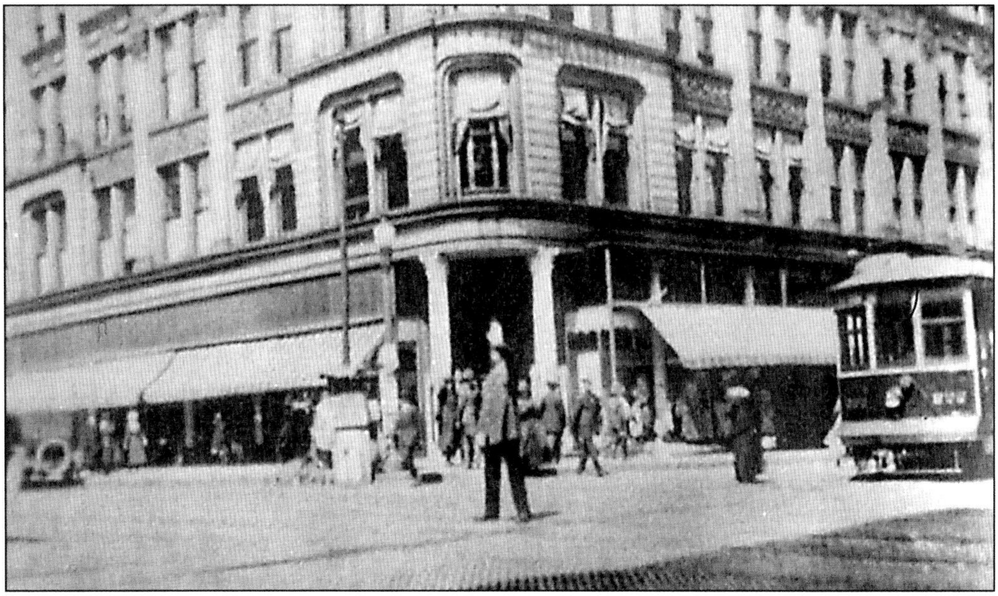

This image shows a police officer directing traffic at Eighth and Main Streets, before Dubuque installed traffic lights.

As if foretelling trolley number 220's future, a touring car passes it effortlessly on Eighth Street's hill. By 1932, the trolleys were gone.

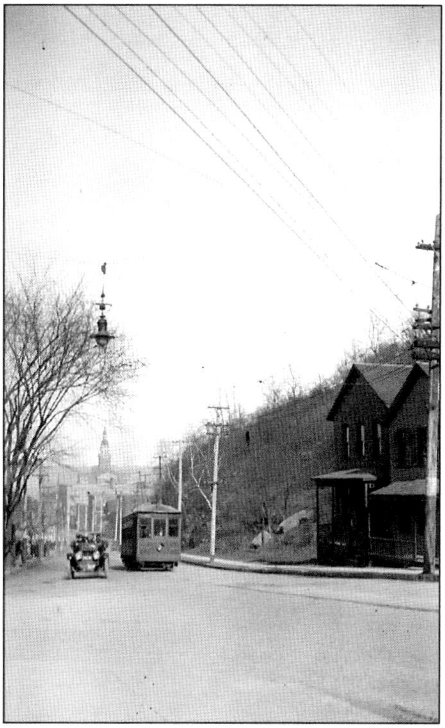

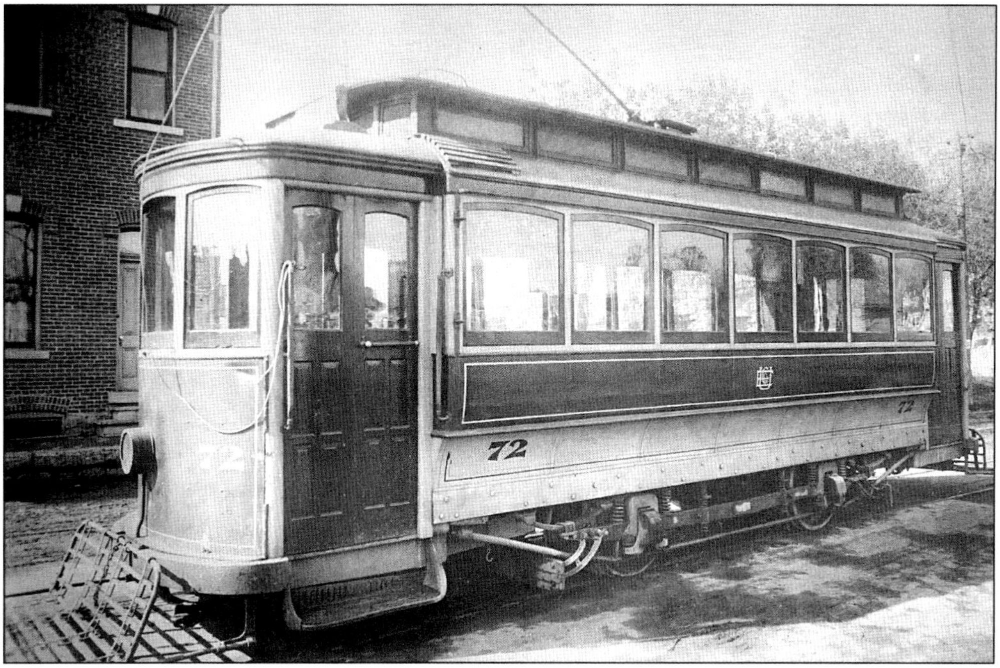

After serving for 64 years, the trolleys of Dubuque, including number 72, pictured here, rumbled into residents' memories, along with the chime of their bells.

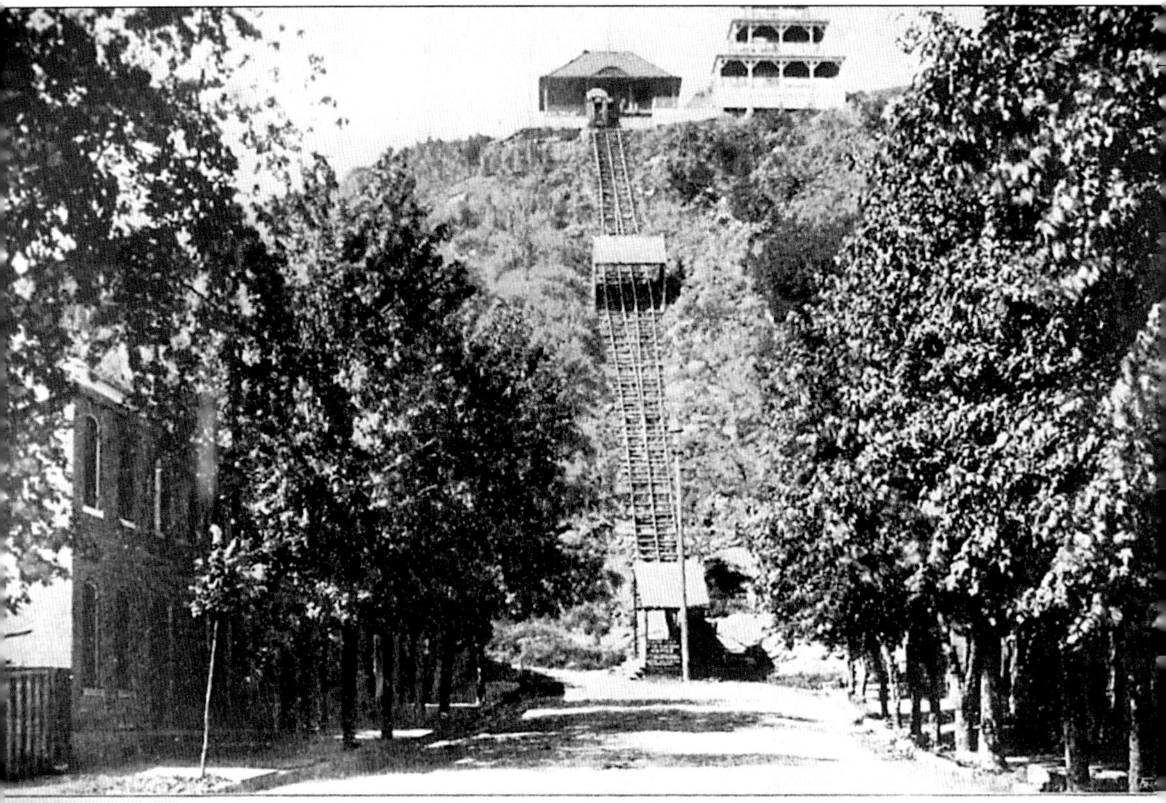

FOURTH STREET ELEVATOR.

On July 25, 1882, J. K. Graves, a banker and entrepreneur began a single-track inclined railway. Graves was acquainted with that type of "lift" from his travels in Europe. It saved him two hours a day, arriving in the business district in a few minutes instead of driving the 30-minute buggy ride from his home through the hills. This image shows the two-car Fenelon Place Elevator that still operates in the 21st century. It is billed as the world's shortest and steepest railway, with a track 289 feet long and a 67.8 percent grade.

The nickel fee charged to travel up or down remained in effect for years. This is a view of the cars and building that operated in 1954.

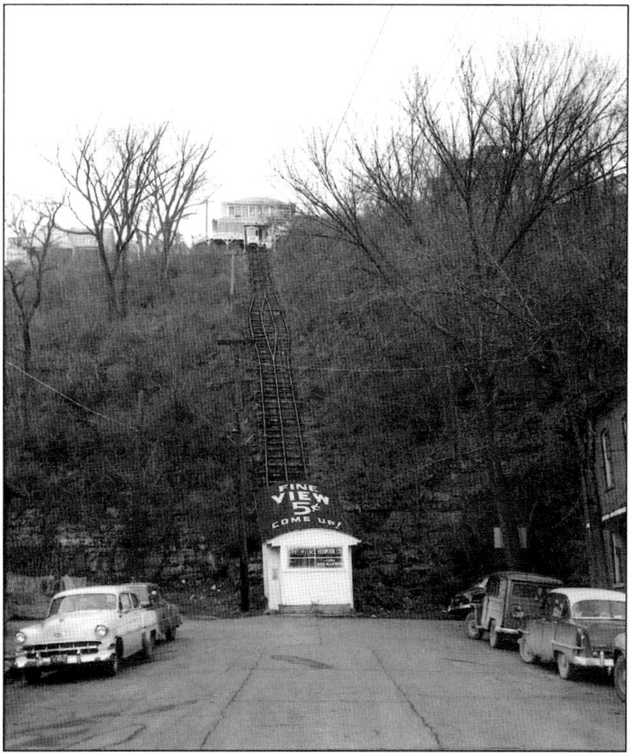

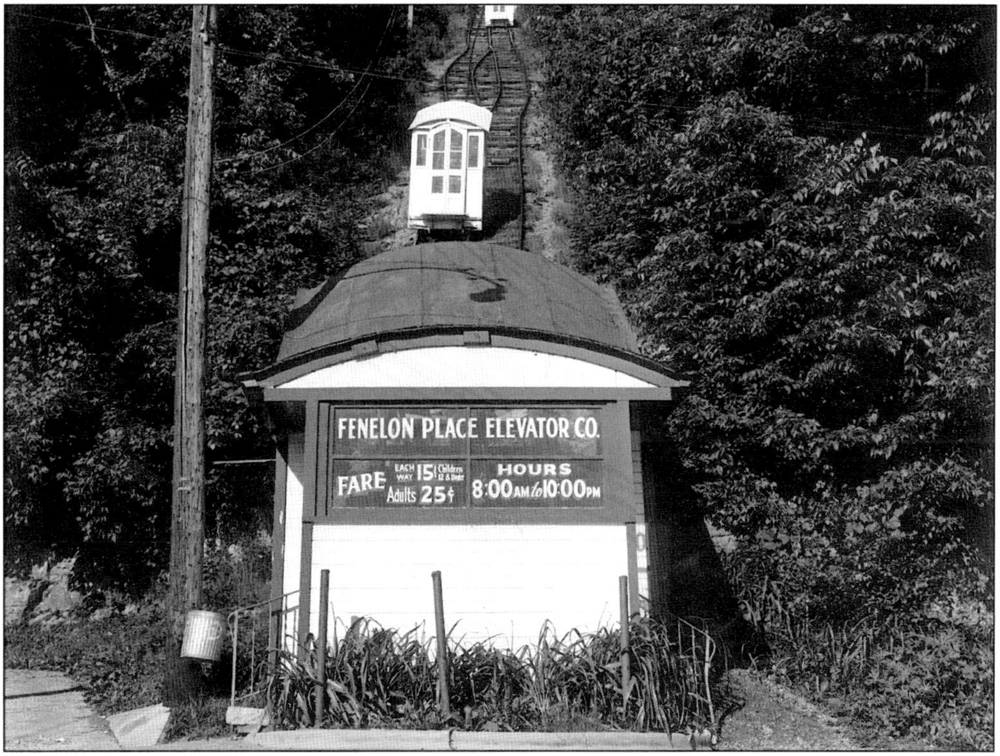

Inflation at work. After a few rate increases, an adult could go one way for a quarter.

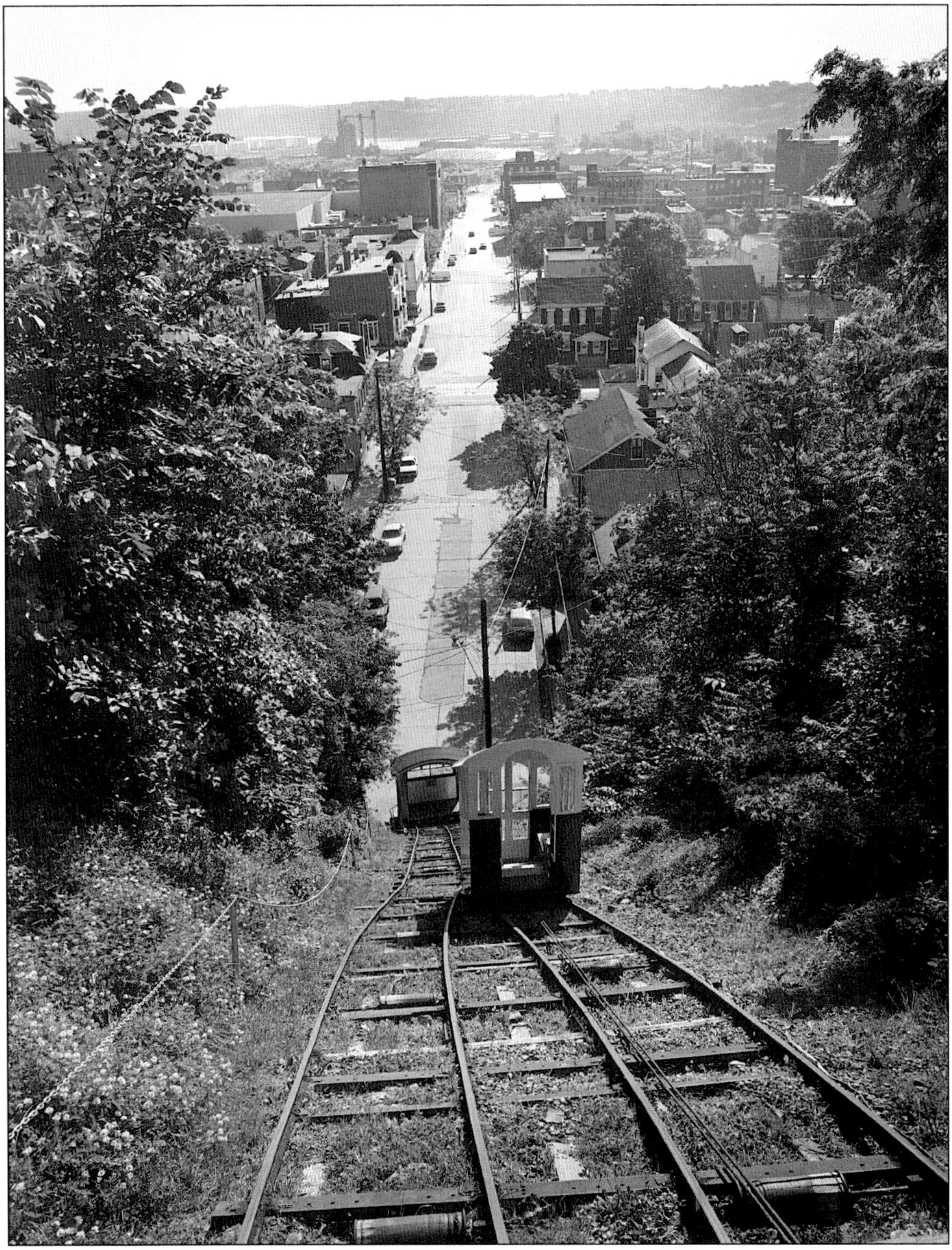

No matter what the cost, the ride is always a thrill. This image shows what the photographer saw on his way up to the top.

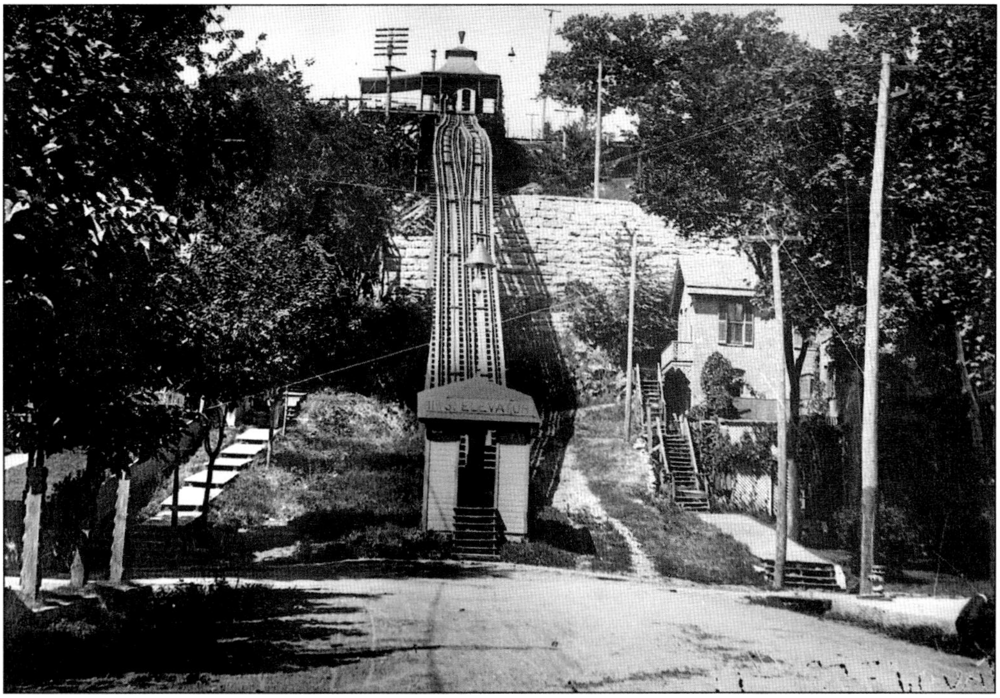

After the success of the Fenelon Place Elevator was well established, another funicular was built at Eleventh Street. The "hump" was a temporary feature when construction of a retaining wall was deemed necessary.

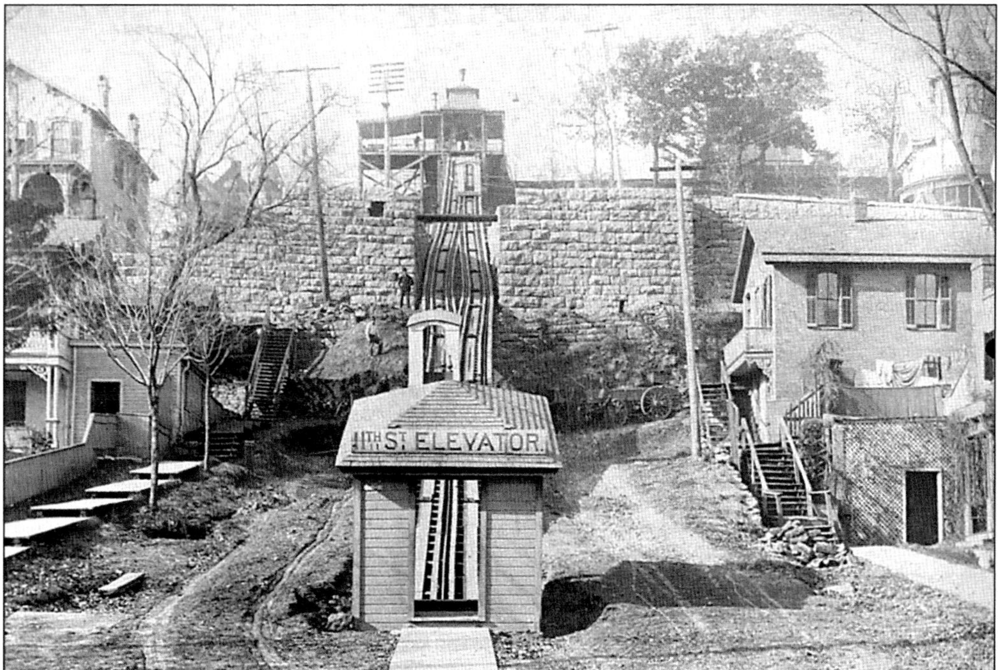

Once the retaining wall was built, the tracks were lowered, doing away with two grades. Compare this image with the photograph at the top of the page.

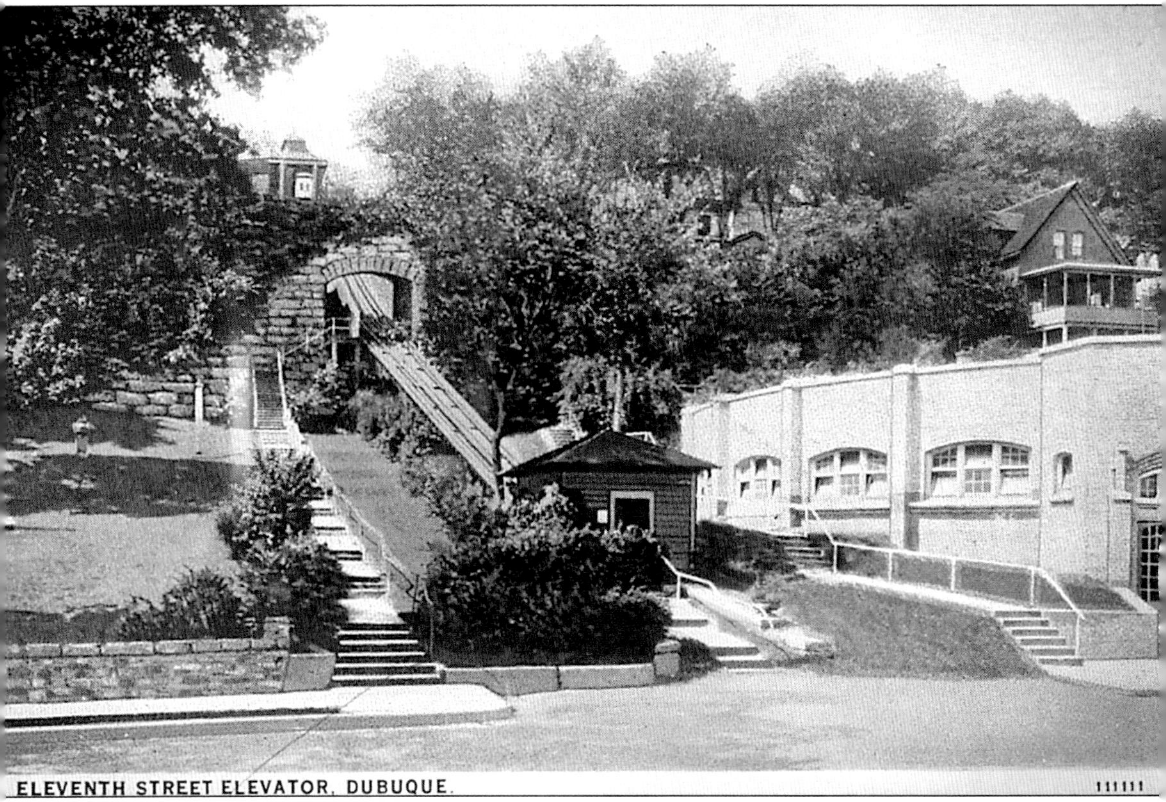

This photograph shows how the completed funicular railway looked when the arch was completed. Today, the arch is about all that is left of the Eleventh Street Elevator.